SPQR

Italian ✕✕

C4

1911 Fillmore St. (bet. Bush & Pine Sts.)

Phone: 415-771-7779
Web: www.spqrsf.com
Prices: **$$$**

Lunch Sat – Sun
Dinner nightly

Ed Anderson

A refined counterpart to the Marina's A16, SPQR (named for the Roman senate and people) offers elevated Italian dining that doesn't sacrifice casual comfort and warmth. Housed in a long, narrow space surrounded by the boutiques of Fillmore Street, the dimly lit dining room offers a handful of closely packed tables surrounding the popular marble counter. It's a lively, energetic place, with a noise level to match.

When in Rome (or San Francisco), you'll always dine seasonally, but options could include suckling pork confit with pickled peppers and charred vegetables, or crisply roasted guinea hen thigh and breast in Alba mushroom *brodo* with buttery delicata squash and young turnips. The superlative pastas are not simply a highlight but a necessary focus to meals here—consider embarking on the six-course pasta tasting menu. Hopefully, it might include the tender *tortelli* filled with earthy-sweet roasted parsnip and tossed with smoked honshimeji mushrooms in espresso-aged cheese.

Desserts may be delicate and contemporary, as in the honey-buttermilk panna cotta topped with spiced Fuyu persimmon cake, sliced persimmons, pomegranate seeds, and a quenelle of toasted black walnut ice cream.

San Francisco ▶ Marina

Spruce ❀

Mediterranean 🍴🍴🍴

3640 Sacramento St. (bet. Locust & Spruce Sts.)

Phone: 415-931-5100
Web: www.sprucesf.com
Prices: $$$

Lunch Mon – Fri
Dinner nightly

Frankie Frankeny

Though it was once an auto-body shop, Spruce for long now has cast off its workaday trappings and transformed into a contemporary getaway for the well-heeled Pacific Heights crowd. With its large, well-spaced tables, lavish brown velvet drapes, and black-and-white framed artwork, it is attractive and casually elegant, just like its engaging, suited staff.

Spruce's cuisine evokes seasonality with a Mediterranean effect. Dishes include *burrata* over tender asparagus, fingerling potatoes, and seascape strawberries; thickly sliced duck breast fanned over a tartlet of white-bean "cassoulet;" and for dessert, a lemon-and-pistachio tart trickled with toasted meringue, pistachio ice cream, and raspberry sauce. Bookending this meal are bonus treats like warm borscht with a fresh-baked *gougére* and rich wedge of cocoa-nib brownie.

The beverage program here is as impressive as the cuisine itself with a lengthy cocktail menu, a smart selection of wines by the glass and bottle, and thorough list of spirits. Even coffee is treated with care, with six single-origin varieties available. Linger long enough in its handsome environs, and it's easy to see why this stud remains an evergreen favorite.

Tacolicious

Mexican ✗

C2

2031 Chestnut St. (bet. Fillmore and Steiner Sts.)

Phone: 415-346-1966   Lunch & dinner daily
Web: www.tacolicioussf.com
Prices: 🍪🍪

Born out of a farmer's market stand, this local mini-chain now has four locations and legions of fans willing to wait in line for its famed tuna tostada. It's still filled with barely seared tuna, crisp leeks, and topped with chipotle mayo, but somehow it tastes better each year. Overstuffed tacos require a head dip to relish the delicious *guajillo*-braised short ribs and crisp rock cod with cabbage slaw. Just remember to douse them with plenty of the smoky, tangy house-made salsas. A solid kids' menu draws families, and some parents can be seen taking advantage of the extensive tequila selection as their youngsters dine.

At the Chestnut Street original, the pressed-copper ceiling and religious votive candles provide a colorful atmosphere.

Terzo

Mediterranean ✗✗

C2

3011 Steiner St. (bet. Filbert & Union Sts.)

Phone: 415-441-3200   Dinner nightly
Web: www.terzosf.com
Prices: $$

The third time's a charm as the saying goes and Terzo, the third restaurant from the group that owns Rose Pistola and Rose's Café, gets it right. Filament bulbs cast a cool light over the dark contemporary interior where chocolate leather covers the banquettes and a central communal table bustles with noshing regulars. Wall-mounted racks display a good selection of global wines, with many available by the glass— de rigueur for washing down these Mediterranean-inspired small plates.

Start with grilled Monterey Bay calamari with lentils, fennel, and a dusting of pimentón; or try the luscious hummus and beet salad. Hearty appetites should look for larger entrées like roasted mahi mahi with garbanzo beans and almonds.
Terzo is romantic, so do bring a date.

The Tipsy Pig

Gastropub ✗✗

C2

2231 Chestnut St. (bet. Pierce & Scott Sts.)

Phone: 415-292-2300
Web: www.thetipsypigsf.com
Prices: $$

Lunch Wed – Sun
Dinner nightly

The Tipsy Pig sports just the right mix of handsome furnishings, pressed-tin ceilings, and exposed brick walls to exude a saloon-like style that combines perfectly with flavorful Californian grub. A constant crowd of Marina hipsters can be found lingering at their front bar pouring a delectable selection of spirits and beers sized from the 10 oz. "Piglet" to the 20 oz. "Tipsy Pig."

Settle into the elevated wood-furnished dining room for the main event, perhaps beginning with a bowl of creamy sweet corn clam chowder drizzled with chili oil. The roster of tasty and fresh gastropub fare may reveal a spicy tuna burger served on a bun smeared with *sambal* and smashed avocado; or bite-size pieces of roasted summer squash tossed in melted butter and herbs.

Viva Goa

Indian ✗

B2

2420 Lombard St. (bet. Divisadero & Scott Sts.)

Phone: 415-440-2600
Web: www.vivagoaindiancuisine.com
Prices: 🍪🍪

Lunch & dinner daily

Cardamom, curry, and the strums of an Indian sitar hang in the air at Viva Goa, the Lombard Street eatery that offers a rich culinary experience thanks to Goa's coastal life where Portuguese influences mingles with the local cuisine. Once you find parking—this neighborhood can be tricky—slide into a burgundy booth and order a Goan specialty. Both the seafood curry and stuffed-and-fried whole pomfret are unexpected standouts.

Indian food lovers will also find tasty executions of such favorites as fried chicken lollipops drenched in a peppery red sauce; spicy *vindaloo*; aromatic *biryani*; chicken *tikka masala*; savory *samosas*, and blistered garlic naans. Spice junkies can ask for extra hot, while budget diners will appreciate the buffet at lunch.

Zushi Puzzle

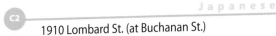

Japanese ✗✗

C2

1910 Lombard St. (at Buchanan St.)

Dinner Mon – Sat

Phone: 415-931-9319
Web: www.zushipuzzle.com
Prices: 💰💰

This packed Lombard Street *sushi-ya* may have the oddest name on the block, but its success is no puzzle: fish is flown in fresh from Japan each day and dozens of specialty maki including the soft shell and snow crab Dynasty roll are both beautifully plated and among the tastiest around. The Best Hand Roll isn't just the flourish of a confident chef, but earns its superlative name.

In fact, Chef Roger Chong is a friendly, funny guy from his post at the back counter. Make a reservation (you'll need one) for a view of the master at work. Adventurous types can relinquish the menus and let the chef steer your course, while safer palates find comfort in bowls of soba and udon noodles. Seafood addicts should check the dry erase board for the day's catch.

Look for our symbol 🍸,
spotlighting restaurants
with a notable
cocktail list.

Mission
Bernal Heights · Potrero Hill

The sun always shines in the Mission, a bohemian paradise dotted with palm trees and home to artists, activists, and a vibrant Latino community. Graffiti murals line the walls of funky galleries, thrift shops, and bookstores; while sidewalk stands burst with fresh plantains, nopales, and the juiciest limes this side of the border.

The markets here are among the best in town: **La Palma Mexicatessen** brims with homemade *papusas*, chips, and fresh Mexican cheeses; **Lucca Ravioli** stocks imported Italian goods; and **Bi-Rite** is a petite grocer popular for fresh flowers and prepared foods. Across the street find **Bi-Rite Creamery**, a cult favorite for ice cream. From cheese and ice cream, turn the page to hipster coffee hangout, **Ritual Coffee Roasters**. What's so stellar about their coffee? Join the line outside the door, order one of their special roasts from the Barista, and you will start to get the picture.

Countless bargain *mercados* and dollar stores might suggest otherwise, but the Mission is home to many an avant-garde hangout. **Dynamo Donuts** on 24th Street is *the* place for delectable flavors like apricot-cardamom, chocolate-star anise, and maple-glazed bacon-apple. **Walzwerk** charms with East German kitsch and is also the go-to spot for Deutsch delights. Mission pizza reigns supreme—thin-crust lovers wait in line at **Pizzeria Delfina** as they serve a wicked pie

with crispy edges blistered just so. Carb addicts cannot (and should not) miss the exceptional breads, pastries, and pressed sandwiches at **Tartine Bakery**. To best experience the flavors of the Mission, forgo the table and chairs and pull up at a curb on Linda Street, where a vigilant street food scene has incited a revolution of sorts. The **Magic Curry Kart** plates $5 steaming rice dishes, while the **Pie Fridays** stand serves up wedges of flaky and freshly baked pies topped with mounds of sweet whipped cream. This alley buzzes with locals also noshing on homemade pastries, empanadas, and Vietnamese spring rolls until the grub runs out.

Additionally, the city's hottest 'hood offers a cool selection of sweets. A banana split is downright retrolicious when served at the Formica counter of 90-year-old **St. Francis Fountain**. The sundaes are made with **Mitchell's Ice Cream**, famous since 1953. Modish flavors—think Grasshopper Pie and Kahlua Mocha Cream—are in regular rotation at the newer **Humphrey Slocombe**. **Mission Pie** is a local jewel that lures all for their sumptuous selection of savory and sweet pies. While their menu spins to the season, it also pays homage to the environment by using only local, sustainable produce sourced from nearby farms, and unveils light savory treats, baked goods, and of course those unforgettable pies.

Dance off your indulgences on Salsa Sunday at **El Rio**, the dive bar with a bustling back patio; or join the hip kids for DJs and live bands at the culturally diverse **Elbo Room**. The lesbian set shoots pool at the **Lexington Club**. On the late night, growling stomachs brave harsh lighting at the numerous taquerias, many of which are open until 4:00 A.M. Go see for yourself: try the veggie burrito at **Taqueria Cancún**; tacos at **La Alteña**; and mind-blowing meats (*lengua* or *cabeza*?) at **El Farolito**. During the day, **La Taqueria**'s carne asada burrito is arguably the best. And the **El Tonayense** taco truck, to quote one blogger, is of course "da bomb!"

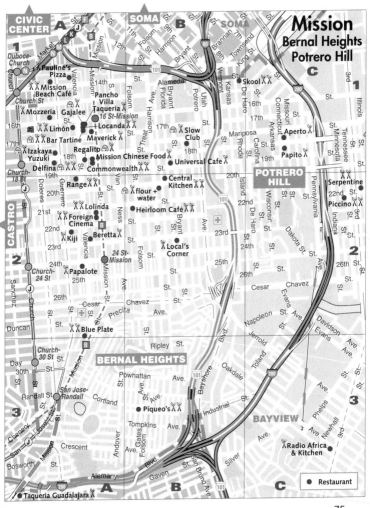

Mission

Bernal Heights
Potrero Hill

Aperto

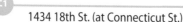
Italian ✗

1434 18th St. (at Connecticut St.)

Phone: 415-252-1625
Web: www.apertosf.com
Prices: $$

Lunch & dinner daily

If only everybody could live next to this cheery Italian café. It has all the trappings of an ideal local haunt from yellow walls and towering windows to a large corner nook, perfect for families to gather round. Servers are hospitable and intent; even line cooks might send smiles your way.

The name of their game is rustic Italian food which consists of a great selection of pastas and daily specials. A meal might start with delicious bruschetta brushed with olive oil, a thick fava bean paste, and artichoke hearts. Carb fiends will savor perfectly al dente orecchiette mingled with asparagus stalks in garlic-infused white wine; while meatheads hanker for tender red wine-braised beef short ribs served over a bed of fresh corn and braised shelling beans.

Bar Tartine

A1

Eastern European ✗✗

561 Valencia St. (bet. 16th & 17th Sts.)

Phone: 415-487-1600
Web: www.bartartine.com
Prices: $$

Lunch Wed – Sun
Dinner Tue – Sun

Bar Tartine's minor revamp resulted in a delightful though diminutive annex. The weekday lunch menu of open-faced rye bread sandwiches topped with smoked trout, chicken liver pâté, or cheeses meets a small menu of snacks and baked goods.

In the evening, the annex closes and the entire wood-ridden restaurant is open for dinner. Friendly servers buzz around the welcoming room with such ambitious creations as a chilled white beet soup with whey, white curry, and coriander, nicely paired with smoky potatoes laid beside a ramp aïoli. Balancing earthy textures with hearty flavors are lentil croquettes served on sesame-*kamut* bread, layered with yogurt, cucumbers, and lentil sprouts. Get your bird on with a chicken stuffed with sausage and crunchy sauerkraut.

Beretta

1199 Valencia St. (at 23rd St.)

Phone: 415-695-1199
Web: www.berettasf.com
Prices: $$

Lunch Sat – Sun
Dinner nightly

A lively vibe, strong cocktail program, and late hours (until 1:00 A.M. nightly) ensure that the crowds have yet to abate at this five-year-old Mission hotspot. The menu is packed with flavorful Italian fare and delicious antipasti like rich and chunky eggplant *caponatina* with oozing *burrata* drizzled in excellent olive oil. Crisp, thin crust pizzas are another highlight, with tangy sauce and cured meats like spicy salami and *coppa*.

A handful of booths offer a more private experience, while a large communal table serves the walk-in crowd. Whether you're spending an evening amid the glow of Edison bulbs and the clink of cocktail shakers or munching on a brunch-time pizza carbonara at a sunny outdoor table, you'll exit both sated and energized.

Blue Plate

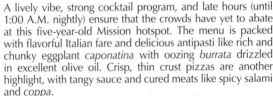

3218 Mission St. (bet. 29th & Valencia Sts.)

Phone: 415-282-6777
Web: www.blueplatesf.com
Prices: $$

Dinner nightly

With nary a dining patio in sight, Missionites make frequent appearances at Blue Plate for its quaint back garden (where potted plants and blossoming fruit trees overhang café tables) and solid American food that dances to the season. Inside the snug dining room, tables are tight-knit and while the best seats are at the back, unique accents like a display of local art keep the skinny-jeaned regulars happy and unhurried.

Long-time Chef/co-owner Cory Obenour's creative flavor combinations sparkle through in such offerings as a green garlic and potato-leek soup bobbing with house-smoked salmon; and pillowy knobs of gnocchi with lamb meatballs. Illustrating classic Americana is a Blue Plate meatloaf served with creamy mashed potatoes and green beans.

Central Kitchen

B2

Contemporary

3000 20th St. (at Florida St.)

Phone: 415-826-7004
Web: www.centralkitchensf.com
Prices: $$

Lunch Sun
Dinner nightly

Central Kitchen, from the team behind flour + water just up the block, shares its older sibling's penchant for farm-fresh ingredients, hip staff, and a loud indie-rock soundtrack. However, this is no overflow spot: the kitchen serves a sophisticated, artful Californian cuisine (including an optional tasting menu) designed to bring out the best of the area's top-notch produce.

The contemporary ethos extends to the space, with plenty of exposed ducting, concrete, and a center atrium festooned with twinkling lights. The staff may be trendy, but they provide a satisfying experience—as does the beautifully roasted hen atop Beluga lentils dabbed with leek-clam relish; or an earthy and hearty plate of rabbit charcuterie with bright green pistachio *gribiche*.

Commonwealth

A1

Californian

2224 Mission St. (bet. 18th & 19th Sts.)

Phone: 415-355-1500
Web: www.commonwealthsf.com
Prices: $$

Dinner nightly

Commonwealth is a restaurant that takes chances, starting with its edgy Mission locale. Yet the interior is minimal and serene, with a bar offering views of the open kitchen and tables spotlit by filaments. There is a sense of purpose here, both among the progressive owners who donate part of every tasting menu to charity, and the buzz of young epicureans.

This kitchen thrills in reformulating ingredients to deliver flavor and textural surprise, as in herring fillets with chicken skin breadcrumbs and beet-miso purée; egg custard with uni, seaweed brioche cubes, and wild greens; and lamb's tongue terrine with gem lettuce, Meyer lemon, artichoke hearts, and pistachio cream. At dessert, chocolate and peanut butter semifreddo tops cloud-like frozen popcorn.

Delfina

Italian 𝕏𝕏

A1

3621 18th St. (bet. Dolores & Guerrero Sts.)

Phone: 415-552-4055   Dinner nightly
Web: www.delfinasf.com
Prices: $$

Delfina is one of those spots that is perennially popular with the Mission locals. The pizzeria next door does a booming business, but this spacious dining room is almost always packed, and highlights a neat arrangement of bare wood tabletops, a narrow counter (perfect for solo diners), and a semi-open kitchen. Mirrors on the side walls and a line of windows in the front give this space a larger and airy feel. There is no need to dress up for this casual, welcoming spot. Expect menu items such as hearty, chewy pappardelle tossed with flavorful pork sugo; tender-roasted and crisp-skinned quail served over creamy polenta; and chicken liver *spiedini* with *guanciale* and aged *balsamico*. Close with a lovely chocolate *budino* with salted caramel ice cream.

flour + water ☺

Italian 𝕏

B2

2401 Harrison St. (at 20th St.)

Phone: 415-826-7000   Dinner nightly
Web: www.flourandwater.com
Prices: $$

In Italian cooking, it all just amounts to flour and water, the two basic ingredients in homemade pasta and pizza dough. And, these are cooked to perfection at this beatnik haunt where artsy twenty-something's are cool with waiting an hour for a blistered pie.

Join the crowd in the standing room bar for a glass of *nebbiolo* as you look around. Concrete floors and a redwood bar lend an industrial vibe, but seafoam walls and aquatic art keeps things oddly warm. The narrow space gets loud with patrons chirping over a squash salad with *lardo*, Brussels sprouts, and pistachios; nightly tastings of seasonal, artisan pastas; and pizzas topped with tasty combos like sunchokes, chanterelles, Taleggio, and horseradish gremolata.
Check out new sib Central Kitchen.

Foreign Cinema

International ✗✗

A2

2534 Mission St. (bet. 21st & 22nd Sts.)

Phone: 415-648-7600
Web: www.foreigncinema.com
Prices: $$

Lunch Sat – Sun
Dinner nightly

Dinner and a movie? Absolutely. And especially at Foreign Cinema where international films are projected onto a brick wall at the back of a garden patio. This is date night at its best and even if you can't snag a coveted table on their patio, the spacious dining room inside beguiles with a soaring ceiling, welcoming vibe, and glass wall of windows.

Indulging your *chéri* with a regal repast of globally-flecked dishes is *sine qua non*. In fact, find couples on the regular sharing the likes of salt cod brandade gratin paired with crunchy grilled bread; or white tuna sashimi touched with an avocado mousse, tobiko, and grapefruit. At brunch, locals give poached farm eggs with crisp duck leg confit, Venetian chicories, and sherry vinaigrette two thumbs up.

Gajalee 👄

Indian ✗✗

A1

525 Valencia St. (bet. 16th & 17th Sts.)

Phone: 415-552-9000
Web: www.gajaleesf.com
Prices: $$

Lunch & dinner daily

Named for the Indian term for an informal gathering, Gajalee may not appear lavish, but it's heavy on traditional flavor and ingredients. The remarkably authentic Southern Indian fare focuses on seafood, creamy curries, and delicate spices. They'll even ask just how hot you like your shrimp chili *tava* and rich, moist fish *kolhapuri*. Portions are generous; the pitch-perfect rice or *chapatti* is a meal unto itself. Finish with the light, meltingly sweet *gulab jamun*.

Though the neon signs out front aren't prepossessing, the dining room is surprisingly cheerful, with yellow walls and colorful murals. Snag a window seat for great people-watching on one of Valencia Street's most bustling corners. Those who'd rather dine at home can order takeout or delivery.

Heirloom Café

Californian ✗✗

B2

2500 Folsom St. (at 21st St.)

Phone: 415-821-2500   Dinner Mon – Sat
Web: www.heirloom-sf.com
Prices: $$$

Though a nice selection of European vintages is a boon to this charming bistro housed in a quiet corner of the Mission, the delicate and seasonal food keeps it bustling. Fresh and elegant Mediterranean-leaning dishes are pure expressions of California's bounty. Sample the likes of seared scallops on a bed of fresh fava beans and frisée with minced bacon and shallot-butter; or pan-roasted cod with cauliflower purée, English peas, and ramps. Simple desserts display a gentle touch, as in polenta cake with macerated strawberries and tarragon cream.

The dining room features communal tables, a marble counter with a close-up view of the open kitchen, whitewashed walls plastered with European wine labels, warm candlelight, and even warmer service.

Izakaya Yuzuki

Japanese ✗

A1

598 Guerrero St. (at 18th St.)

Phone: 415-556-9898   Dinner Wed – Mon
Web: www.yuzukisf.com
Prices: $$

Izakaya Yuzuki's tantalizing array of grilled and fried bites is made with palpable authenticity. Note the number of dishes that are prepared with *koji* (fermented rice mixed with water and salt) to impart umami. Taste this in *yaki surume ika*, marinated Hokkaido squid—the body grilled until tender with crisped, chewy tentacles—served with excellent yuzu mayonnaise for dipping. Morsels of dark meat chicken are also marinated in *koji* and then fried until golden for enticing *kara-age*. House-made tofu or *nukazuke*, vegetables pickled in fermented rice bran, are among the delightful *otsumami* to savor with sake or frosty sweet potato beer.

The modest interior showcases simple white walls hand-painted with vegetable outlines and an amicable staff.

Kiji

A2

1009 Guerrero St. (bet. 22nd & 23rd Sts.)

Phone: 415-282-0400
Web: www.kijirestaurant.com
Prices:

Dinner Mon – Sat

Less is more at Kiji, a super-simple neighborhood sushi joint on a busy stretch of Guerrero Street, in the heart of the Mission. With just a handful of tables and a tiny sushi counter, Kiji is perennially packed: have patience—a table will turn over soon—or make like the locals and call in your order to-go.

While an array of maki are available for Americanized tastes, the menu is best represented by traditional Japanese fare such as hamachi *kama*, a broiled yellowtail collar served with ponzu sauce; and a nightly list of nigiri that may include melt-in-your-mouth *aji*, *tai*, escolar, and ocean trout. Everything here is fresh and good, rather than fancy. Try the Kiji roll, stuffed with snow crab and asparagus and topped with tuna, *tobiko*, and spicy sauce.

Limón

A1

524 Valencia St. (bet. 16th & 17th Sts.)

Phone: 415-252-0918
Web: www.limon-sf.com
Prices: $$

Lunch & dinner daily

Reinvented as Limón Rotisserie, this location of Limón resides on Valencia Street in the heart of the bustling Mission district. In keeping with its handle, the décor features orange and lime accents along taupe walls hung with colorful paintings. The setting is *mucho* casual and walk-ins are welcome.

Limón features the *pollo a la brasa*, an absolutely worthy focus: this Peruvian slow-roasted bird is perfectly juicy and moist, marinated with garlic and herbs, and paired with a side of *aji*. Other solid hits may include *ensalada ruca*, fresh root vegetables mixed with *choclo*, green peas, and tossed in a creamy mustard dressing; crispy and addictive golden brown yucca fries; or *tacu-tacu*, a fragrant and delicious mixture of rice, beans and *aji amarillo* sauce.

Local's Corner

Californian   ✗

B2

2500 Bryant St. (at 23rd St.)

Phone: 415-800-7945   Lunch Tue – Sun
Web: www.localscornersf.com   Dinner Tue – Sat
Prices: $$

Local's Corner is exactly that—a neighborhood café set upon a corner and geared toward local foodies. This vintage-esque respite contains only a handful of tables and counter seats. Service is laid-back, but it's so much fun to watch the animated (read: skilled) team in the open kitchen.

The menu of light, well-crafted Californian fare spins to the season, so check out the framed mirror listing daily oysters and cheeses. Then embark on dishes that might feature a refreshing chicken salad mingled with yogurt, toasted almonds, raisins, and fresh cilantro; or beef tartare crowned with a quail egg and pickled cauliflower. That smoked salmon salad sandwich with a side of peppery arugula is just begging to be paired with a homemade Meyer lemon lemonade.

Locanda

Italian   ✗✗

A1

557 Valencia St. (bet. 16th & 17th Sts.)

Phone: 415-863-6800   Dinner nightly
Web: www.locandasf.com
Prices: $$

Locanda is a well-loved offspring of the highly successful team behind popular Delfina, so it's sure to be a hit. This osteria takes its inspiration from Rome. Chic and casual, the space is defined by wood furnishings and floors, an open kitchen, and a communal table. It's a little bit traditional and a little bit contemporary.

Antipasti like shaved raw artichokes with grilled ricotta and a refreshing salad with endive, crème fraîche, and cured salmon, are a great way to begin before moving on to heartier pastas and charcoal-grilled dishes. Don't be fooled by the simple-sounding menu, since there's also a selection of offal plates like chilled tongue with salsa verde, tripe with tomato, mint, and pecorino, or fried sweetbreads and artichokes.

San Francisco ▲ Mission

83

Lolinda

A2

2518 Mission St. (bet. 21st & 22nd Sts.)

Phone: 415-550-6970

Web: www.lolindasf.com

Prices: $$

Dinner nightly

Equal parts contemporary steakhouse and small plates spot, Argentine-inspired Lolinda is fun and sexy, loaded with twenty- and thirty-somethings gabbing over cocktails and sips of malbec. The soaring dining room with its wagon-wheel chandeliers and tufted-leather banquettes leads to a bustling second-floor mezzanine; whereas El Techo, a heated and more casual roof deck, offers sweeping views of the skyline. Here, sharing is encouraged and groups can be found divvying up plates of silky ono ceviche, flaky chicken empanadas, or sweet, caramelized pork belly.

Bull sculptures and murals remind diners that the chargrilled steak or crosscut beef short ribs with chimichurri are must-orders—tender and smoky, they'll transport you to Buenos Aires instantly.

Maverick

A1

3316 17th St. (bet. Hoff & Mission Sts.)

Phone: 415-863-3061

Web: www.sfmaverick.com

Prices: $$

Lunch Sat – Sun

Dinner nightly

Its name suggests culinary iconoclasm, but Maverick is all about classic Americana—as one bite of the tender-crisp fried chicken with spicy green beans and buttery biscuits ably demonstrates. Comfort food abounds, from a starter of *gougéres* with French onion dip to a finale of brownie sundae with Bourbon-caramel ice cream. If that isn't enough, the aura is equally relaxed, drawing couples and families with children in tow.

The simply dressed dining room is bifurcated with a main area full of tight-knit tables and a smaller communal room near the open kitchen that churns out chicken buckets to-go on special nights. Weekend brunch is also popular with braised duck hash and a Vermont cheddar omelet that will ease any transgressions from the night before.

Mission Beach Café

American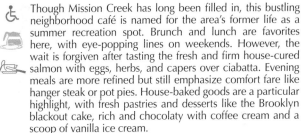

A1

198 Guerrero St. (at 14th St.)

Phone: 415-861-0198
Web: www.missionbeachcafesf.com
Prices: $$

Lunch daily
Dinner Mon – Sat

Though Mission Creek has long been filled in, this bustling neighborhood café is named for the area's former life as a summer recreation spot. Brunch and lunch are favorites here, with eye-popping lines on weekends. However, the wait is forgiven after tasting the fresh and firm house-cured salmon with eggs, herbs, and capers over ciabatta. Evening meals are more refined but still emphasize comfort fare like hanger steak or pot pies. House-baked goods are a particular highlight, with fresh pastries and desserts like the Brooklyn blackout cake, rich and chocolaty with coffee cream and a scoop of vanilla ice cream.

The modern space with big windows and leather chairs, looks formal, but the friendly, casual service keeps things down to earth.

Mission Chinese Food

Chinese

A1

2234 Mission St. (bet. 18th & 19th Sts.)

Phone: 415-863-2800
Web: www.missionchinesefood.com
Prices:

Lunch & dinner Thu – Tue

Some people say it's the most over-hyped spot around, yet Mission Chinese Food is as popular as ever. And the craze has even spread to the East Coast, but this original well-worn dining gem remains the same: strangely set within the defunct Lung Shan Restaurant, and decked with a red dragon that looms overhead.

Servers move around with brusque efficiency as they present flavor-packed, contemporary interpretations of Chinese dishes like smoky, fatty *kung pao* pastrami strewn with shaved potato and peanuts; sizzling cumin lamb chili joined with pickled long beans; or a unique dish of wild pepper leaves swirled with tofu ribbons and pumpkin slices dressed in a chili broth. Reservations are not accepted, so be prepared to stand around in your skinny jeans.

Mozzeria

Pizza ✗

A1

3228 16th St. (bet. Dolores & Guerrero Sts.)

Phone: 415-489-0963
Web: www.mozzeria.com
Prices: ⊛⊛

Dinner Tue – Sun

Oh, the pies at Mozzeria! Whether it's the traditional Margherita, oozing with mozzarella and fresh basil; the California-style slathered with decadent blue cheese, caramelized onions, and thyme; or the Asian-style crowned with roast duck, hoisin sauce, and spring onions, there's a pleaser for every palate.

Specializing in those Neapolitan-style, thin-crust pizzas (fired at a thousand degrees), this brilliant newbie's deaf owners attract a largely non-hearing patronage. But don't fret if you're not proficient in sign language as the wonderful and accommodating staff will steer your way. Though pizza is their main affair, other tasty options abound like flaky, delicate salmon topped by salsa verde, served with tangy fried capers and rosemary potatoes.

Pancho Villa Taqueria

Mexican ✗

A1

3071 16th St. (bet. Mission & Valencia Sts.)

Phone: 415-864-8840
Web: www.sfpanchovilla.com
Prices: ⊛⊛

Lunch & dinner daily

Around the corner from the 16th and Mission BART stop, this long-running taqueria earns high marks from locals. Upon entering, take a moment to step back and examine the menu board; the vested attendants working the flat-tops and grills will be quizzing you on the beans, condiments, and choice of 10 meats you desire. That line moves quickly, so be ready. After loading up your burrito, perhaps filled with thinly sliced steak and butterflied prawns, select an *agua fresca* from the glass barrels, and hit the salsa bar. It features award-winning varieties in every range of heat and sweet to complement their thin, ultra-crispy tortilla chips. Ambience is nil and tables can be hard to snag, but the reward is a fresh and flavorful taste of the Mission.

Papalote

Mexican 🍴

 A2

3409 24th St. (bet. Poplar & Valencia Sts.)

Phone: 415-970-8815
Web: www.papalote-sf.com
Prices: 💰💰

Lunch & dinner daily

For a lighter, more Californian take on classic taqueria fare, head to this tiny joint slightly off the Mission's beaten track. There, you'll find tortillas packed with flaky and perfectly cooked fish, plump shrimp, and flavorful carne asada, available in either burrito or taco form. (Be sure to go "super" for a hearty dose of freshly made guacamole.) Order at the counter, then snag a table and try not to fill up on chips.

Whatever you order, top it with a heaping helping of the outstanding roasted-tomato salsa, good enough to merit licking the ramekin—take-home jars are sold on-site and online. Throw in an *agua fresca* or a cold beer from the fridge, and prepare to leave stuffed and smiling from a chat with the friendly owner.

Papito

Mexican 🍴

 C1

317 Connecticut St. (at 18th St.)

Phone: 415-695-0147
Web: www.papitosf.com
Prices: 💰💰

Lunch & dinner daily

Owned by the team behind nearby Chez Papa and Chez Maman, this taqueria has a French touch that complements its sunny, bistro-like environs on the slope of Potrero Hill. The colorful walls and tightly packed tables lead to a semi-open kitchen full of energy and movement, while servers may be snappy without sacrificing timely presentations.

Start with the zippy *ensalada* Papito, packed with avocado, crispy tortilla strips, and cilantro dressing. Then, dig into the giant mushroom quesadilla with Oaxaca cheese or crisp rock cod tacos with chipotle mayo and cabbage slaw. Well-crafted Mexican entrées, a flavorful salsa selection, and a fully-stocked bar further cement Papito's status as a neighborhood favorite spot for a quiet lunch or bustling dinner.

Pauline's Pizza

Pizza

 260 Valencia St. (bet. Duboce Ave. & 14th St.)

Phone: 415-552-2050   Dinner Tue – Sat
Web: www.paulinespizza.com
Prices: **$$**

Housed in a sunny yellow building on vibrant Valencia St., Pauline's maintains its reputation as a Mission favorite for California-style pizzas topped with heaps of organic vegetables. Like its array of food, this family-friendly haunt is comfortable, simply decked with a semi-open kitchen and large, airy windows.

Pizza is their game, and they offer several varieties (like butternut squash with rosemary, shallots, and Gruyère) along with a nightly selection of specials. With pre-baked shells available to-go, you may try to recreate their pies at home, but their signature pizza slathered with pesto and pine nuts is best enjoyed in-house. By rule, the spicy Louisiana andouille pizza must be chased by a cool, creamy ice cream sundae.

Piccino

Pizza

 1001 Minnesota St. (at 22nd St.)

Phone: 415-824-4224   Lunch & dinner Tue – Sun
Web: www.piccinocafe.com
Prices: **$$**

 First impressions do matter and with Piccino, you'll be charmed at first sight. Settled on the first floor of a Victorian building painted bright yellow with green trim, Piccino isn't as cutesy inside as it is on the outside. Instead, this chic restaurant employs raw wood planked floors, sleek chocolate brown chairs, and Eames stools at the counter to rather cool effect.

Headed by a skilled cadre of cooks, the kitchen turns out Italian food with California punch. Thin-crust crispy pizza is the shining star, though panini and pastas are a close second. Refreshing salads whet your appetite for the deliciously chewy and crispy pizzas, served on wooden, parchment paper-lined boards. For dessert try the *affogato* made with Pink Squirrel ice cream.

Piqueo's

Peruvian ✗✗

830 Cortland Ave. (at Gates St.)

Phone: 415-282-8812   Dinner nightly
Web: www.piqueos.com
Prices: $$

Experience the diversity of Peruvian cuisine with a trip to this popular Bernal Heights small-plates spot, where influences range from Japanese (ahi tuna ceviche with ginger and hoisin); and Spanish (paella with seafood, olives, and black mint); to Andean (yucca balls stuffed with cheese and ham). A welcoming staff paces the flow of dishes well, ensuring each complex flavor gets to stand on its own. Add on a bottle of robust Portuguese red wine with dinner and thick dulce de leche parfait topped with fresh berries, and Port-spiked cream for dessert.

Piqueo's is a neighborhood favorite among families and couples of all ages packing the tightly spaced tables. Large windows let in plenty of light, illuminating chalkboards full of appealing specials.

Radio Africa & Kitchen

International ✗

4800 3rd St. (bet. Oakdale & Palou Aves.)

Phone: 415-420-2486   Dinner Tue – Sat
Web: www.radioafricakitchen.com
Prices: $$

Bayview may be one of the most crime-ridden areas in the city, however, the arrival of hot spots like Radio Africa & Kitchen strutting a unique bill of fare and bright setting, have been hugely sought-after.

This well-received haunt features Ethiopian-born Chef Eskender Aseged's original style of Afro-Mediterranean food mingled with Cali flair—the ingredients come from a local community garden. A healthy dish of green lentils is topped with roasted red beets, goat cheese, arugula, and shredded red cabbage; and baked white fish is deliciously seasoned with a fragrant spice blend and crowned with tomato confit. Heartier appetites will return time and again for the leg of lamb massaged with a unique *berbere* blend and coupled with roasted vegetables.

Range

San Francisco ▶ Mission

A2 Contemporary ✗✗

842 Valencia St. (bet. 19th & 20th Sts.)

Phone: 415-282-8283   Dinner nightly
Web: www.rangesf.com
Prices: $$

It may have been one of the first higher-end restaurants to colonize this stretch of the Mission, but Range's crowds haven't abated, despite the influx of new local dining options. Its popularity is thanks to the focused menu of seasonal cuisine that manages to be uncomplicated yet reliably delicious. Expect dishes like grilled asparagus drizzled with *harissa* and cumin-laced yogurt; pan-roasted medallions of rabbit loin with natural jus and minty gremolata; and milk-chocolate mousse cake.

This industrial-chic space combines worn wood floors, contemporary fixtures, and leather seating; knowledgeable servers are cordial and hip. The wine list may be packed with interesting choices, but innovative cocktails draw their own crowds to the light-studded bar.

Regalito

A1 Mexican ✗

3481 18th St. (at Valencia St.)

Phone: 415-503-0650   Lunch Sat – Sun
Web: www.regalitosf.com   Dinner nightly
Prices: $$

With a bright and colorful address just off busy Valencia, Regalito evokes the feel and flavors of Mexico at every turn, from the art-packed chartreuse walls to the handmade, hot-off-the-press tortillas that grace many of the dishes. The service is endearing, the kitchen is gleaming, and the ingredients are top-notch—as the row of perfect avocados lining the counter will confirm.

Start off with crisp potatoes topped with crema and crumbled chorizo, or freshly made chips with thick house guacamole. A top entrée is the lovingly slow-roasted *cochinita pibil*, rich pork tempered by a tangy citrus sauce and bright pickled onions. Given the popularity of this tiny neighborhood mainstay, the only downside of dining at Regalito can be the wait for a table.

Serpentine

Californian ✗✗

C2

2495 3rd St. (at 22nd St.)

Phone: 415-252-2000
Web: www.serpentinesf.com
Prices: $$

Lunch daily
Dinner Mon – Sat

Located in the Dogpatch, Serpentine is typically SF: an urban-industrial space with worn wood floors, loft-like ceilings, and exposed ductwork. The setting coupled with Californian fare that features fresh, local, and seasonal ingredients, equals a very popular spot among locals for a business lunch, dinner, or weekend brunch.

Sociable servers may bring you an arugula salad tossed with crunchy sugar snap peas, shaved carrots, Easter Egg radishes, sliced almonds, and *ricotta salata* in a tangy red wine vinaigrette. The relaxed atmosphere is ideal for enjoying fresh food prepared with skill—that might even include a fluffy pork *rillette* sandwich heaped with deliciously griddled crispy pork and topped with a tangy shaved fennel- and pepper-relish.

Skool

Seafood ✗✗

B1

1725 Alameda St. (at De Haro St.)

Phone: 415-255-8800
Web: www.skoolsf.com
Prices: $$

Lunch & dinner daily

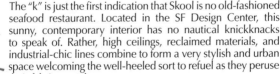

The "k" is just the first indication that Skool is no old-fashioned seafood restaurant. Located in the SF Design Center, this sunny, contemporary interior has no nautical knickknacks to speak of. Rather, high ceilings, reclaimed materials, and industrial-chic lines combine to form a very stylish and urban space welcoming the well-heeled sort to refuel as they peruse their fabric swatches.

Both Californian and Japanese inflections are to be found in the light, bright fare turned out from the open kitchen. Nosh on house-cured salmon pastrami Benedict with fresh arugula and a yuzu-hollandaise sauce; a modern Niçoise salad with sesame-crusted tuna and cucumber-anchovy vinaigrette; or mussels and smoked bacon in Point Reyes blue cheese broth.

Slow Club

Californian ✗

2501 Mariposa St. (at Hampshire St.)

Phone:	415-241-9390	Lunch daily
Web:	www.slowclub.com	Dinner Mon – Sat
Prices:	$$	

Slow Club is one of those Mission restaurants that makes you work for it. But you'll want to score that parking spot, or wait for brunch, because a meal at Slow Club is worth it. The restaurant itself is minimally dressed and industrial, with a small open kitchen and sidewalk patio for sun-soaked days. While the food is not contrived or pretentious, it shows consistent and delicious Californian fare crafted from fresh and local ingredients. A seasonal menu may reflect grilled flatbread with sheep's milk mozzarella, roasted tomato sauce, and applewood-smoked ham; followed by *berbere*-spiked marinated beef skewers served over fluffy quinoa with caramelized turnips and carrots. A yummy butterscotch pecan pie with whipped cream makes for a stellar finale.

Taqueria Guadalajara

Mexican ✗

4798 Mission St. (at Onondaga Ave.)

Phone:	415-469-5480	Lunch & dinner daily
Web:	N/A	
Prices:		

Mission Street has no end of authentic Mexican taquerias, but Guadalajara nearly always has a (short) line thanks to its flavorful meats, rich carnitas, substantial ceviches, and those huge burritos filled with sweet-salty *al pastor* pork. Tacos may be stuffed with smoky-tender strips of grilled chicken, chopped onion, and a splash of salsa verde. The salsa bar impresses with spicy and savory options, plus pickled vegetables. Cool the burn with an *agua fresca* or *horchata* that is creamy, cinnamony, and not overly sweet.
The vibe is flat-out casual, with counter service and murals depicting the Mexican countryside. The crowd is mostly locals and budget-minded bohemians, who stroll in or take the bus instead of battling the metered street parking.

Universal Cafe

Californian ✗

B1

2814 19th St. (bet. Bryant & Florida Sts.)

Phone: 415-821-4608   Lunch & dinner Tue – Sun
Web: www.universalcafe.net
Prices: $$

Set amid warehouses in a quieter more residential part of the Mission, this popular café draws large crowds for reinvented classics featuring pastas and local fish. However, brunch is the major draw, with lightly toasted English muffin sandwiches stacked with melted cheese, over-easy eggs, crisp bacon, and tasty avocado salsa. Then, indulge in sweet and firm little beignets with lightly whipped cream and tangy-sweet marmalade. Drinks are notable, including a spicy-tart ginger lemonade.

Chef/owner Leslie Carr Avalos prides herself on serving organic fare. Her open kitchen allows diners to watch the staff at work. The semi-industrial design is hip without being oppressive, and encourages lingering—if there isn't a line of people eyeing your table.

Look for the symbol 🛏
for a brilliant breakfast to
start your day off right.

Nob Hill
Chinatown · Russian Hill

In company with the Golden Gate Bridge and Alamo Square's "Painted Ladies," Nob Hill is San Francisco at its most iconic. Historic cable cars chug up the dramatic grades that lead to the top, with familiar chimes tinkling in the wind, and brass rails checking tourists who dare to lean out and take in the sights. The Powell-Mason line offers a peek at Alcatraz; and the California Street car stops right at the gilded doors of Grace Cathedral.

Once a stomping ground for Gold Rush industry titans, this urbane quarter—sometimes dubbed "Snob Hill"—echoes of mighty egos and ancestral riches. It is home to white-glove buildings, ladies who lunch, and opulent dining rooms. Named for the 1800s railroad magnates, the **Big 4** is a stately hermitage known for antique memorabilia and nostalgic chicken potpie. Extravagant **Top of the Mark** is beloved for bounteous brunches and panoramic vistas. **Bacchus Wine Bar** is an elegant and alluring Italian-style hideaway lauded for its stylized interiors and incredible wine, beer, and sake selections. For a total departure, kick back with a Mai Tai (purportedly invented at Oakland's Trader Vic's in 1944) at the **Tonga Room & Hurricane Bar**, a tiki spot with a live thunderstorm inside the Fairmont Hotel.

RUSSIAN HILL

Slightly downhill, toward Polk Street, the vibe mellows as heirloom splendor gives way to Russian Hill, chockablock with boutiques, dive bars, and casual eateries that cater to regular groups of mostly twenty-something singles. Good, affordable fare abounds at popular haunts like **Caffé Sapore** and **Street. Nick's Crispy Tacos**, the tacky taqueria turned nighttime disco, is a perennial favorite. And, for dessert, try the sinful chocolate earthquake from **Swensen's Ice Cream** flagship parlor, which is still *so* 1948. A handful of haute foodie shops fortuitously whet the palates of resident young professionals. **Cheese Plus** showcases more than 300 international cultures, artisan charcuterie, and chocolate. Across the street, **The Jug Shop** is a mecca for micro-brew beers and southern hemisphere wines. Dining at the eternally delicious and inexpensive **House of Nanking** is a rare experience. Don't bother ordering from the menu—the owner often takes menus out of diner's hands and orders for them.

CHINATOWN

For a change of pace, head to Chinatown, whose authentic markets, dim sum palaces, and souvenir emporiums spill down the eastern slope of Nob Hill in a wash of color and Cantonese characters. Here you'll find some of the city's finest and most crave-worthy barbecue pork buns at the area's oldest dim sum house, **Hang Ah Tea Room**, and a bevy of quirky must-sees. Fuel up on oven-fresh, creamy custard tarts at **Golden Gate Bakery**, but also save room for samples at **Golden Gate Fortune Cookie Company**, where you can watch the prophetic little

sweets in the making. The Mid-Autumn Moon Festival brings mooncakes, a traditional pastry stuffed with egg yolk and lotus seed paste. Gastronomes should unwind (and take home a taste of Chinatown) at the family-owned and operated Wok Shop for unique Asian cookware, linens, and tools. Their stock of rare products encompasses nearly every facet of Asian cooking.

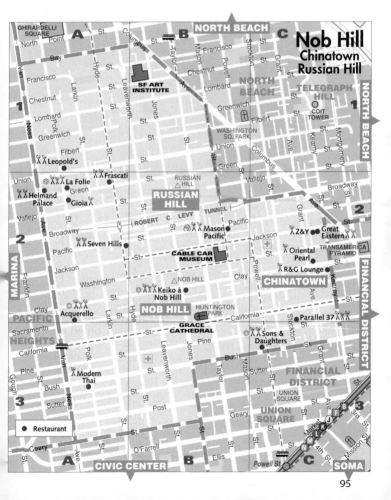

Acquerello

San Francisco ▶ Nob Hill

1722 Sacramento St. (bet. Polk St. & Van Ness Ave.)

Phone: 415-567-5432
Web: www.acquerello.com
Prices: $$$$

Dinner Tue – Sat

Daniel Morris

Acquerello's rather nondescript beige exterior belies its former life as a chapel. Yet once inside, the space is an arresting mix of vaulted ceilings, gold walls, and alcoves. The elegant and traditional chamber suits the sophisticated clientele, who are of a certain age and perfectly at home among old-school luxuries like the suited staff, crystal stemware, and formal service. The wine list is an honorable tome.

The variety of tasting and prix-fixe menus may be reliably classic, but seasonal ingredients and contemporary inspiration keep each course absolutely delicious. Begin with such delights as a soup combining tender coins of octopus, creamy diced potatoes, and garbanzo beans in smoked paprika broth with floral hints of basil. Then, move on to "baked potato" gnocchi that are caramelized on the outside, almost melting within, and served with morsels of outstanding golden brown sweetbreads in a pool of rich mushroom jus. Savor the Cusié cheese accented with mushroom crumble and chestnut-honey meringue, as a prelude to desserts like orange-vanilla panna cotta.

Just remember to save room for the mignardise cart laden with exquisite cookies, chocolates, lollipops, and caramels.

Frascati

Mediterranean XX

A2

1901 Hyde St. (at Green St.)

Phone: 415-928-1406
Web: www.frascatisf.com
Prices: $$

Dinner nightly

Frascati is one of Russian Hill's most desirable treasures. Named for a bucolic hilltop town overlooking Rome, this convivial haven boasts prime vistas of passing cable cars via comfortable tables by the front window. Those looking for more intimacy may prefer the romantic mezzanine with a pretty view of the dining room.

Speaking of which, the interior bursts with boisterous regulars who can be seen devouring the seasonal Mediterranean fare. Begin with Monterey Bay sardines brushed with Meyer lemon aïoli and chili oil; or sample a hearty plate of fresh pappardelle mixed with pork sugo and baby spinach. Other front-runners include maple leaf duck breast with herb spätzle, nicely cinched by vanilla bean panna cotta crowned with caramelized bananas.

Gioia

Pizza X

A2

2240 Polk St. (bet. Green & Vallejo Sts.)

Phone: 415-359-0971
Web: www.gioiapizzeria.com
Prices: $$

Lunch & dinner Tue — Sun

This San Francisco spot is the sibling to its very popular and petite Berkeley location. The décor is stylish and blends rustic with contemporary elements—a long marble dining counter, reclaimed barn wood wainscoting, and shiny metal lanterns and light fixtures. Guests can walk-in and order takeout... pizza by the slice? But the majority of diners choose to settle down amid this bustling scene of local business groups and cheery residents.

Start with a salad of arugula with almonds, pecorino, and Banyuls vinaigrette. Then it's pie time: a thin, chewy pizza slathered with *prosciutto cotto*, chili flakes, and minced garlic layered in tangy aged provolone; or thin-crust topped with savory sliced asparagus, red onion, clouds of ricotta, and melted pecorino.

Great Eastern

San Francisco ▲ Nob Hill

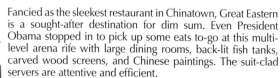

Chinese ✗✗

C2

649 Jackson St. (bet. Grant Ave. & Kearny St.)

Phone: 415-986-2500
Web: www.greateasternsf.com
Prices: ⊕⊕

Lunch & dinner daily

Fancied as the sleekest restaurant in Chinatown, Great Eastern is a sought-after destination for dim sum. Even President Obama stopped in to pick up some eats to-go at this multi-level arena rife with large dining rooms, back-lit fish tanks, carved wood screens, and Chinese paintings. The suit-clad servers are attentive and efficient.

And while dim sum may be where its capability lies, the à la carte menu is equally remarkable with dishes like crispy skinned half Peking duck strutting a silky fat layer and smoky meat, paired with steamed, fluffy buns—*hao chi*! Chicken sautéed with cashews in a fragrant garlic sauce is delectable; and you can finally enjoy your veggies with perfectly cooked Chinese broccoli glazed in a salty-and-smoky oyster sauce.

Helmand Palace

Afghan ✗✗

A2

2424 Van Ness Ave. (bet. Green & Union Sts.)

Phone: 415-345-0072
Web: www.helmandpalacesf.com
Prices: $$

Dinner nightly

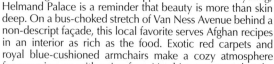

In a neighborhood where appearances are everything, Helmand Palace is a reminder that beauty is more than skin deep. On a bus-choked stretch of Van Ness Avenue behind a non-descript façade, this local favorite serves Afghan recipes in an interior as rich as the food. Exotic red carpets and royal blue-cushioned armchairs make a cozy atmosphere for warming up with spicy fare. Newbies can trust that the murals depicting Afghani life are a promise of authenticity.

Here meals begin with hearty oven-fresh bread served with a trio of dips, then go on to include traditional appetizers such as *kaddo*, baked pumpkin with spicy ground beef and yogurt-garlic sauce; or tasty *seek kabab*, a charbroiled leg of lamb with sautéed eggplant, tomato, and raisins.

98

Keiko à Nob Hill ✿

1250 Jones St. (at Clay St.)

Dinner Tue – Sun

Phone: 415-829-7141
Web: www.keikoanobhill.com
Prices: $$$$

Timothy Gordon

Perfectly discreet and easy to miss—just a small brass plaque marks the restaurant—Keiko à Nob Hill manages to be as opulent as it is intimate. The interior has that classy-clubby look of a bygone era, when big elegance trumped fussy accents, tablecloths knew no creases, and waiters cut a better suit. It is where wealthy people go when they want to dress up and (quietly) hit the town. The small number of tables keeps the mood comfortable.

The smart and skillful kitchen prepares a menu that is as luxurious as the surrounds, yet much more global in combining French, Californian, and Asian flavors. Every element plays a key role in the velvety cauliflower mousse with trout roe, scallops, sea-salty uni, and cherry blossom smoke. Then, savor an intense yet more traditional pea soup with mint, bacon, and *fromage blanc* mousse. A nugget of Colorado lamb might be encased in a layer of sausage, alongside eggplant gratin and a green disc of chrysanthemum powder.

Come dessert, smash through the delicate sugar tuile topping a mango-pineapple parfait with coconut mousse. The wine list may bring tears of joy (and fearful pricing), with particular respect to excellent Burgundy and American vintages.

La Folie

French ΧΧΧ

2316 Polk St. (bet. Green & Union Sts.)

Phone:	415-776-5577
Web:	www.lafolie.com
Prices:	$$$$

Dinner Mon – Sat

Dan Peek

Its name may mean "the folly," but a meal at Roland Passot's longstanding French gem has been a safe bet for many years. Timelessly understated, La Folie's curtained dining room features lofty ceilings, richly upholstered banquettes, and polished wood; the more casual lounge next door feels airy and open.

Classic French technique gets a California twist on Passot's menus, available in a variety of configurations (including a vegetarian option). Meals begin with a spread of canapés including rich foie gras bonbons, egg shells stuffed with mushroom fondue, and creamy salmon-mascarpone pinwheels. Then it's on to the main event with courses like warm pig's feet, sweetbreads, and lobster terrine over lentil salad; a duo of tender duck breast and rich leg confit with citrus, baby turnips, and passion fruit gastrique; or a warm Edam cheese soufflé with *fromage blanc* sorbet, bacon, and sesame tuile.

As is to be expected from an upscale French establishment, the wine list focuses on Gallic labels with a soupçon of Californian vintages. A sizable and gracious staff keeps treats coming between courses, resulting in a moderate and pleasantly romantic buzz among couples out for a special evening.

Leopold's

Austrian ✕✕

A1

2400 Polk St. (at Union St.)

Phone: 415-474-2000
Web: www.leopoldssf.com
Prices: $$

Lunch Sat – Sun
Dinner nightly

Beer lovers are saying *Prost*! to Leopold's, an authentic Austrian *gasthaus* that is the toast of the town. And it's no wonder: two- three- and five-liter beer steins and boots hold lots of liquid to cheers with. Word to the wise: non-diehards coming for the food should slip in before it gets too crowded. Reservations? *Nein*.

With Alpine décor and all manner of fried, cheesy, and meaty fare, Leopold's is an honest restaurant ideal for the genuinely hungry. Dinner might include rich *kasespatzle* gratin seasoned with fragrant nutmeg, garnished with crisp onions, and served with a warm cabbage and bacon salad; and the extra-hearty *choucroute garnie* platter loaded with smoky pork and bratwurst with sauerkraut and caraway-roasted potatoes.

Mason Pacific

American ✕✕

B2

1358 Mason St. (at Pacific Ave.)

Phone: 415-374-7185
Web: www.masonpacific.com
Prices: $$

Dinner Tue – Sun

Though it debuted in 2013, this smart American bistro is already the darling of Nob Hill with swarms of Teslas and Maseratis lining up at the valet station. The stylish occupants, from tech millionaires to white-haired society matrons, stream into the light-filled dining room where they angle for a seat at the semi-private banquette facing the street or in the front room at the marble bar.

The menu is prepared with skill and top-notch ingredients and includes a note-perfect fried chicken and caramelized Alaskan halibut with grated cauliflower and *peperoncini*. The burger, served on a pretzel bun with smoked tomato, is also a terrific choice. And while the friendly, smartly attired staff keeps the handful of tables moving, reservations are still a must.

Modern Thai

Thai

1247 Polk St. (at Bush St.)

Phone: 415-922-8424
Web: www.modernthaisf.com
Prices: $$

Lunch & dinner daily

Cheery flowers, greenery, and walls painted in shades of lime and raspberry make this spot look like a tropical oasis, complete with affordable lunch specials and flavorful Thai. Grab a seat on the enclosed porch (weather permitting) and check out the ample vegetarian offerings or specialties like pad Thai. Start with "golden bags," six deep-fried egg wrappers stuffed with a yellow curried mix of sweet potatoes, peas, and taro, served with refreshing cucumber salad; or crisp-fried calamari, tossed with fresh vegetables and peanuts in a dynamic chili-fish sauce. Craving a kick of spice? Request a hot sauce caddy, stocked with three fiery condiments made from different chilies.

Desserts venture into the less exotic, with pan-fried blueberry roti.

Oriental Pearl

Chinese

760 Clay St. (bet. Grant Ave. & Kearny St.)

Phone: 415-433-1817
Web: www.orientalpearlsf.com
Prices: $$

Lunch & dinner daily

Named to honor Hong Kong "The Pearl of the Orient," Oriental Pearl is more elegant than its Chinatown brethren: white tablecloths, intricately carved chairs, and polite servers make for a pleasant atmosphere. Street parking is at a premium, so park at Portsmouth Square Garage across the street.

This sparkling "pearl" offers an array of dim sum, à la carte, and set combo menus. Lauded as a signature for good reason, meatballs of minced chicken, mushrooms, and ham are wrapped in egg white crêpes and tied at the top with chive slivers—like tasty little beggar's purses. Wide, chewy *chow fun* are tossed with tender beef in a savory black pepper-black bean gravy; while flash-fried string beans with tofu doused in a chili-garlic sauce is a fab veggie option.

Parallel 37

Californian  𝗫𝗫𝗫

C2

600 Stockton St. (bet. California & Pine Sts.)

Phone: 415-773-6168

Lunch & dinner daily

Web: www.parallel37sf.com

Prices: $$$

The recently renovated dining room of The Ritz-Carlton has taken a more comfortable, brasserie-style turn but remains upscale with leather sofas and glowing walls. The menu is less classic French, with more of a contemporary farm-to-table philosophy and hints of Asian influence. Hotel guests and locals alike can be seen grabbing cocktails at the busy bar, while the adjoining dining room is slightly more sedate. The food traverses a range of culinary styles and influences, as in roasted Alaskan halibut with yuzu and stinging nettle flatbread; or sautéed lamb with chorizo and bamboo rice. The professional staff will happily guide you through selecting one of the innovative entrées and the perfect Napa wine. A tasting menu is available by request.

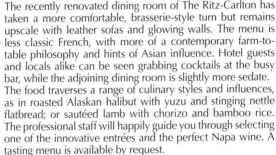

R & G Lounge

Chinese 𝗫

C2

631 Kearny St. (bet. Clay & Sacramento Sts.)

Phone: 415-982-7877

Lunch & dinner daily

Web: www.rnglounge.com

Prices: ⓔⓢ

R & G Lounge has been a longtime Chinatown fave for Cantonese food. The space is clean, while the service is a bit better than mediocre. Sure the décor is dated and the dropped ceiling of beige ribbons is rather strange, but really who's looking up when delicacies (like tender, falling-off-the-bone honey spare ribs glazed in a sweet and tangy sauce) await down, on your plate?

Tanks of fish signal fresh seafood and fittingly, their signature dish is salt & pepper crab. At lunch, the wood-paneled den downstairs is crammed with families and businessmen. Find them chowing on fresh mixed vegetables delicately stir-fried in garlic sauce; or lamb sautéed with leeks in a mildly-spiced, aromatic gravy of ginger and garlic, teamed with steamed *bao*.

Seven Hills

A2

Italian XX

1550 Hyde St. (at Pacific Ave.)

Phone: 415-775-1550
Web: www.sevenhillssf.com
Prices: $$

Dinner Tue – Sun

Shrouded by the rustling trees of Hyde Street and the ding-ding of the passing cable car, Seven Hills is an obscure Italian eatery that has become a local favorite. And how could locals not flock to this bambino-sized *ristorante* where a cozy vibe, jovial staff, and just four seats at the bar make Seven Hills a perfectly low-key neighborhood haunt.

Two petite wood-clad dining rooms host a consistent crowd where those in the know opt for pasta, the specialty of the house, in either half- or whole portions. Seasonal recipes might include delish scallop ravioli with sweet corn and English peas. Other delightfully unembellished fare may include seared calamari with tangy caponata to start, and house-made ricotta studded with candied pistachios to finish.

Z & Y

C2

Chinese X

655 Jackson St. (bet. Grant Ave. & Kearny St.)

Phone: 415-981-8988
Web: www.zandyrestaurant.com
Prices: $$

Lunch & dinner daily

This precious Chinatown pearl is loved and lauded for its bold-flavored, tasty Chinese food. Attention spice addicts: when Z & Y's menu indicates that a dish will be chili-hot, *trust* them—fiery flavors aren't toned down for gun shy American palates. By virtue of its tempting Chinese, this long and slender restaurant with tight-knit tables aglow with red Chinese lanterns, is forever packed.

Nailing the red-hot motif are brusque servers robed in red and carrying savory dishes like golden brown scallion pancakes sprinkled with sesame seeds; tender pork strips bathing in a garlic sauce pungent with dried Sichuan chilies; and Mongolian beef flavored with oyster and soy sauce. Also joining the fan faves is a deliciously sticky black sesame rice ball soup.

Sons & Daughters ✿

Contemporary XX

C3

708 Bush St. (bet. Mason & Powell Sts.)

Phone: 415-391-8311
Web: www.sonsanddaughterssf.com
Prices: $$$$

Dinner Wed – Sun

Rachel Garrison

A chic, modern crowd braves the less desirable trappings of the Tendernob for dinner in this unique and elegant space, where a young, hip staff does fine dining their way. Stroll past the tiny open kitchen in front and settle into a cushy brown leather chair; then try to guess which foods are pictured in the abstract black-and-white photos that adorn the walls.

A multi-course tasting menu (modifiable for vegetarians) is the sole option with contemporary plates like roasted beet salad with whipped, *vadouvan*-spiced goat cheese; buttery braised chanterelles over crispy potato *pavé*; and rare squab breast perfectly balanced with sweet Marcona almond butter and grapefruit. Throughout the meal, delicious house-made breads arrive in procession, from brioche to buckwheat toast, to a pretzel roll. Meyer lemon curd with grapefruit meringue, or dark chocolate ganache with mint and eucalyptus provide a satisfying conclusion.

Along the way, sips arrive from the carefully selected wine list, and are gracefully presented by a knowledgeable steward. Interesting serving pieces made of slate and cross-cut raw wood speak to the innovative vibe, as do the indie-rock soundtrack and tattooed chefs.

North Beach
Fisherman's Wharf · Telegraph Hill

Nestled between bustling Fisherman's Wharf and the steep slopes of Russian and Telegraph Hills, North Beach owes its lively nature to the Italian immigrants who settled here in the late 1800s. Many of these were fishermen from the Ligurian coast; the seafood stew they made on their boats evolved into the quintessential San Francisco treat, cioppino—a must-order in this district. Though Italians may no longer be in the majority here, dozens of pasta places, pizzerias, coffee shops, and bars in North Beach attest to their idea of the good life. At the annual North Beach Festival in mid-June, a celebrity pizza toss, Assisi Animal Blessings, and Arte di Gesso (chalk art) also nod and pay homage to the neighborhood's Italian heritage. **Pier 23 Cafe** remains a popular stop for tourists after a ferry to Alcatraz, or a walk along The Embarcadero.

Today the majority of North Beach's restaurants and bars lie along Columbus Avenue. Be sure to check out the quarter's Italian delis, like **Molinari**'s, whose homemade salami has been a local institution since 1896. Pair some imported meats and cheeses with a bottle of wine for a perfect picnic in nearby Washington Square Park. Hanging out in North Beach can be a full-time job, which is what attracted a ragtag array of beret-wearing poets to the area in the 1950s. These so-called beatniks—Allen Ginsberg and Jack Kerouac among them— were eventually driven out by

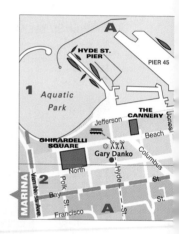

busloads of tourists. Bohemian spirits linger on at such landmarks as the City Lights bookstore and next door at **Vesuvio**, the original boho bar.

Feasting in Fisherman's Wharf

You won't find many locals here, but Fisherman's Wharf, the mile-long stretch of waterfront at the foot of Columbus Avenue, ranks as one of the city's most popular tourist attractions. It may teem with souvenir shops, street performers, and rides, but you should go if only to feast on a sourdough bread bowl filled with clam chowder, and fresh crabs cooked in huge steamers right on the street. Sample a piece of edible history at **Boudin Bakery**. This old-world respite has bloomed into a modern operation, complete with a museum and bakery tour; and yet, they still make their

B SAN FRANCISCO BAY **C**

D 1

PIER 41

PIER 39

PIER 43½

FISHERMAN'S WHARF

AQUARIUM OF THE BAY

The Embarcadero

Point

Bay St.

Taylor St.

Mason St.

Powell St.

Stockton St.

Kearny St.

PIER 29

SAN FRANCISCO BAY

● Restaurant

Francisco St.

Ave.

●Albona ⋇⋇

Chestnut St.

Grant St.

Stockton St.

LEVI'S PLAZA

St.

St.

Lombard St.

NORTH BEACH

TELEGRAPH HILL

Sansome St.

⋇2

Greenwich St.

⋇

COIT TOWER

Montgomery St.

Battery St.

WASHINGTON SQ. PARK ⋇⋇⋇●Park Tavern

Kearny St.

⋇⋇ Piperade

Filbert St.

⋇Trattoria Contadina ●Tony's Pizza Napoletana

⋇ Café Jacqueline

The Embarcadero

Union St.

⋇⋇ Rose Pistola

●Maykadeh ⋇ ⋇

Jones St.

Taylor St.

Mason St.

Powell St.

Columbus

Stockton St.

Green St.

St.

St.

Front St.

Davis St.

PIER 7

RUSSIAN HILL

△HILL

Vallejo St.

the house ⋇

Broadway

RUSSIAN HILL

Broadway

⋇⋇⋇Coi ⊛⊛

St.

⋇⋇⋇⋇

ROBERT C. LEVY TUNNEL

⊛⋇⋇Cotogna ●●Quince

⊛⋇⋇ St. Kokkari Estiatorio

3

Leavenworth St.

Pacific St.

Pacific Ave.

Grant Ave.

⋇⋇⋇●Roka Akor Jackson St.

Drumm St.

Washington St.

JACKSON SQUARE

EMBARCADERO PLAZA

Jackson St.

TRANSAMERICA PYRAMID

St.

EMBARCADERO CENTER

Washington St.

NOB HILL

Clay Ave.

CHINATOWN

FINANCIAL DISTRICT

Sacramento St.

NOB HILL

△NOB HILL

sourdough bread fresh every day, using the same mother first cultivated here from local wild yeast in 1849. Nearby, Ghirardelli Square preserves another taste of old San Francisco. This venerable chocolate company, founded by Domenico "Domingo" Ghirardelli in 1852, now flaunts its delectable wares at the noteworthy **Ghirardelli Ice Cream and Chocolate Manufactory**. While here, ogle the original chocolate manufacturing equipment while enjoying a rich hot fudge sundae. Don't leave without taking away some sweet memories in the form of their chocolate squares.

Albona

B2 Italian

545 Francisco St. (bet. Mason & Taylor Sts.)

Phone: 415-441-1040
Web: www.albonarestaurant.com
Prices: $$

Dinner Wed – Mon

This brightly painted mid-century bungalow is nestled on a street with high-rises. Inside, find a petite, cozy, and brasserie-like dining room outfitted with velvet curtains and effusive waiters donning traditional waistcoats. Photographs on the walls depict the Istrian village from which the restaurant takes both its name and cuisine inspiration: the focus here is on the peninsula's cooking, where classic Roman-Venetian styles meet Croatian influences.

The menu reveals delicious but somewhat unfamiliar dishes like pork *involtini* stuffed with sauerkraut and enhanced by preserved-fruit sauce; or cured sardines with raisins and pine nuts. While presentations aren't overly refined, it's the ultimate in comfort fare—deeply satisfying and very flavorful.

Café Jacqueline

C2 French

1454 Grant Ave. (bet. Green & Union Sts.)

Phone: 415-981-5565
Web: N/A
Prices: $$$

Dinner Wed – Sun

This petite bistro specializes in soufflés—and what incredibly light and flavorful creations they are. Her space may not dazzle with tables packed like sardines, but Café Jacqueline's faithful French treats certainly will.

Not ideal for large gatherings or groups-on-the-go (meals here may take hours), the café is patronized by those who have time on their hands—and delicious, fluffy soufflés on their mind. Start with the staple French onion soup, but with such a surfeit of savory soufflés on offer, it seems only right to follow suit with a towering chanterelle mushroom rich with Gruyère; or lobster soufflé that is at once decadent and fresh. Moving on—the warm dark chocolate is so plush and moist, you may wonder how you lived before it.

Coi ⚖⚖

🍴🍴

C3

373 Broadway (bet. Montgomery & Sansome Sts.)

Phone: 415-393-9000
Web: www.coirestaurant.com
Prices: $$$$

Dinner Tue – Sat

Dwight Eschliman

Coi's serene interior feels peacefully removed from the world, reflecting a Japanese aesthetic of muted colors, small wood-grain tables, and rice-paper screens casting a soft light overhead. The unique glazed and earthenware ceramics are of noteworthy beauty. The servers are flawless, effortless, and casually cool.

Chef Daniel Patterson's deft hand and creative intellect is clear throughout the very contemporary prix-fixe menu. To begin, sample an artistic dish of "earth and sea" combining tofu mousseline seasoned with sea water and bright orange steelhead trout roe, garnished with oxalis flowers. The "fried" egg is not actually fried; the yolk is cooked sous-vide, rolled in tempura, and placed on a bed of broccoli, cauliflower, and Brussels sprouts with smoked onions and herbs. Monterey Bay abalone is firm, fresh, and thinly shaved, then mixed with sautéed new onion and pea shoots.

For dessert, the whipped coconut is stark white and stunning, with smooth and creamy textures to complement the blood orange, olive oil, rhubarb, and oyster leaf garnishes. Spice cake is equally impressive, prepared as a mille-feuille layering thin rounds of date cake, yogurt, and sesame tuiles.

Cotogna ☺

C3

Italian ✕✕

490 Pacific Ave. (at Montgomery St.)

Phone: 415-775-8508
Web: www.cotognasf.com
Prices: $$

Lunch & dinner daily

Lack the funds to fork over for dinner at Quince? Head to Chef Michael Tusk's less expensive, but very tasty outpost just next door. Cotogna is a rustic eatery aimed at the Roman heart. Here you'll find straightforward, well-prepared fare such as salt-and-pepper Monterey squid over chopped *puntarelle* salad; pillowy beet *tortelloni* with poppy seeds in butter; and skirt steak with grilled radicchio and balsamic.

Grab a $10 glass of *vino* at the copper-topped bar and swirl while you spy the goings-on in the kitchen. Here find the pizza furnace and green enamel oven fired by almond wood where the staff labors over grilled meats and esoteric Neapolitan pies (like sea urchin and cauliflower). Take a seat at one of the communal tables for a quieter experience.

the house

C3

Asian ✕

1230 Grant Ave. (bet. Columbus Ave. & Vallejo St.)

Phone: 415-986-8612
Web: www.thehse.com
Prices: $$

Lunch Mon – Sat
Dinner nightly

This perennially popular, 20-year-old Asian bistro provides a welcome alternative to the Italian-heavy streets in North Beach. The décor is minimal with blonde wood tables and there's no menu, so listen closely to the efficient staff as they recite the bounties of the day. A versatile drinks list completes the enticing spread in addition to offering a happy reprieve to those who've endured a long wait for limited tables.

Dishes like delicately prepped scallops in saffron sauce, and crispy halibut tempura propped atop roasted cauliflower may vary by the day. But, a playful, fusion element remains a steady feature in all items including house-specialties, of which warm wasabi noodles topped with flank steak or teriyaki-glazed salmon are perfect examples.

Gary Danko 🏵

A1

800 North Point St. (at Hyde St.)

Dinner nightly

Phone: 415-749-2060
Web: www.garydanko.com
Prices: $$$$

San Francisco ▶ North Beach

Gary Danko

The blackened windows of this legendary restaurant near Fisherman's Wharf mean that only those lucky enough to dine here have seen those stately and private wood-paneled rooms. Nonetheless, Chef Danko is widely recognized as one of the city's greats. His French culinary chops are evident in dishes like a crispy, panko-crusted farm egg, its yolk adding richness to a bowl of creamy polenta with plump mushrooms. Yet his kitchen readily delves into more international flavors, like a Middle Eastern-inspired herb-crusted lamb loin with mouthwatering flavors of spicy *chermoula*, dates, and Israeli couscous.

The petite space is textbook-romantic, filled with flowers, starched linen, and couples celebrating special occasions. Gracious, old-school service adds to the classic appeal, as does an outstanding wine list boasting more than 12,000 bottles (and many half-bottles) from around the globe.

Customizable tastings allow diners to mix and match their own three- four- or five-course menus, ensuring that a meal here will satisfy every palate and price point. Whatever tasting you choose, don't miss the outstanding cheese plate heaped with artisanal *fromage*, plenty of walnut bread, and sweet grapes.

Kokkari Estiatorio

D3

Greek ✕✕

200 Jackson St. (at Front St.)

Phone: 415-981-0983
Web: www.kokkari.com
Prices: $$

Lunch Mon – Fri
Dinner nightly

Praise the Greek Gods as Kokkari is one of those places that consistently serves delicious food—no wonder this ample space is forever packed. Roaring fireplaces, wood accents, and iron light fixtures give the tavern an old-world feel that complements its fresh and flavorful carte.

In keeping with its spirit, warm servers cradle such exquisite Greek dishes as a mixed green salad mingling apple shavings, golden beets, and salty feta with oregano-infused vinaigrette; or large chunks of grilled yogurt- and herb-marinated chicken souvlaki and red bell peppers served with cool, creamy *tzatziki* and warm homemade pita strewn with herbs and sea salt. End with a filo shell filled with sweet semolina custard, topped with tangy blood orange segments.

Maykadeh

C2

Persian ✕✕

470 Green St. (bet. Grant Ave. & Kearny St.)

Phone: 415-362-8286
Web: www.maykadehrestaurant.com
Prices: $$

Lunch & dinner daily

Tucked on the inclines leading to Telegraph Hill, this Persian tavern can be a parking challenge for some, but those who've perfected their 90-degree skills will be rewarded with a Middle Eastern oasis in pasta-heavy Little Italy. For 20 years, families have gathered at Maykadeh's linen-lined tables for warm flatbreads spread with a classic mix of onion, basil, and feta; followed by juicy chicken kebabs; lamb and beef skewers; or hearty lamb stew beside fragrant saffron-infused basmati rice.

With tunes and a crowd to match, the aura here is homey featuring dreamy lighting and red roses atop each table. Sour chicken with roasted walnuts and pomegranate may sound esoteric to some palates, but don't fret—like Maykadeh itself, it's surely worth trying.

Park Tavern

American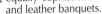

C2

1652 Stockton St. (bet. Filbert & Union Sts.)

Phone: 415-989-7300
Web: www.parktavernsf.com
Prices: $$$

Lunch Fri – Sun
Dinner nightly

From the team behind Marlowe and newcomer The Cavalier in SoMa, Park Tavern is a welcome respite from the bustle of North Beach. The see-and-be-scene crowd is almost always packed with affluent locals, young professionals, and power brokers plus their trophy wives. The voluminous tavern is equally sophisticated with beamed ceilings, mosaic floors, and leather banquets.

Start with appetizers like *lardo*-wrapped smoked prawns with remoulade; or try some Brussels sprouts chips. Tender Cornish game hen is all heart and soul brined in truffle stock and presented whole on the stand surrounded by wilted spinach and peewee potatoes. A successful combo of wood fire-roasted strawberry and rhubarb shortcake with vanilla ice cream completes this tasty experience.

Piperade

Basque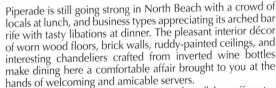

D2

1015 Battery St. (bet. Green & Union Sts.)

Phone: 415-391-2555
Web: www.piperade.com
Prices: $$

Lunch Mon – Fri
Dinner Mon – Sat

Piperade is still going strong in North Beach with a crowd of locals at lunch, and business types appreciating its arched bar rife with tasty libations at dinner. The pleasant interior décor of worn wood floors, brick walls, ruddy-painted ceilings, and interesting chandeliers crafted from inverted wine bottles make dining here a comfortable affair brought to you at the hands of welcoming and amicable servers.

The Basque menu may reveal items such as flaky puff pastry topped with a mélange of wild mushrooms and fresh thyme; and a juicy herb-marinated roasted rack of lamb joined with garlicky lamb sausage and a fennel bulb. For a special finale, plunge into a *gâteau Basque*—creamy custard surrounded by puff pastry and covered with plump Amarena cherries.

Quince ✿ ✿

C3

Italian

470 Pacific Ave. (bet. Montgomery & Sansome Sts.)

Phone: 415-775-8500

Web: www.quincerestaurant.com

Prices: $$$$

Dinner Mon – Sat

Marion Brenner

Notably welcoming and warm, Quince is upscale yet conveys a distinct northern Californian personality. The airy and attractive room features brick walls and elegant everything, yet nothing is stuffy or heavy. There are no poseurs or loud crowds. Everyone is just happy to be here and celebrating a special occasion, business deal, or vacation. This sounds simple, but Quince has attained an easy grace that other restaurants don't realize they lack.

The menu favors a more contemporary Italian cuisine, which is creative and delicious. The nightly prix-fixe may begin with a slow-cooked farm egg in a complex vegetable broth with seasonal accents like pristine micro-turnips, shaved asparagus, and bits of paper-thin bacon. This might be followed by perfectly cooked pasta like *casoncelli* with roasted, shaved, and blanched asparagus in brown butter; or house-made *strichetti* in a powerfully reduced squab sauce with shredded loin, truffles, and *Parmigiano Reggiano*.

Finish with an ambitious and modern sweet, like a rectangular *millefoglie* layering chocolate cake and mousse with pistachios, alongside a scoop of intense pistachio ice cream with lemon confit, crumbled honeycomb, and toasted nuts.

Roka Akor

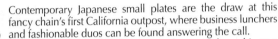 Japanese

C3

801 Montgomery St. (at Jackson St.)

Phone: 415-362-8887
Web: www.rokaakor.com
Prices: $$$

Lunch Mon – Fri
Dinner nightly

Contemporary Japanese small plates are the draw at this fancy chain's first California outpost, where business lunchers and fashionable duos can be found answering the call.

Whether diners are craving an omakase, steak, sushi, or a snack with cocktails, there's something for everyone on their vast menu. From crunchy chicken *karaage* to *robata*-grilled black-cod skewers and meaty tiger prawns, flavors are terrific and consistent. Sleek and retro, the décor emphasizes soothing blonde woods amid this noisy space. The downstairs lounge offers a darker, sexier vibe. And while this address has housed several restaurants over the years, Roka Akor will hopefully be the last tenant for a while given their extensive, innovative, and very thrilling array of items.

Rose Pistola

 Italian

C2

532 Columbus Ave. (bet. Green & Union Sts.)

Phone: 415-399-0499
Web: www.rosepistolasf.com
Prices: $$$

Lunch & dinner daily

Settle into classy and comfy Rose Pistola to relish a menu inspired by North Beach's original Northern Italian (Ligurian) residents. The wood-fired oven plus sleek open kitchen run the length of the dining room, whereas cheery yellow walls and friendly service add to the warmth of this diner.

The menu is skewed towards seafood featuring products from independent farmers and fishermen. Patrons come in droves to revel in flavorful seafood-stuffed calamari set upon a tomato-rich *puttanesca*. Chicken *al mattone* is grilled under a brick and served tender and moist with a dollop of shallot-and herb-butter. Pair this with deep-fried potato wedges infused with Marash chile and...smile.

Dog owners favor the table-lined sidewalk for sneaking focaccia to Fido.

Tony's Pizza Napoletana

Pizza ✗

1570 Stockton St. (at Union St.)

Phone: 415-835-9888
Web: www.tonyspizzanapoletana.com
Prices: $$

Lunch & dinner Wed – Sun

Tony's is a local institution that churns out a large menu of Neapolitan- Sicilian- and American-style pizzas. It is also well liked by all who flock here—not just for the pizza, but also for the buzzing social scene. You may think you've done well by arriving early, yet find herds waiting for a coveted seat here.

The bar is fair game and flanked by crowds hungry for the prized Margherita, a wood-fired crust slathered with San Marzano tomatoes, mozzarella, and basil. Tony's boasts a pizza for every palate, so come with friends to sample selections like the coal-fired New Yorker (pepperoni, sausage, and ricotta); or Californian style: "Fear and Loathing" with tamarind-glazed pork, jalapeños, and agave.

Deep-dish sibling Capós is equally beloved.

Trattoria Contadina

Italian ✗

1800 Mason St. (at Union St.)

Phone: 415-982-5728
Web: www.trattoriacontadina.com
Prices: $$

Lunch Sat – Sun
Dinner nightly

This old-school charmer dispenses Italian-American dishes in a quaint trattoria donning a faux-balcony overhead. Rife with a nostalgic vibe (framed photos of celebs hang throughout), it's no wonder that this homey tavern has such a loyal following. But, don't be surprised if the occasional visitor wanders in looking for an escape from the Italian tourist traps nearby.

The rustic menu is concise, but the portions are hearty. Start with *rigatoncelli* swirled with caramelized pancetta, porcini mushrooms, and sun-dried tomatoes in a tomato-cream sauce; before tucking into a juicy chicken breast covered with smoked mozzarella, prosciutto shavings, and served in a pool of Madeira wine sauce. Still need a drop of sweet? The lemon cheesecake is exemplary.

COLVMBVS DISI

Richmond & Sunset

Here in the otherworldly outer reaches of San Francisco, the foggy sea washes up to the historic Cliff House and Sutro Baths. In spring, cherry blossoms blush at the breeze in gorgeous Golden Gate Park; and whimsical topiaries wink at pastel row houses in need of fresh paint. Residents seem inspired by a sense of Zen not quite found elsewhere in town, whether you happen upon a Japanese sushi chef or a Sunset surfer dude. A melting pot of settlers forms the culinary complexion of this quiet though urban pocket. Find them lined up for an excellent selection of meats, smoked delicacies, sausages, pickles, sauerkraut, and other European specialty ingredients at **Seakor Polish Delicatessen and Sausage Factory**. Nearby, the steam wafting from bowls of piping hot *pho* is nearly as thick as the marine layer, while many of the neighborhoods' western accents hail from across the pond.

New Chinatown

The Richmond District, however, has earned the nickname "New Chinatown" for a reason. A big exposition for the adventurous cook, Clement Street bursts with cramped sidewalk markets where clusters of bananas sway from the awnings and the spices and produce are as vibrant as the nearby **Japanese Tea Garden** in bloom. While the Bay Area mantra "eat local" doesn't really

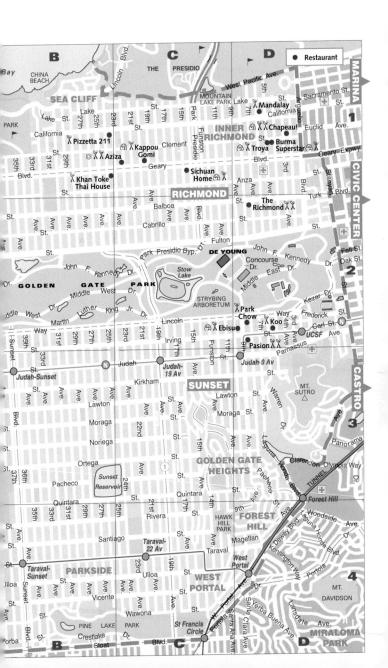

B   Bay   CHINA BEACH

THE PRESIDIO   **C**

D   ● Restaurant

MARINA

SEA CLIFF

PARK ►

Lake   St.   27th   25th

California

Lake   St.   23rd   21st   19th   17th   15th

MOUNTAIN LAKE PARK   Park   11th

West Pacific Ave.

Lake   St.   7th   5th

Sacramento St.

Arguello

✕ Mandalay

Euclid   Ave.

35th   33rd   31st   29th

Blvd.

✕ Pizzetta 211

✕✕ Aziza

✕ Kappou Gomi

Clement

INNER RICHMOND

✕ Chapeau!

California

Presidio

St.

✕ Troya

Burma Superstar

Geary   Expwy.

St.

✕ Khan Toke Thai House

Geary

Funston

St.

Ave.

Sichuan Home

Anza

3rd

Slanyan   Blvd.

Turk   Blvd.

CIVIC CENTER

RICHMOND

St.

Ave.   St.   Ave.   St.   Ave.

Balboa

The Richmond ✕✕

Ave.

Cabrillo

Blvd.

St.

Ave.

Fulton

Ave.

St.

Park Presidio Byp.

Dr.

John   F.

DE YOUNG

Concourse

Kennedy

Oak St.

Fell St.

2

GOLDEN   GATE   PARK

John   F.   Kennedy   Dr.

Middle   West   Dr.

Stow Lake

Dr.

East

Middle

Kezar Dr.

Middle   West

Luther   King   Jr.   Dr.

STRYBING ARBORETUM

Way

Frederick

3rd

Carl St.

Martin

Lincoln

Way

✕ Park Chow

✕ Koo

UCSF

Way   31st   29th   27th   25th   23rd   21st   19th   17th   15th

Irving

✕ Ebisu

St.

3rd

Ave.

Parnassus

Funston

11th

✕✕ Pasion

CASTRO

35th   33rd

St.

Sunset

Judah-Sunset

Judah

Judah-19 Av

Judah-9 Av

St.

MT. SUTRO △

3

Kirkham

Lawton

SUNSET

Lawton   St.

Warren

Ave.

Ave.   Ave.   Ave.   22nd

Moraga

Moraga   St.

Laguna

Dr.

Blvd.

Noriega

St.

15th

Honda

Panorama

37th   36th

Ortega

Sunset Reservoir

24th

GOLDEN GATE HEIGHTS

Pacheco

Clarendon   Olympia Way

St.

Pacheco

Quintara

St.

21st

Quintara

14th

TUNNEL

Blvd.

35th   33rd   31st   29th   27th   25th

Rivera

9th

HAWK HILL PARK

FOREST HILL

Forest Hill

Woodside   Ave.

St.   Ave.

Santiago

Taraval-22 Av

23rd

Ulloa

19th

Magellan

St.

Taraval

West Portal

Kensington Way

Dewey Blvd.

Laguna Honda Blvd.

Portola

Dr.

4

Taraval-Sunset

PARKSIDE

Ave.   St.   Ave.

Vicente

WEST PORTAL

St.

Mt.

Portola

Dr.

Santa Ana Ave.

Yerba Buena Ave.

Lansdale   Ave.

MT. DAVIDSON

Jiloa   Sunset   St.

Wawona

PINE LAKE PARK

St Francis Circle

Santa Clara Ave.

Portola

MIRALOMA PARK

Yorba   Blvd.

Crestlake   Dr.

Sloat   Blvd.

B   **C**   **D**

apply here, sundry international goods abound—think kimchi, tamarind, eel, live fish, and pork buns for less than a buck. Curious foodies find global delicacies: this is *the* place to source that 100-year-old egg. A gathering place for sea lovers, **Outerlands** is perfect when in need of warmth, food, shelter, and "community." Here, there is a mom-and-pop joint for every corner and culture. The décor is nothing to write home about and, at times, feels downright seedy, but really, you're here for the cuisine, which is usually authentic: Korean barbecue at **Brother's Restaurant**; Burmese at **B Star Bar**; *siu mai* at **Shanghai Dumpling King** and **Good Luck Dim Sum**. Not to mention a thrilling offering of tequila and mescal at **Tommy's Mexican Restaurant**. For a sip that refreshes, crowds collect at family-owned **Aroma Tea Shop**. This little gem features such exclusive, custom blends of individually-sourced teas from around the world. The owners even encourage free tea tastings. For young kids out on the late night, Hong Kong–style delights can be found at **Kowloon Tong Dessert Cafe**.

SUNSET

A touch more gentrified than neighboring Richmond, Sunset—once a heap of sand dunes—retains a small-town vibe that's groovy around the edges. In the early morning, locals line up for fresh bread and pastries at **Arizmendi Bakery**, then wash down their scones at the **Beanery** around the corner. Asian-devotees flock to **Izakaya Sozai** for their gratifying yakitori specialties, sashimi, and other faithful treats. Tourists taking in the sights at the de Young Museum or the Academy of Sciences might also choose to linger over lunch at **Academy Café** for their slow-cooked specials, crunchy tacos, or pasta platters. If tacos are not your thing, find more delicious Mexican treats like tortas loaded with flavorful meats, beans, cheese, avocado, and onions at the humble **La Fonda** on Irving Street. Finally, don't miss dinner at **The Moss Room**, boasting a plethora of unique and delicious dishes made with local, seasonal, and healthy ingredients. Speaking of delicious preparations, **San Tung** on Irving Street has amassed a cult following of locals who seem more than happy to wait in line for their famously crispy dry fried chicken wings. Meanwhile, residents in the Outer Sunset who aren't in the mood for long lines and endless lingering do not have to worry about making it to the local farmer's market. **Noriega Produce** lives just around the corner and is an excellent bazaar for fresh, seasonal, and organic produce. Of course, no regal repast is complete without some sweet. **Holy Gelato!** is a quirky shop that sells coffee, teas, as well as the namesake gelato in a wide range of interesting flavors like crème brûlée, goat cheese, and honey lavender. Keep your sweet tooth satiated with a dab of Asian kitsch: **Polly Ann Ice Cream** has served such flavors as durian, jasmine tea, and taro for years.

Aziza ✿

Moroccan 🍴🍴

C1

5800 Geary Blvd. (at 22nd Ave.)

Phone: 415-752-2222

Web: www.aziza-sf.com

Prices: $$$

Dinner Wed – Mon

Eric Wolfinger & Kelly Puleio

Far in the foggy reaches of the Outer Richmond, Mourad Lahlou's contemporary Moroccan restaurant continues to draw crowds to its exotic dining room, where intricate wooden tables, red glass chandeliers, and Moorish archways contribute to a casual, yet sensual dining experience.

Whether you opt for an à la carte affair or the tasting menu, Aziza's creations surprise and thrill—from the spherified Castelvetrano olive that may begin a meal to inventive mains like sous-vide duck over potato and chard with spiced granola crumble. Confits like lamb placed atop baby artichokes, sweet dates, garlic, and ground pistachio, or the famous duck *basteeya* with plum sauce have known to cause swooning. A concise wine list has known to give way to such artistic concoctions like vodka infused with strawberries and Fresno chili.

Desserts are a highlight and include a black currant curd with fennel meringue and vanilla mousse; or spongy semolina cake with a coffee reduction and sesame ganache. Sharply dressed servers offer expert descriptions of each dish with a grace and ease that reflects the stellar kitchen. Be sure to allow extra time for street parking or valet in this residential area.

Burma Superstar 🐶

D1

309 Clement St. (bet. 4th & 5th Aves.)

Phone: 415-387-2147
Web: www.burmasuperstar.com
Prices: 💰💰

Lunch & dinner daily

  ♿

Any foodie worth their cilantro in San Francisco has made the trek to Clement Street to jot their name on a clipboard and wait it out at Burma Superstar, the now cult classic with everything going for it. Seriously, Chinatown restaurants wish they were this cool.

The massive menu wants for large parties that like to share—narrowing down the options can be a bit of a task. Have faith, an über-friendly staff is on hand to help. You'll find a mix of Asian flavors, but seek out the genuine Burmese recipes noted by asterisks on the menu. Mild-mannered fare includes a tea leaf salad with roasted peanuts and fish sauce. The star of Superstar is the *mohinga*—a divine noodle soup with ground catfish and Asian veggies spiked with lemon and lemongrass.

Chapeau! 🐶

D1

126 Clement St. (bet. 2nd & 3rd Aves.)

Phone: 415-750-9787
Web: www.chapeausf.com
Prices: $$

Dinner Tue – Sat

  ♿

For an oh-so-French experience on Asian food-centric Clement, denizens head to Philippe Gardelle's authentic bistro, where tightly spaced tables and paintings of the titular hats create a convivial atmosphere. Packed with regulars receiving *bisous* from the chef, Chapeau is warm and generous, a vibe that's aided by its strong Gallic wine list.

Dishes are traditional with a bit of Californian flair, like fingerling potato chips in a frisée and duck confit salad or salted-caramel ice cream that tops the *pain perdu*. The cassoulet, wholesome with braised lamb, rich with smoky sausage, and earthy with white beans, is perfect for a foggy night in the Avenues. Come before 6:00 P.M. for the $30 early bird prix-fixe, or create your own from their many set menus.

Ebisu

D2

Japanese ✗

1283 9th Ave. (at Irving St.)

Phone: 415-566-1770
Web: www.ebisusushi.com
Prices: 💰💰

Lunch & dinner Tue – Sun

For wholly unauthentic but wonderfully satisfying sushi, locals have headed to Steve and Koko Fujii's neighborhood gem for over thirty years. The kitchen routinely gets creative with quirkily named rolls like Hanukkah, Potato Bug, and Tootsie Roll; while purists select from the daily rotating nigiri and sashimi. Be sure to check all the chalkboards, lest you miss one of the several specials like live scallop, *mochiko*-crusted sand dabs, or steamed monkfish liver.

The sleek wood-heavy space is very contemporary, and well-chosen but less expensive sake samplers liven up the atmosphere. (There's also a premium list, with premium prices.)

Travelers should also note their location in SFO Terminal G, and sister noodle spot, Hotei, housed across the street.

Kappou Gomi 😊

C1

Japanese ✗

5524 Geary Blvd. (bet. 19th & 20th Aves.)

Phone: 415-221-5353
Web: N/A
Prices: $$

Dinner Tue – Sun

Kappou Gomi feels a world away from the city's popular Japanese eateries and, as a sign in the window makes clear, seekers of bento boxes and trendy maki need not apply. This is one of San Francisco's rare *kappou* restaurants, which specializes in more delicate and authentic food.

The small, subdued space features an extensive menu organized by ingredients and intricate preparations that draw a house full of Japanese diners. Look for such exotic dishes as *namayuba*, a salad of fresh favas in creamy *yuba*; raw *tai* with pickled celery in chrysanthemum blossom dressing; and whole *aji tataki*. Once you've finished the fillets, the kitchen will deep-fry the head, bones, and tail for a crunchy finish. You won't find that at your local sushi hot spot!

Khan Toke Thai House

Thai

B1

5937 Geary Blvd. (bet. 23rd & 24th Aves.)

Phone: 415-668-6654

Web: N/A

Prices:

Lunch & dinner daily

 Word on the street is that Khan Toke offers *the* most unique Thai in SF. Surely this isn't a stretch given that guests relinquish their shoes at the door as is customary; and the "House's" décor screams authenticity by way of low carved tables frilled with diners seated on floor cushions, dangling their legs in sunken wells beneath. Wood paneling and carvings adorn the walls and faithful artifacts complete the exotic backdrop. In the same vein, diners can look forward to classic, shareable fare like *sur rong hai* (deliciously tender beef tips marinated in tamarind and finished with cilantro); *gaeng kheaw wan* (spicy green chicken curry with potatoes, sweet basil, and lush coconut); and *moo ga prou* (pork sautéed with scallions and splashed with chili sauce).

Koo

D2

Japanese

408 Irving St. (bet. 5th & 6th Aves.)

Phone: 415-731-7077

Web: www.sushikoo.com

Prices: $$

Dinner Tue – Sun

Koo is praised and preferred for its delicate tempura and pristine nigiri, but this local darling also advertises an array of maki which, although mighty innovative, are created for an American palate. Enter the pleasant wood-trimmed dining room, dotted with tight-knit tables and hints of classic Japanese architecture, to find a cool Richmond set engrossed in their traditional nightly specials.

Take your cue from them, and order off of the list of fresh fish before the droves in line deplete such specials as *saba tataki*, thin slices of mackerel dressed with scallion and ponzu; top-notch nigiri topped with expertly cut and sourced fish; and an U2 roll filled with lacy shrimp tempura, creamy avocado, and crowned with spicy tuna and tobiko beads.

Mandalay

Burmese

D1

4348 California St. (bet. 5th & 6th Aves.)

Phone:	415-386-3895	Lunch & dinner daily
Web:	www.mandalaysf.com	
Prices:		

A block from the hustle and bustle of Clement Street, this long-running single room flaunting various Burmese influences provides a quieter alternative to its jam-packed neighbors. Though the '70s-style décor is a bit worn-out, you'll gain renewed energy from the earnest staff dressed in classic sarongs who eagerly attend to a spate of regulars. Beer and wine are available, but don't count out a ginger-mint lemonade or iced tea with condensed milk.

Steer clear of the Chinese dishes and dive straight into a pickled ginger salad with toasted lentil seeds; followed by the nation's favorite food—*mohinga*—ground catfish chowder floating noodles, fried onions, and dried chilies; or *nan gyi dok*, round rice noodles paired with spicy coconut chicken curry.

Old Mandarin Islamic

Chinese

A4

3132 Vicente St. (bet. 42nd & 43rd Aves.)

Phone:	415-564-3481	Lunch Fri – Mon & Wed
Web:	N/A	Dinner nightly
Prices:		

At first glance, Old Mandarin Islamic may seem like a generic Chinese mainstay with a no-frills décor of carpeted floors and mirrored walls. With further scrutiny, you will find that it is in fact anything but average. This little sanctum dedicates itself to Halal Chinese food, following the Islamic dietary code, yet there is no lack of flavor in these boldly seasoned and truly delicious Mandarin dishes.

Lamb is clearly a favorite here and plays the lead in their signature stir-fry in hot oil with cumin seeds and fresh chili paste. True spice-heads will relish the extremely hot pepper chicken with pickled chilies, garlic, and scallions; while flour dumplings sautéed with vegetables in silky garlic sauce are uniquely chewy and deeply flavored.

Park Chow

D2

1240 9th Ave. (bet. Irving St. & Lincoln Way)

Phone: 415-665-9912   Lunch & dinner daily
Web: www.chowfoodbar.com
Prices: $$

Welcome to Park Chow, the inner Sunset neighborhood joint where you can truly have it your way. In the mood for spicy Thai noodles tossed with cilantro and peanuts? You got it. Wild mushroom *pizzette* with chewy crust and thyme? Sure thing. Pork chops, deviled eggs, and home-baked coconut cream pie? (You get the picture.)

With such a diverse menu and an equally eclectic staff, Park Chow succeeds at pleasing everyone. A crackling fire warms the homey, two-story spot where a retractable roof lets the sunshine in. Daily sandwiches come with heartwarming soup or fries and healthy salads are bountiful. There's even a menu of pint-sized burgers and chicken strips for the kiddos to fuel up before a walk in Golden Gate Park, just a block away.

Pasion

D2

737 Irving St. (bet. 8th & 9th Aves.)

Phone: 415-742-5727   Lunch & dinner daily
Web: www.pasionsf.com
Prices: $$

In a neighborhood loved for authentic international flavors, Pasion is causing a stir with Latin American ingredients and an ambience as fiery as the food. But while the name suggests a sultry vibe, couples seeking romance may be met with a boisterous after-work scene: squeeze into the bar for an alluring drink and get ready to make a night of it. Luckily, the kitchen has just the thing to pair with that pisco sour.

Helmed by Chef/owner Jose Calvo-Perez of the popular Peruvian restaurant Fresca, Pasion serves zesty ceviches alongside more creative items. Belly up to bold lamb *albondigas* with Manchego cheese and chilies in a savory foie gras broth, or a double-cut pork chop in mango-cilantro sauce. Duck confit empanadas are ideal for sharing at the bar.

Pizzetta 211

 Pizza

 B1

211 23rd Ave. (at California St.)

Phone: 415-379-9880

Web: www.pizzetta211.com

Prices: $$

Lunch & dinner daily

 This shoebox-sized pizzeria may reside in the far reaches of the Outer Richmond, but it's easily identifiable by the crowds hovering on the sidewalk to score a table. Once inside, you'll be greeted by *pizzaiolos* throwing pies in the tiny exhibition kitchen—ask for a counter seat to get a better view.

The thin, chewy, blistered *pizzettas* each serve one, making it easy to share several varieties. Weekly specials utilize ingredients like seasonal produce, house-made sausage, and fresh farm eggs, while standbys include a pie topped with wild arugula, creamy mascarpone, and San Marzano tomato sauce. Whatever you do, arrive early: once the kitchen's out of dough, they close for the day, and the omnipresent lines mean the goods never last too long.

The Richmond

American

D2

615 Balboa St. (bet. 7th & 8th Aves.)

Phone: 415-379-8988

Web: www.therichmondsf.com

Prices: $$

Dinner Mon – Sat

Its far-flung locale makes quaint and unassuming The Richmond a no-brainer for neighborhood types, but John and Thu Ha's thoughtful cuisine puts the restaurant on the map for any SF foodie seeking fine dining on a dime.

After visiting the de Young Museum or Academy of Sciences in Golden Gate Park a few blocks south, head to The Richmond for a five-course tasting menu for less than $50. À la carte offerings are available for those who prefer to steer their own course, including crab cakes with smooth avocado purée or poached yellowfin tuna. A highball of coffee semifreddo is a sweet and speedy cap to the meal. Pine wine crates that double as wall panels and bar tops remind of the rewards of dining here: good wines by the glass start around $7.

Sichuan Home 😊

C1

5037 Geary Blvd. (bet. 14th & 15th Aves.)

Phone: 415-221-3288
Web: N/A
Prices: $$

Lunch & dinner daily

The snug Sichuan Home lures diners far and wide to its bright, clean room with walls covered in shellacked wood panels and shiny mirrors. Décor aside, it's really all about their superb range of Sichuan food. Above the tables, find such smart accents as framed photos and descriptions of some of their more prized items.

A sampling should include tender, bone-in rabbit with scallions, peanuts, and a perfect dab of scorching hot peppercorns, cooled down by pickled cabbage bathed in rice wine vinegar and star anise. Dried red chilies are the star in a savory, aromatic composition of crispy fried string beans with tender, flavorful ground pork; while an enormous and cracklin' hot Dungeness crab sautéed with garlic and ginger is festive and very tasty.

Sutro's

A1

1090 Point Lobos Ave. (at Ocean Beach)

Phone: 415-386-3330
Web: www.cliffhouse.com
Prices: $$$

Lunch & dinner daily

Care to dine while gazing at the glorious Pacific? Make your way to Sutro's during daylight hours and snag any seat—tables are arranged to face a serene wall of windows, offering stunning views of the ocean. Housed on the lower level of the Cliff House, reservations are necessary here, so plan in advance. Dine on Dungeness crab cakes generously filled with fresh meat, over Cara Cara oranges and shaved fennel salad dressed in tangy vinaigrette; or pistachio-crusted scallops and orange-glazed pork belly with parsnip purée, butternut squash, and red wine syrup.

Be sure to save room for one (or two) of the outstanding desserts, as in the divinely rich butterscotch *pot de crème* garnished with a lacey and buttery tuile, infused with *garam masala*.

Troya

Mediterranean 🍴

D1

349 Clement St. (at 5th Ave.)

Phone: 415-379-6000

Web: www.troyasf.com

Prices: $$

Lunch & dinner daily

♿

If it weren't for the Asian supermarkets just outside, you could be forgiven for thinking you were in the Mediterranean upon arriving at delightful Troya with its tiled terra-cotta floors and gently worn wooden furniture. Neighborhood regulars are cheerfully greeted by a squadron of swift yet very friendly waiters, who bustle by patrons as the aromas of rich spices fill the room.

The vibrant Turkish food includes tender, almost pearl-like *manti* dressed in paprika-infused yogurt; crisp flatbreads topped with an aromatic blend of ground beef, lamb, and tomato; gently fried zucchini cakes; juicy kebabs; as well as lighter wraps and salads for lunch. Meze like plump dolmas and creamy hummus are a great addition to that late-afternoon glass of wine.

Bib Gourmand 🙂
indicates our inspectors'
favorites for good value.

SoMa

Peek behind the unassuming doors of the often-gritty façades prevalent in SoMa, the neighborhood South of Market, and discover a trove of creative talent. While you won't find a flood of sidewalk cafés and storefronts ubiquitous to more obviously charming enclaves, SoMa divulges gobs of riches (from artistic diamonds in the rough to megawatt culinary gems) for the tenacious urban treasure seeker.

Residential Mix

A diverse stomping ground that defies definition at every corner, SoMa is often labeled "industrial" for its hodgepodge of converted warehouse lofts. Additionally, with a mixed troupe of artists, photographers, architects, dancers, and designers now occupying much of SoMa's post-industrial real estate, you might also call it "artsy." In reality, dynamic SoMa wears many faces: youths in concert tees navigate their skateboards around the pitfalls of constant construction, fueled by "Gibraltars" from cult classic **Blue Bottle Cafe**. Sports fans of a different sort converge for Giants baseball and sandwiches at **Crazy Crab'z** in AT&T Park. In the Sixth Street Corridor, an immigrant population enjoys tastes of home at such authentic dives as **Tu Lan**, the Vietnamese hole-in-the-wall also favored by the late Julia Child. Just blocks away, a towering crop of luxury condominiums draws a trendy yuppie set keen to scoop up modern European furnishings at the SF Design Center and dine at equally slick restaurants—think of **Roe**, which doubles as an after-hours nightclub.

Arts and Eats

Since SoMa is perhaps most notable for its arts scene, this nook is also home to the San Francisco Museum of Modern Art, countless galleries, Yerba Buena Center for the Arts, and the unique Daniel Libeskind-designed Contemporary Jewish Museum. Naturally, neighborhood foodies crave stylish culinary experiences to match their well-rounded worlds. Art and design play a key role in the district's most distinctive dining and nightlife venues; and, the neighborhood is fast welcoming new and avant-garde restaurant concepts. Not far from the Jewish Museum, is **Mint Plaza**—step into this charming gathering spot for a bite, perhaps a respite, or to simply read a book. Post-dinner, art evangelists hit **111 Minna**, a gallery turned late-night DJ bar, or the chic wine lounge **Press Club** for its first-rate array of Californian wines and beers. Down the street, **MaSo** serves fresh Californian fare in a sophisticated yet retro setting. Speaking of MaSo, the restaurant inside the Westin Market Street, hip hotel restaurants and bars are supremely prolific in SoMa, in part because of its proximity to the Moscone Convention Center. While there are a number of upscale watering holes to choose from, a batch of casual joints has sprung up of late. **Custom Burger**, at Best Western Plus Americania, piles gourmet toppings such as Point Reyes Blue Cheese and black olive tapenade onto patties of Kobe beef, salmon, and lamb. **Perry's**, the "meet market" made famous in Armistead Maupin's *Tales of the City*, is enjoying a second home in the upscale boutique Hotel Griffon on Steuart Street. On the lobby level of the InterContinental San Francisco, **Bar 888** pours more than 100 *grappe* to taste. And if that isn't enough, SoMa is also home to a veritable buffet of well-known restaurants with famous toques at the helm. But the fact that these boldface names can also be found in the food court at the mall is testament to the area's democratic approach to food: there is high-quality cuisine to be had here at workaday prices. Likewise, wondrous things can be found between two slices of bread. Tom Colicchio's **'wichcraft** is a popular lunch spot among area professionals, and former Rubicon star Dennis Leary can actually be spotted slinging sandwiches at **The Sentinel**. Take a break from shopping at the Westfield San Francisco Centre to fuel up at **Buckhorn Grill**. This mini-chain was launched in the Bay Area and specializes in aged and marinated tri-

tip, deliciously charred over a wood fire. For budget foodies, SoMa overflows with cheap eats. Westfield Centre houses an impressive food court with plenty of international options. Nearby, museumgoers can refuel with a fragrant cup of tea at **Samovar** or try a micro-brew beer at **Thirsty Bear Brewing Company**. Take a peaceful stroll around South Park, and make sure you stop by **Mexico au Parc**, where the *sopes* run out by noon. Ballpark denizens get their burger fix at brewpub **21st Amendment**, and **Citizen's Band** is renowned for its casual vibe and seasonal American fare.

Nightlife

This is all to say little of SoMa's buzzing nightlife, whose scene traverses the red carpet from sports bars to DJ dens, hotel lounges to ultra-lounges, and risqué dinner theater—imagine drag (at **AsiaSF**) to Dutch (the Amsterdam import **Supperclub** that serves a racy mixed plate of performance art and global cuisine in bed.) Oenophiles should definitely swing by **Terroir**, the witty little wine bar on Folsom that stocks more than 700 organic and old-world varietals. And, for more rowdy imbibing, **Bossa Nova** bursts with the flavors of Rio. Soak up your *cachaça*, SoMa-style, with a decadent Nutella banana pancake from the 11th Street trailer, **Crêpes a Go-Go**.

SoMa

NOB HILL

Restaurant

CHINATOWN

NOB HILL

UNION SQUARE

UNION SQUARE

TENDERLOIN

Bluestem Brasserie

Fifth Floor

M.Y. China

Lark Creek Steak

OLD MINT

MOSCONE CENTER WEST

54 Mint

Luce

CIVIC CENTER

ASIAN ART MUSEUM

CITY HALL

UN PLAZA

SF PUBLIC LIBRARY

SF WAR MEMORIAL & PERFORMING ARTS CENTER

Civic Center

AQ

MISSION

Una Pizza Napoletana

1601 Bar & Kitchen

Basil Canteen

Manora's Thai Cuisine

Bar Agricole

Sushi Zone

Cathead's BBQ

MARINA

CIVIC CENTER

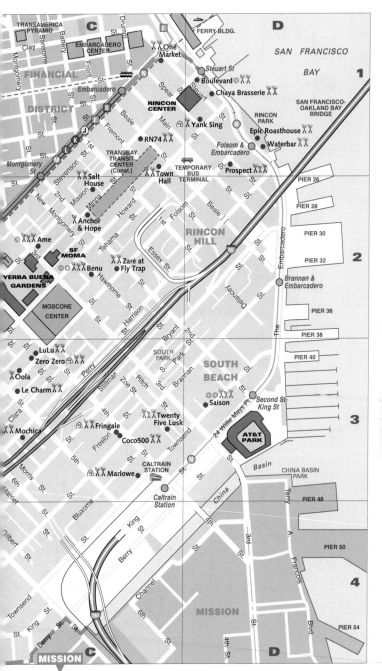

TRANSAMERICA
PYRAMID
Clay

C

EMBARCADERO
CENTER

XX One
Market

F

FERRY BLDG.

D

SAN FRANCISCO

BAY

1

FINANCIAL

Embarcadero

Steuart St

Boulevard XX

Chaya Brasserie XX

SAN FRANCISCO–
OAKLAND BAY
BRIDGE

DISTRICT

RINCON
CENTER

XX Yank Sing

RINCON
PARK

Epic Roasthouse XX

Waterbar XX

RN74 XX

Montgomery
St

TRANSBAY
TRANSIT
CENTER
(Const.)

Folsom &
Embarcadero

Prospect XXX

XX Town
Hall

TEMPORARY
BUS
TERMINAL

XX Salt
House

PIER 26

PIER 28

X Anchor
& Hope

RINCON
HILL

PIER 30

XXX Ame

SF
MOMA

XXX Benu

XX Zaré at
Fly Trap

Brannan &
Embarcadero

PIER 32

2

YERBA BUENA
GARDENS

MOSCONE
CENTER

PIER 36

PIER 38

LuLu XX

Zero Zero

SOUTH
PARK

SOUTH
BEACH

PIER 40

X Oola

Le Charm XX

Saison

XXX

Second St-
King St

3

X Mochica

XX Fringale

XXX Twenty
Five Lusk

AT&T
PARK

Coco500 XX

Basin

CHINA BASIN
PARK

XX Marlowe

CALTRAIN
STATION

PIER 48

Caltrain
Station

China

MISSION

PIER 50

4

MISSION

PIER 54

C

D

133

Ame

 Contemporary

689 Mission St. (at 3rd St.)

Phone: 415-284-4040
Web: www.amerestaurant.com
Prices: $$$

Dinner nightly

Joe Fletcher

Located in the tony St. Regis hotel, Ame is the cityside effort from Terra and Bar Terra Chefs Hiro Sone and Lissa Doumani; and features their signature blend of European, Japanese, and American influences. Chic and contemporary, the dining room moves to the tune of their open kitchen, with a small raw bar and dim lighting setting the scene. The well-trained, stylish staff knows how to cater to the diverse, jacketed crowd that lands here—usually to power-lunch at the raw bar or sit down to a relaxed evening meal.

Whether you pick items from the menu or sample a five-course tasting, you'll assuredly enjoy the delicate flavors in seared yellowfin tuna *tataki*; or fried soft-shell crab over creamy lobster bisque with parsley coulis. Be sure to peruse their excellent wine list featuring an extensive sake selection that has been known to find its way into Ame's subliminal cooking—sake-marinated Alaskan black cod with shrimp dumplings in shiso broth is a perfect sample.

Desserts like tangy rhubarb tart with tangerine sorbet or coconut panna cotta with a complex mango-pineapple-kiwi compote and macadamia nuts, add a tropical element that sends the meal out on a light graceful note.

Anchor & Hope

Seafood

 C2

83 Minna St. (bet. 1st & 2nd Sts.)

Phone: 415-501-9100
Web: www.anchorandhopesf.com
Prices: $$$

Lunch Mon – Fri
Dinner nightly

A maritime theme hangs in the salty air and conjures an east coast seaside shack at Anchor & Hope, sister restaurant to Salt House and Town Hall. This converted early 1900's auto shop now echoes a warehouse on the wharf, with thick ropes hanging from the high-pitched ceiling while a mounted garfish keeps a watchful eye. Like any bustling pier, Anchor & Hope is a boisterous place to dock.

Still, everyone is here for seafood. Blackboards boast the day's fresh oysters and shellfish, while a classic shrimp cocktail or apple-ginger cured salmon tartare are tasty starts. At lunch, try a tuna melt with Gruyère and tomato confit or Smithwicks beer-battered cod with rosemary potato wedges. Finish with a caramel mousse bar with chewy nougat.

AQ

Contemporary

 B3

1085 Mission St. (bet. 6th & 7th Sts.)

Phone: 415-341-9000
Web: www.aq-sf.com
Prices: $$$

Lunch Sun
Dinner Tue – Sun

On this edgy block of Mission Street, AQ's elegant exterior stands out immediately. The interior is even more impressive with a soaring loft, exposed brick, and sleek furniture. The décor (like the menu) changes with each season, so a spring visit may reveal sprigs of cherry blossom, hydroponic herbs growing at the wood-topped bar, and bushels of yellow tulips. The beauty extends to superbly arranged contemporary plates like soft-shell crab with dulse *pistou*; or slow-cooked beef tongue, peppery and pastrami-like, with béarnaise and poached egg over tarragon sponge cake. Whether you choose à la carte or go with the tasting menu, the hip staff is friendly and engaging. The outstanding cocktails (fig leaf fizz infused with egg whites) alone merit a visit.

Bar Agricole

Californian

B4

355 11th St. (bet. Folsom & Harrison Sts.)

Phone: 415-355-9400   Lunch Sun
Web: www.baragricole.com   Dinner nightly
Prices: $$

Bar Agricole is coveted, especially for Sunday brunch. Settled in SoMa, this warehouse-like set features rough concrete surfaces, stacked plank walls, and skylights framed by sculptural glass "curtains" that hang like art installations.

Revered as a foodie haven for its menu of shareable small plates, diners come in droves to sample crispy rye toast points layered with rich salmon gravlax, horseradish crème fraîche, and shallots, finished with a tasty micro herb garnish; or tender lamb shoulder laid beside roasted eggplant, crumbled feta, and a fried egg trickled with an herb-rich pesto. Dinner unveils an *agri-cool* spread of roasted chicken with squash blossoms and tomatillo, thrillingly finished with a lavender meringue capped lemon-ricotta tart.

Basil Canteen

Thai

B4

1489 Folsom St. (at 11th St.)

Phone: 415-552-3963   Lunch Mon – Fri
Web: www.basilthai.com   Dinner nightly
Prices: $$

Basil Canteen is a pioneer of sorts in the former Jackson Brewery landmark building. This voluminous Thai restaurant keeps company with its surrounds by sporting an industrial look through brick walls, oversized windows, metal stairs, and rising ceilings. Find a communal table downstairs and a smattering of smaller seats on the upstairs mezzanine.

Groups of suits at lunch and locals by night come for the likes of *pau pia yuan*, paper-thin rolls of crunchy cucumber, bean sprouts, herbs, and shrimp in lime vinaigrette; and sizzling drunken beef with Kaffir lime, chili, and lemongrass. The *kang kua goong*, sweet prawns and tender chunks of Japanese pumpkin stewed in red coconut curry, is at once spicy, creamy, tangy, and absolutely delicious.

Benu ✿✿

Contemporary ✕✕✕

22 Hawthorne St. (bet. Folsom & Howard Sts.)

Phone: 415-685-4860   Dinner Tue – Sat
Web: www.benusf.com
Prices: $$$$

Benu

A brick archway leading to a courtyard and vine-covered trellis may be the entrance, but most passersby would probably prefer to jump right through those sidewalk windows into the bright open kitchen. Inside, the skylit dining room features plush dove-grey carpets, high-backed banquettes, and exceptionally attentive service. Dark tables are laden with bespoke everything, from the opening *chawan mushi*'s porcelain lid right down to the tiered blackwood box of mignardises. The crowd is pretty, international, and rife with gourmands who add a note of seriousness to dining here.

A full tour of the kitchen's talent is best explored through the tasting menu, where Korean, Chinese, Japanese, and French influences are on wondrous display. Memorable dishes include a rich and velvety medallion of monkfish liver with grated daikon, fennel, and very buttery brioche. A humble-sounding pumpkin tofu is a silky, warm sphere of house-made tofu infused with pumpkin flavor, suspended in an elegant pumpkin consommé.

Desserts may sum up an entire season as in a wintery reflection of tangy cider, tart cranberries, eggnog custard, spiced tuiles, and more with fluffy pumpkin cake and frozen custard "snow."

Bluestem Brasserie

American

B2

1 Yerba Buena Ln. (at Market St.)

Phone: 415-547-1111
Web: www.bluestembrasserie.com
Prices: $$

Lunch & dinner daily

Bluestem Brasserie is a pleasant haunt that welcomes both locals and passersby from nearby Market Street. The voluminous space features loft-like ceilings, a sweeping staircase, and a lounge frequented for after-work cocktails. The somewhat bumbling service doesn't quite match the classy ambience, but it's nothing that a menu rife with the best of Californian ingredients can't fix. Start with an arugula salad with grilled sweet corn, fresh apricots, and goat's milk cheese, tossed in a Meyer lemon *citronette*. Barbecue-spiced chicken is super juicy bathed in a fragrant garlic-rosemary jus; while dessert is a successful pairing of butterscotch-tapioca pudding with a salty-smoky bacon butter cookie shaped like a…you guessed it…pig!

Cathead's BBQ

Barbecue

A4

1665 Folsom St. (bet. 12th & 13th Sts.)

Phone: 415-861-4242
Web: www.catheadsbbq.com
Prices:

Lunch & dinner Wed – Mon

A bright red building as bold as its barbecue and as fiery as its habanero sauce could only be Cathead's. This hot spot has already generated quite a buzz, so expect to wait in line. After ordering and paying, take a seat—preferably at the counter which offers the best views of the brick smokers. The space is tiny, making takeout big business here.

The menu features smoldering delights, plus locally inspired items like cornmeal-crusted tofu, or a dandelion-and-potato salad. But really, you're here for the meat combo starring St. Louis ribs, slow-smoked pulled pork, delicious sweet tea barbecue chicken, and Coca-Cola-smoked brisket. Sides (purple cabbage-habanero slaw or pimento mac and cheese) are so delish you'll wish they were a meal on their own.

Boulevard ✿

D1

1 Mission St. (at Steuart St.)

Phone: 415-543-6084
Web: www.boulevardrestaurant.com
Prices: $$$

Lunch Mon – Fri
Dinner nightly

Boulevard

The boulevard is nothing less than the Embarcadero at this charming Californian restaurant, whose home in the historic Audiffred Building affords diners a view of the Bay Bridge spanning cold waters, and a bustling street. Boulevard takes its style cues from the Belle Époque with blown-glass wall sconces, a tri-colored marble floor, and a humming open kitchen with counter seating that's perfect for solo guests.

Homey flavors and unexpected touches commingle on the seasonal menu which has featured chorizo batons with seared scallops over roasted fingerling potatoes and sherry cream; or toasted pecans that top a braised Kurobuta pork short rib with kabocha squash and bacon marmalade. Grilled halibut gets a Mediterranean finish from tabbouleh and hummus, and for dessert, a butternut squash cake with maple-sugar cream features the clever additions of sage ice cream and a salted, dried squash tuile.

The lunch crowd includes suits sealing deals, but the vibe turns romantic in the evening as locals and tourists enjoy a cocktail beneath the soft lighting. An attentive staff echoes the elegance of the room, and those who swoon for sips will want to swan dive into the remarkable list.

Chaya Brasserie

D1

132 The Embarcadero (bet. Howard & Mission Sts.)

Phone: 415-777-8688 Lunch Mon – Fri
Web: www.thechaya.com Dinner nightly
Prices: $$$

Few evening views can top these of the twinkling Bay Bridge, so grab a table in the front of the dining room against the window to secure this picturesque scene. Inside, find steel beams and leather banquettes fashioning a perfectly comfortable ambience for their crowds of local business people gathering here. Contemporary Asian art reflects the Japanese-influenced fare.

In addition to a daily sushi menu, find pan-roasted wild King salmon with carrots, hearts of palm, creamed baby potatoes, Romesco sauce, and green olive relish; yellowfin tuna tataki salad with garlic soy dressing; and squid ink fettuccine with fresh sea urchin and white shrimp. Sinful endings have included the milk chocolate croissant bread pudding with caramel ice cream.

Coco500

C3

500 Brannan St. (at 4th St.)

Phone: 415-543-2222 Lunch Mon – Fri
Web: www.coco500.com Dinner Mon – Sat
Prices: $$

In an area that abounds with grab-and-go spots, Coco500 remains a cherished establishment. With a light-filled dining room decorated with a blue-tiled bar, modern accents, and friendly service, this place attracts a classic blend of Blackberries by day and local residents for dinner.

The kitchen cobbles a Californian menu rife with local, seasonal ingredients, homemade pastas, and wood-fired pizzas. There are small dishes for sharing, like flatbread topped with grated Parmesan melted into mushroom *duxelles* and drizzles of truffle oil; or memorable ricotta cavatelli tossed in a herb-rich lamb Bolognese studded with fresh peas and torn mint leaves. A Meyer lemon semifreddo served with poppy seed-studded shortbread begs the question, one spoon or two?

Epic Roasthouse

Steakhouse ✗✗

D1

369 The Embarcadero (at Folsom St.)

Phone: 415-369-9955
Web: www.epicroasthousesf.com
Prices: $$$

Lunch Wed – Sun
Dinner nightly

Not surprisingly, this ravishing roasthouse has some of *the* most epic views along the iconic Embarcadero. Reminiscent of a club of sorts and featuring dining room windows that overlook the beautifully lit Bay Bridge, other dapper details like leather banquettes and plush carpets serve to seal this handsome deal.

While the views are expansive, the food can be expensive, so embrace your expense account while savoring a full-bodied merlot alongside all things "red." Start with house-cured meats before moving to wood oven-roasted marrow bones with tomato jam. Spend some time with the star of the show (juicy prime rib) without ever forgetting about the tasty sides, but always save a smack of space for their hot beignets caressed with mascarpone cream.

Fifth Floor

Contemporary ✗✗✗

B2

12 4th St. (at Market St.)

Phone: 415-348-1555
Web: www.fifthfloorrestaurant.com
Prices: $$$$

Dinner Tue – Sat

Elegantly set on the fifth floor of Hotel Palomar, it seems only fitting that beautiful Fifth Floor's bar and lounge is well-loved by corporate barons and other ritzy revelers. The adjacent dining room is sedate and outfitted with drum lights casting a sultry glow on inlaid wood floors, leather armchairs, and a lavish wine cellar.

A casual dining experience can be had amidst the refined servers and wood tables dressed with sparkling silverware. Such flush accessories keep fine company with contemporary plates of oysters done five ways (béarnaise, caviar, rouille, cucumber, chowder, and mignonette); Mendocino uni flan with Dungeness crab "fondue" and saffron; lamb married with rye berries, pickled raisins, and yogurt; and a milk chocolate mousse bombe.

54 Mint

B2

Italian

16 Mint Plaza (at Jessie St.)

Phone:	415-543-5100	Lunch Mon – Fri
Web:	www.54mint.com	Dinner Mon – Sat
Prices:	$$	

Though several of its compatriots in Mint Plaza have gone under, this contemporary trattoria remains strong, with passionately made, authentic Italian fare. From house-cured *salumi* to asparagus topped with *burrata* and truffle oil, a meal could be made out of starters alone. However, that would mean missing delicious entrées like pillowy gnocchi with rich oxtail ragù and grilled octopus with fingerling potatoes.

Original brick walls, cream leather bar stools, and polished concrete floors give 54 Mint a contemporary, industrial feel that's heightened by the shelves of balsamic vinegar, pasta, and other Italian pantry staples available for purchase. Alfresco dining on the plaza is also a must, whether for warm evenings or sunny $20 prix-fixe lunches.

Fringale 😋

C3

French

570 4th St. (bet. Brannan & Bryant Sts.)

Phone:	415-543-0573	Lunch Tue – Fri
Web:	www.fringalesf.com	Dinner nightly
Prices:	$$	

Housed in a cheery yellow building on SoMa's restaurant-lined Fourth Street, unassuming Fringale is just the sort of intimate bistro this neighborhood needs: petite, hospitable, utterly charming, and delicious every time. The menu satisfies with authentic Basque cuisine and a decidedly French accent. A perfect beginning is found in the spicy Monterey calamari grilled *a la plancha* with *piment d'Espelette* and briny olives. Other bistro favorites might include crispy duck confit paired with French lentils, salty bacon, and drizzled with a tangy red wine sauce; sautéed prawns in Pastis; and heart-warming daily specials like bœuf Bourguignon.

For dessert, try Mme. Angèle's *gâteau Basque*, a buttery almond torte filled with custard cream.

Lark Creek Steak

Steakhouse ✗✗

B2

845 Market St. (bet. 4th & 5th Sts.)

Phone: 415-593-4100   Lunch & dinner daily
Web: www.larkcreek.com
Prices: $$$

After a long day sizing up the sales racks at the Westfield San Francisco Centre, this steakhouse provides a welcome respite for footsore shoppers to savor hearty American fare. From crisp salads to thick Porterhouses, there are options for every palate. A farm-to-table philosophy makes this one of the better restaurants you'll encounter in a mall.

From the moment you enter, the friendly staff will put you at ease, drawing your focus into the elegant dining room with its bevy of leather banquettes. Indulge in a "pastrami" burger with Swiss, bacon, and spicy sauce, followed by an ice cream sundae topped with caramel-bacon popcorn, and you'll be geared up for another few hours of shopping—if you don't decide to stay and linger over a glass of wine.

Le Charm

French ✗✗

C3

315 5th St. (bet. Folsom & Shipley Sts.)

Phone: 415-546-6128   Dinner Tue – Sat
Web: www.lecharm.com
Prices: $$

Set in SoMa, Le Charm is indeed a *très* charming boîte. Closely spaced tables topped with bistro paper cluster together in the persimmon-hued dining room rife with wood floors and illuminated by pretty lamp sconces. A petite bar upfront offers an ideal respite to the likes of expats on a budget or novices to the cuisine.

The open kitchen resides next to this bar and turns out a tandem of venerable French classics like excellently seasoned chicken liver salad drizzled with tart sherry vinegar; followed by supremely tender osso bucco fortified by Porto, grapes, and gnocchi *à la Parisienne* flavored with garlic and parsley. The staff is happy to converse *en français*, likely about the richness behind a warm, whipped cream-crowned apple tarte Tatin.

Luce ✿

B3

888 Howard St. (at 5th St.)

Phone: 415-616-6566

Web: www.lucewinerestaurant.com

Prices: $$$

Lunch & dinner daily

Rien van Rijthoven

As one might expect from its home on the ground floor of the towering InterContinental hotel, this is an elegant, fine-dining establishment. Shining inlaid floors and enormous windows make Luce seem like an extension of the marble-clad lobby. Yet, it flaunts its own unique, modern design with a few funky touches like purple and white orb lights, thin silver curtains, and calla lilies in a black vase on each table.

By day, Luce caters to its hotel guests with respectable breakfasts and lunches. Come night, this admirable kitchen cuts loose and begins to truly shine with contemporary American cooking. A three-course prix-fixe may reveal fresh, plump ravioli filled with truffled ricotta and minced sweetbreads in Muscovy duck jus, served with more crisp and golden-fried sweetbreads, baby greens, and slices of black truffle. Follow this with a trio of guinea hen, prepared sous-vide with salted butter, pressed-leg confit, house-made sausage, and coupled with smoked-date purée, new potatoes, and spring onions.

Every element of each dish is synchronized to the end, which may reveal puffy rounds of rosemary-infused Pavlova with macerated huckleberries, lemon mousse, and pine nut ice cream.

LuLu

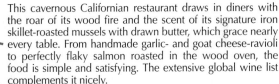

Mediterranean ✗✗

C3

816 Folsom St. (bet 4th & 5th Sts.)

Phone: 415-495-5775
Web: www.restaurantlulu.com
Prices: $$

Lunch & dinner daily

This cavernous Californian restaurant draws in diners with the roar of its wood fire and the scent of its signature iron skillet-roasted mussels with drawn butter, which grace nearly every table. From handmade garlic- and goat cheese-ravioli to perfectly flaky salmon roasted in the wood oven, the food is simple and satisfying. The extensive global wine list complements it nicely.

Floor-to-ceiling windows bathe the room in natural light and provide a cheerful view onto bustling Folsom Street. The crowd of families and groups is here for a leisurely meal, and service is paced accordingly. One item that won't linger for long is the crisp, golden profiterole filled with rich espresso ice cream and topped with chocolate and butterscotch sauce.

Manora's Thai Cuisine

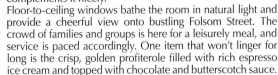

Thai ✗

A4

1600 Folsom St. (at 12th St.)

Phone: 415-861-6224
Web: www.manorathai.com
Prices:

Lunch Mon – Fri
Dinner Mon – Sat

A firmly rooted dining destination in this otherwise underdeveloped part of town, Manora's has been a source for authentic Thai dishes since the '80s. Crowds flock here for the affordable lunch specials, which include gems like pad Thai topped with plump shrimp and a golden fried egg, fragrant lemon chicken soup, and moist, perfectly charred satay skewers surrounded by fresh vegetables.

The pace at dinner is more relaxed, with endearing service that makes customers truly feel at home amid the wood carvings of the dining room. The fresh, zingy flavors of dishes like spicy green papaya salad draw diners through the well-aged wooden door again and again. Meals are all the better when cooled off with a creamy cold coffee or sweet Thai iced tea.

Marlowe

Californian 𝕏𝕏

C3

330 Townsend St. (bet. 4th & 5th Sts.)

Phone: 415-974-5599
Web: www.marlowesf.com
Prices: $$

Lunch Mon – Fri
Dinner nightly

This attractive spot is known and loved for its scene. In other words, reservations are a must, though with some luck you may find some open seats at their small "communal table." Marlowe's urban style has a rustic demeanor evident in its cozy arrangement of dark wood tables; the pleasant staff lends extra warmth.

The menu is fun, creative, and has wide appeal with a lot of California and a bit of France. Starters reveal Dungeness crab and rock shrimp in a *Louie* bath. Most tables have a basket of fries that pair perfectly with a Marlowe burger crowned with cheddar and bacon. Desserts are all the rage and layer on the decadence—a silky TCHO chocolate cream pie is quaintly served in a glass jar.

Check out British-themed baby sib The Cavalier also in SoMa.

Mochica

Peruvian 𝕏𝕏

C3

937 Harrison St. (bet. 5th & 6th Sts.)

Phone: 415-278-0480
Web: www.mochicasf.com
Prices: $$

Lunch & dinner Wed – Mon

Mochica is the first of Chef Carlos Altamirano's prized and popular Peruvian eateries in the Bay Area. Rich hues, slate floors and well-set communal tables offer a tasty glimpse through oversized windows.

The belly-sating cuisine is nearly always perfectly prepared and flavorful, with tastes of authenticity in each bite. Meals here may begin with dishes such as the buttery corn cake, *pastelito choclo*, made with potato, *queso fresco*, and crunchy bits of Peruvian corn alongside *salsa blanca* and *sarsita d'choclo*; or *causa limena*, a ring of creamy mashed potatoes flavored with *aji amarillo* and lime juice topped with cilantro-marinated tiger shrimp. Tasty endings include a sweet *arroz con leche* drizzled with delicious *chicha morada* sauce.

M. Y. China 😋

Chinese ❌❌

B2

845 Market St. (bet. 4th & 5th Sts.)

Phone: 415-580-3001
Web: www.mychinasf.com
Prices: $$

Lunch & dinner daily

Martin Yan's China is a glitzy showstopper located under the dome of the Westfield shopping center. Glossy wood panels separate the sprawling series of rooms, dominated by a marble and white-tiled open kitchen where one can watch as dough is pulled, twisted, and cut into noodles.

The famed chef honors his menu with focus and clarity. Try the wild boar juicy dumplings—presented in a bamboo steamer, cradled in a ceramic spoon, and stuffed with a luscious meatball afloat in hot broth wrapped in a delicate casing and accompanied by slivered ginger root in red vinegar. The Beijing knife-cut noodles are equally memorable, served as a hearty bowl of toothsome wheat flour strands topped with diced tofu in hoisin vinaigrette, cool vegetables, and micro basil.

One Market

Californian ❌❌

C1

1 Market St. (at Steuart St.)

Phone: 415-777-5577
Web: www.onemarket.com
Prices: $$

Lunch Mon – Fri
Dinner Mon – Sat

Located at the very end of Market Street facing the Ferry Building, this perennial power-lunch spot draws crowds for its bright, bustling vibe, and Bay views. High ceilings and a busy open kitchen catch the eye, while efficient bow-tied waiters attend to the booths and banquettes.

Chef Mark Dommen's contemporary Californian food is fresh and seasonal, starting with Nantucket Bay scallops sautéed in brown butter with baby mustard greens in a pool of fermented black bean sauce, garnished with apple and puffed rice. This might lead to a colorful composition of seared flounder over flavorful black-eyed peas with smoky bacon and tart *sofrito* vinaigrette. Traditional desserts like pear galette are sized as "traditional" or "singular" (half) portions.

147

Oola

C3

Californian

860 Folsom St. (bet. 4th & 5th Sts.)

Phone: 415-995-2061 Lunch & dinner daily
Web: www.oola-sf.com
Prices: $$

Long and narrow Oola is hugely sought after by corporate groups and after-work revelers for its stellar combo of tasty treats and quenching cocktails. Furnished with delightful bar seating in the front and an elevated dining area at the back, the restaurant is further beautified by sultry, low lighting, exposed brick walls, white bar stools, and contemporary-chic suede banquettes.

The food is the real draw here and may uncover a fresh salad of arugula, baby spinach, walnuts, and apple with tangy blue cheese dressing; and soy-glazed baby back ribs garnished with cilantro and served over a zesty red cabbage-apple slaw. Even a small plate of Swiss chard sautéed with salty pancetta, or a well-prepared vanilla crème brûlée will have you going *oo la la*!

Prospect

D1

American

300 Spear St. (at Folsom St.)

Phone: 415-247-7770 Lunch Sun
Web: www.prospectsf.com Dinner nightly
Prices: $$$

Prospect is still living up to all the hype. Its large bar and lounge is always humming with well-dressed, young, professional clusters; the dining room attracts power brokers; while the private room is forever hosting a fête. The restaurant is as sophisticated and stylish as the food, so dress suitably.

Interpretations of American dishes are prepared with skill and may reveal perfectly seasoned fried green tomatoes served with frisée, plump white prawns, and a streak of red pepper aïoli. A crisp-skinned roasted chicken breast and confit thigh placed over a bed of *farro* dotted with crunchy cauliflower florets is stunningly trailed by an elegant version of strawberry shortcake—buttery, thin biscuits sandwiched with jam and tangy Greek yogurt.

RN74

Californian XX

C1

301 Mission St. (at Beale St.)

Phone: 415-543-7474
Web: www.rn74.com
Prices: $$$

Lunch Mon – Fri
Dinner nightly

Named for the Burgundy region "Route Nationale 74" in France, RN74 is part restaurant and part wine bar. At the base of the Millennium Tower, set amidst office buildings, it draws a large corporate crowd, particularly for lunch and after-work drinks. Architectural basics like high ceilings and concrete pillars are balanced with unique design elements like train station-style boards that list available wine bottles.

There is also a large bar-lounge area, but most flock here for the Californian menu infused with French accents. Expect such flavorful and harmonious preparations as *garganelli* tossed with artichoke hearts, peas, and wild nettles; and supremely moist fried chicken paired with foraged mushrooms—a dish as solid and stylish as the place itself.

Salt House

American XX

C2

545 Mission St. (bet. 1st & 2nd Sts.)

Phone: 415-543-8900
Web: www.salthousesf.com
Prices: $$

Lunch Mon – Fri
Dinner nightly

Housed on the ground floor of a former printing warehouse, this industrial but comfortable spot is a refuge in the sea of glass-fronted skyscrapers that surround it. The owners, who are also behind nearby Town Hall and Anchor & Hope, know exactly what diners want. Inside, the atmosphere is quiet and business-friendly at lunchtime, but amplifies when the after-work crowd streams in.

The food also reflects a duality between bolder, more ambitious dinners and simple, elegant lunchtime salads, tossing earthy and sweet beets with creamy goat cheese and crunchy pistachios; or sandwiches like the succulent Waldorf chicken on a crusty roll. Inventive desserts, like a grapefruit cake with semifreddo and pink peppercorn meringue, are also not to be missed.

Saison ✿ ✿

D3

Californian 𝄪𝄪𝄪

178 Townsend St. (bet. 2nd & 3rd Sts.)

Phone: 415-828-7990

Web: www.saisonsf.com

Prices: $$$$

Dinner Tue – Sat

Bonjwing Lee

Dining at Saison is like going to an idyllically California-casual dinner party at someone's impossibly cool brick warehouse. The gorgeous interior is vast, yet divided almost equally between the kitchen, lounge, and dining areas, which lends an airy feel. The décor bears an authentic, unique aspect with wood beams, Nordic-style chairs, and chef's table.

No menus are provided and the price is not set until the time of your seating. Convivial servers guide diners through meals, providing instructions like "this is to be eaten in one bite" or "please use your fingers." This is when the forks briefly disappear. It's also when the staff may turn from engaging to didactic.

Under Chef Joshua Skenes, the kitchen presents each course like a gift that not only demonstrates outrageous skill but unmitigated ambition—often with extraordinary results. Meals begin with an utterly refreshing rhubarb soda with edible flowers; or Parmesan custard with favas, gold leaf, and hearth-grilled pea sauce with subtle smokiness. This may lead to perfectly cooked rock cod in coconut curry with plantain chips and Thai spices, or morels stuffed with pigeon farci. Desserts, like sesame soufflé, are memorable.

1601 Bar & Kitchen

Sri Lankan ✗✗

 A4

1601 Howard St. (at 12th St.)

Phone: 415-552-1601
Web: www.1601sf.com
Prices: $$

Dinner Tue – Sat

In a sleepy corner of western SoMa, this small plates spot stands out for its fusion of Chef/owner Brian Fernando's French training and Sri Lankan heritage. Tastes are exciting and yet traditional, as in the soft-cooked egg "hopper" folded with *sambols* into a coconut and fermented rice flour crêpe, or a creamy, peppery mulligatawny soup with roulade of chicken confit. French wines are delicious and smartly chosen, but it's the finesse of the unusual ingredients like black curry or chai foam that will linger on the palate the longest.

A few different seating options are available, from marble-topped tables to black leather banquettes. Interesting accents like the paintings of women with ram heads adorning the walls are sure to spark conversation.

Sushi Zone

Japanese ✗

 A4

1815 Market St. (at Pearl St.)

Phone: 415-621-1114
Web: N/A
Prices: $$

Dinner Mon – Sat

Sushi connoisseurs looking for the city's best aren't likely to find it at Sushi Zone, but that doesn't stop locals from lining the sidewalk to wait for one of a handful of tables or an old chrome stool at the counter. Situated at the spot where SoMa, the Mission, and Hayes Valley collide, Sushi Zone is a convenient spot for dinner after work.

Check the board for nightly specials, which may include hot items like baked mussels with spicy mayo and scallions or baked seabass with mango. Sushi meanwhile is fresh and simple: albacore, yellowtail, mackerel, and salmon nigiri are above average and served over well-prepared rice; sweet papaya balances smoky *unagi* in a simple roll; and a spicy hamachi maki is studded with avocado, jalapeño, and lime.

Town Hall

C1

342 Howard St. (at Fremont St.)

Phone: 415-908-3900
Web: www.townhallsf.com
Prices: **$$**

Lunch Mon – Fri
Dinner nightly

Though the elegant red brick exterior of Town Hall makes it seem like it's been on Howard Street for ages, it's merely a decade old. This is surprising given the deeply satisfying, tried-and-tested Southern flavors on offer. Expect garlic-herb toast topped with barbecue shrimp, St. Louis-style ribs, and spicy shrimp and flounder étouffée. It's all about simple pleasure and hearty portions here.

Given the delicious fare, know that Town Hall is always buzzing, whether it's the office lunch crowd angling for a table or after-work groups of friends hitting the bar for a Vieux Carré cocktail. The outdoor patio provides a quieter experience, and is perfect for savoring every bite of the signature butterscotch-chocolate *pot de crème* if you still have room.

Twenty Five Lusk

C3

25 Lusk St. (bet. 3rd & 4th Sts.)

Phone: 415-495-5875
Web: www.25lusk.com
Prices: **$$$**

Lunch Sun
Dinner nightly

As one of the sleekest and chicest respites in town, Twenty Five Lusk is *the* scene for the well-dressed, well-connected, and well-to-do. An after-work cosmo crowd quickly fills in the lower-level bar and lounge decked with rounded settes surrounding hanging fireplace orbs. Upstairs, slick modern surfaces meet brick-and-timber warehouse.

A glassed-in kitchen returns the focal point to cooking which may include dishes like tomato and fennel bisque poured over lobster morsels; grilled prawns posed atop carrot purée and a mound of grits sprinkled with *togarashi*; or a hearty braised pork shoulder served over wilted kale and sided with cornbread and green tomato salsa. Try the classic *baba* inventively soaked in strawberry syrup and coupled with basil sorbet.

Una Pizza Napoletana

 Pizza ✕

A4

210 11th St. (at Howard St.)

Phone: 415-861-3444   Dinner Wed – Sat
Web: www.unapizza.com
Prices: $$

 You get what you pay for at Una Pizza Napoletana, the New York to SoMa transplant that serves purely authentic pies at import prices. But, a bevy of regulars who race in to claim their tables clearly believe that Una Pizza is worth the premium.

There is no décor to speak of unless you count the assemblage of pizzas a product of high design. Make do with white walls and concrete floors, and don't expect your pizza to get any fancier. Just a few choices of 12-inch rounds come fire-licked and lightly topped. Try the Margherita with San Marzano tomatoes, basil, and buffalo mozzarella; or the smoky *Ilaria* topped with arugula and cherry tomatoes, and named for the chef's own wife. Finish with an intense Neapolitan coffee served with a hunk of dark chocolate.

Waterbar

 Seafood ✕✕

D1

399 The Embarcadero (at Harrison St.)

Phone: 415-284-9922   Lunch & dinner daily
Web: www.waterbarsf.com
Prices: $$$

 Stunning views of the Bay Bridge is the chief draw at this Embarcadero fave for sipping wine on the lovely terrace and slurping oysters at the enormous raw bar. Though the polished, modern dining room can seem serious (as can the expense account-rocking prices), warm and thoughtful service brings things back down to earth.

Seafood-centric entrées make global use of the local waters' bounty including tender squid almost bursting with chorizo alongside candy-like chickpeas. Perfectly crisp pan-roasted striped bass atop flavorful wild rice oozes with delish flavors and textures; and an Americana-influenced dessert menu (think carrot cake ice-cream sandwiches with rum-raisin sauce) is the final touch in ensuring that Waterbar stays packed to the gills.

Yank Sing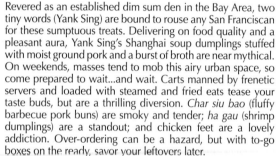

San Francisco ▶ SoMa

Chinese

101 Spear St. (bet. Howard & Mission Sts.)

Phone: 415-781-1111   Lunch daily
Web: www.yanksing.com
Prices: $$

Revered as an established dim sum den in the Bay Area, two tiny words (Yank Sing) are bound to rouse any San Franciscan for these sumptuous treats. Delivering on food quality and a pleasant aura, Yank Sing's Shanghai soup dumplings stuffed with moist ground pork and a burst of broth are near mythical. On weekends, masses tend to mob this airy urban space, so come prepared to wait...and wait. Carts manned by frenetic servers and loaded with steamed and fried eats tease your taste buds, but are a thrilling diversion. *Char siu bao* (fluffy barbecue pork buns) are smoky and tender; *ha gau* (shrimp dumplings) are a standout; and chicken feet are a lovely addiction. Over-ordering can be a hazard, but with to-go boxes on the ready, savor your leftovers later.

Zaré at Fly Trap

Middle Eastern

606 Folsom St. (bet. 2nd & 3rd Sts.)

Phone: 415-243-0580   Dinner Mon – Sat
Web: www.zareflytrap.com
Prices: $$

Nearly 20 years since Hoss Zaré emigrated from Iran and found a job at the Fly Trap to help pay for medical school, the chef/owner is still pursuing his passion in the kitchen he has long called home. A red awning marks this SoMa favorite where the spice-hued interior is as warm as the food. Zaré himself can be found in the dining room nearly every evening, often serving his flavorful Mediterranean-infused Middle Eastern fare himself, much to the delight of his regulars. The chef's kitchen turns out such mouthwatering dishes as a salmon-and-lentil salad studded with roasted bell peppers, fennel, and endive; braised duck with walnuts and pomegranate; or lamb shank with black-eyed peas. Conclude with the best baklava in San Francisco.

Zero Zero

Pizza ✗✗

C3

826 Folsom St. (bet. 4th & 5th Sts.)

Phone:	415-348-8800	Lunch & dinner daily
Web:	www.zerozerosf.com	
Prices:	**$$**	

A modish neighborhood pizzeria, Zero Zero is named for the imported Neapolitan flour that gives these crusts their character. But for a taste of these bubbling Italian masterpieces, be prepared to wait and brave the din: reservations are elusive; and the bar (known for creative and carefully crafted drinks) is inevitably packed.

If you make it to a table beneath the colorful mural in the close-knit upstairs dining room, take advantage of the opportunity to feast. Start with antipasti or local squid *a la plancha*, then meander through a range of pies, many of which are named after San Francisco streets. The Margherita "Extra" is heaped with buffalo mozzarella, while the Fillmore forgoes the sauce in favor of leeks, fontina, and garlic.

Do not confuse ✗ with
❀ ! ✗ defines comfort,
while ❀ are awarded for
the best cuisine. Stars
are awarded across all
categories of comfort.

Joshua Winzeler/Visit Oakland

East Bay

East Bay

Berkeley is legendary for its liberal politics and lush university campus that launched the 1960s Free Speech Movement. Among foodies, this is a Garden of Eden that sprouted American gastronomy's leading purist, Alice Waters, and continues to be a place of worship. Waters' Chez Panisse Foundation has nurtured the Edible Schoolyard, an organic garden and kitchen classroom for students. She also founded Slow Food Nation, the country's largest festival of slow and sustainable foods. Since Waters is credited with developing Californian cuisine, her influence can be tasted in myriad restaurants.

But, one needn't look much further than Berkeley's "gourmet ghetto." The North Shattuck corridor satiates with fresh and meticulously prepared food and/or takeout from **Grégoire** and **Epicurious Garden**. This strip also houses co-ops like the **Cheese Board Collective**; the **Cheese Board Pizza Collective**; and the **Juice Bar Collective**. On Thursday afternoons, the **North Shattuck Organic Farmer's Market** is crammed with local produce. **La Note**'s brioche *pain perdu* is lovely; **Tomate Café** proffers a Cuban breakfast on a pup-friendly patio; and **Caffe Mediterraneum** is the San Francisco birthplace of the caffè latte. Berkeley is also home to **Acme Bread Company** and Chef Paul Bertolli's handcrafted **Fra'Mani Salumi**. Oakland doesn't quite carry the same culinary panache of neighboring Berkeley, but the workaday city has seen a revival of its own with new businesses and condos. **Jack London Square** has stunning views of the bay, and crows the area's chief tourist destination for dining, nightlife, and a **Sunday Farmer's and Artisan Market**. **Fentons Creamery** has served ice cream for over 119 delicious years. Taco junkies congregate on International Boulevard for a taco feast; while **Tacos Sinaloa** and **Mariscos La Costa** are known for their chorizo and fish tacos. Downtown, crowds nosh on po'boys at **Café 15**; and in Temescal, **Bakesale Betty** serves crispy chicken sandwiches atop ironing board tables. For post-work revelry, the **Trappist** pours over 160 Belgian and specialty beers.

On Sundays, oyster mongers line up at **Rudy Figueroa's** in the **Montclair Farmer's Market** for bivalves shucked to order. In August, the Art & Soul Festival brings a buffet of world flavors, as does the Chinatown Streetfest with curries galore and barbecue eats. And in Rockridge, the quaint shopping district between Oakland and Berkeley, boutiques and eateries abound. **Tara's Organic Ice Cream** boasts unique flavors (chile pistachio or basil) in compostable cups. **Market Hall** is a gourmet shopper's paradise with sustainable catch at **Hapuku Fish Shop**, specialty groceries at **Pasta Shop**, a bakery, produce market, and coffee bar.

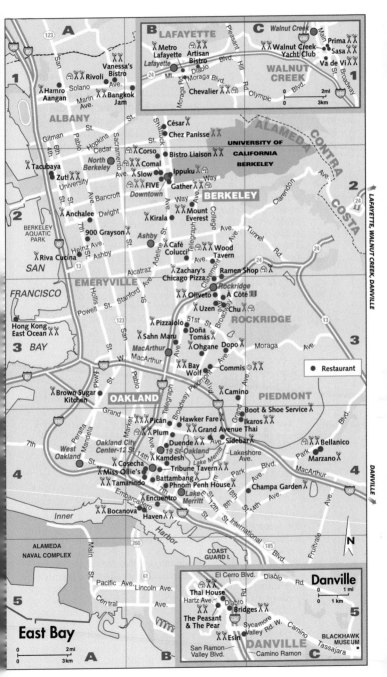

À Côté

B3

Mediterranean

5478 College Ave. (bet. Lawton & Taft Aves.), Oakland

Phone: 510-655-6469   Dinner nightly
Web: www.acoterestaurant.com
Prices: **$$**

A long-running small-plates icon set within the posh stores of Rockridge, À Côté nearly always requires a wait—only a handful of seats are available for reservations. But, after settling into a cozy wood table or perhaps at the granite bar, a lively, very communal vibe will ease any irritation. Forty-plus wines offered by the glass augment their appeal.

The seasonal menu has a French effect, discernable in plump fava bean falafel set atop tart tahini and pickled turnips; or green-garlic soup with a *fromage blanc* crouton. Entrées like seared yellowtail Jack brightened with asparagus, spring onion, and a Meyer lemon-blood orange relish perk up the palate; while a wood-fired oven and heated patio provide comforting warmth for indoor and outdoor meals.

Anchalee

A2

Thai

1094 Dwight Way (at San Pablo Ave.), Berkeley

Phone: 510-848-4015   Lunch & dinner daily
Web: www.anchaleethai.com
Prices:

Anchalee inhabits a brick building with large front windows. It's a cozy spot that eschews kitschy Thai accents for soft green walls and contemporary paintings. Locals love the mellow vibe.

In addition to the regular menu, explore their list of organic vegetarian specials and dishes made with all natural hormone-free meats (à la Berkeley). Organic vegetable rolls wrap up fresh herbs like mint, cilantro, and basil, with a crunch of cabbage, carrots, and soy-tamarind or creamy peanut sauces for dipping. Red curry with cubes of firm tofu, vegetables, and fresh basil is best savored with a refreshing Thai iced tea. An order of their nutty brown rice is de rigueur. Everything is flavorful but mild, so feel free to ask for extra heat.

Artisan Bistro

French ✗✗

B1

1005 Brown Ave. (at Mt. Diablo Blvd.), Lafayette

Phone: 925-962-0882
Web: www.artisanlafayette.com
Prices: $$

Lunch & dinner Tue – Sun

Hearts carved into the exterior shutters are your first clue that this Craftsman cottage is an ideal hideaway for canoodling lovers. Duck into the cluster of cozy dining rooms where warm Dijon mustard walls, local artwork, and a stone hearth work together to set the mood; or, on sunny days, bask in the cool umbrella-shaded patio.

No matter the season, Chef/owner John Marquez's Cal-French cuisine is right on cue. At lunch, roasted lamb shoulder and grilled portobello mushrooms make for fancy sandwiches; dinners are swankier. One might begin with a creamy corn soup or vibrant baby beets, endive, and apples made decadent with herbed goat cheese. Entrées are hearty—think rabbit three ways or roasted chicken with a terrine of leg, apples, and mustard.

Bangkok Jam

Thai ✗✗

B1

1892 Solano Ave. (bet. Fresno Ave. & The Alameda), Berkeley

Phone: 510-525-3625
Web: www.bangkokjamberkeley.com
Prices:

Lunch & dinner daily

Do not be deterred by the plain façade sandwiched amid retail stores. Inside, this long and narrow space is contemporary and stylish with glittering chandeliers, dark wood tables, and brick wainscoting. A sweet, attentive staff keeps things casual and kid-friendly.

Whet the appetite with a plate of crispy vegetable spring rolls stuffed with carrots, cabbage, and onion, served with a tangy sweet and sour dipping sauce. Follow this with organic lemongrass chicken breast, tender and smoky, served over rice and complemented by a duo of spicy lime and sweet tamarind sauces. However, curries are the true standout here, with choices ranging from pumpkin to sweet and spicy mango stewed in coconut red curry with cabbage, peas, carrots, bell peppers, and tofu.

Battambang

B4

850 Broadway (bet. 8th & 9th Sts.), Oakland

Phone: 510-839-8815
Web: N/A
Prices:

Lunch Mon – Sat
Dinner nightly

Surrounded by a collection of Chinese restaurants, markets, and grocers, this unassuming spot sings to its own tune. It's all about authentic Cambodian here at Battambang, where true-blue ingredients like *prohuk* (fermented fish paste) and savory lime-based sauces make their way into the dishes.

Golden hues, wood wainscoting, and glass-topped tables outfit the diminutive space, swarming with local families relishing a good meal at great price. To get your appetite going, watch them load up *bangkair aing*, fresh jumbo prawns grilled and served with a pickled veggie relish and lime juice; *saramann*, sliced beef, green beans, sweet potato, and fresh coconut floating in a fragrant red curry; or spicy baked eggplant stuffed with diced prawns and ground pork.

Bay Wolf

B3

3853 Piedmont Ave. (at Rio Vista Ave.), Oakland

Phone: 510-655-6004
Web: www.baywolf.com
Prices: $$

Dinner nightly

Bay Wolf has been a Bay Area icon since the mid 1970's. As the restaurant approaches its 40th birthday, the kitchen is still successfully preparing food the way it always has—excellent ingredients are treated with simplicity and care. True to the local philosophy, this oft-changing menu spotlights seasonal and local ingredients.

Set in a converted house with a small bar and dining rooms on either side, patrons can be seen nibbling on fried ricotta-stuffed squash blossoms, before proceeding to a pork loin roulade with toasted pistachios spiraling through it, deliciously paired with wild rice pilaf. But, the real scene is on the front porch where local artists, intellectuals, and retirees spend hours lingering over buttery apricot upside down cake.

Bellanico

Italian ✖✖

C4

4238 Park Blvd. (at Wellington St.), Oakland

Phone: 510-336-1180
Web: www.bellanico.net
Prices: $$

Lunch & dinner daily

Neighborhood favorite Bellanico serves up consistently good, rustic Italian fare. Large windows overlook Park Boulevard, while inside, persimmon-colored walls, wood furnishings, and an open kitchen welcome regulars. Lunches are low-key, frequented by business people. Dinners are filled with local couples and families appreciative of the "bambini" dishes—apropos in a place named for the owners' daughters.

As at its sister, Aperto, this seasonal, ingredient-driven menu features local, organic products. Start with a selection of *cicchetti* and antipasto of cauliflower fritters with garlic *aglioli* before moving on to other items including spicy *tagliolini pepati* with bacon. Smoke fiends adore the grilled pork chop adorned with well-seasoned *brodo*.

Bistro Liaison

French ✖✖

B2

1849 Shattuck Ave. (at Hearst Ave.), Berkeley

Phone: 510-849-2155
Web: www.liaisonbistro.com
Prices: $$

Lunch & dinner daily

This slice of Paris in Berkeley, just two blocks from campus, draws regulars with its authentic bistro vibe, complete with closely spaced tables and cheerful yellow walls displaying vintage French posters and artwork. On warm days, diners scramble to score one of the sidewalk tables, though the traffic on busy Shattuck Avenue might dispel any fantasies of the Champs-Élysées.

The fare, like the décor, is classic French, with dishes like escargots in garlic butter and a croque-monsieur oozing with Emmenthaler cheese. At dinner, hearty bœuf bourguignon and steamed mussels in garlic and white wine send diners into Gallic reveries. Finish with a buttery, flaky apple tarte Tatin, drowned in caramel and topped with a scoop of rum-raisin ice cream.

Bocanova

Latin American

55 Webster St. (at Jack London Square), Oakland

Phone: 510-444-1233

Web: www.bocanova.com

Prices: **$$**

Lunch & dinner daily

Located in lively Jack London Square, everything is big at Bocanova—several dining rooms, a massive (and admired) bar, and the spacious patio overlooking the harbor. The industrial-chic space highlights soaring ceilings, funky light fixtures, and stained glass accents amid fine wood furnishings. Adding to the allure is an open kitchen starring a competent lineup of chefs.

Unlike mere mortals, Bocanova aces the art of compartmentalizing. Whether *From the Pantry*, *From the Raw Bar*, or *From the Feidora*, dishes are sure to gratify. Expect the likes of a *huarache* topped with crumbled Oaxaca cheese and ghost chili salami; grilled Pacific cod tacos capped with a zesty tomato-avocado relish; and chicken enchiladas smeared with an aromatic tomatillo salsa.

Boot and Shoe Service

Pizza

3308 Grand Ave. (bet. Lake Park Ave. & Mandana Blvd.), Oakland

Phone: 510-763-2668

Web: www.bootandshoeservice.com

Prices: **$$**

Lunch & dinner Tue – Sun

Can't get a table at Oakland's popular Pizzaiolo? Well, you may not have much luck at sister pizzeria, Boot and Shoe Service, either. Nevertheless, it's still well worth the wait. On a bustling stretch of Grand Avenue, this crammed casual eatery is also a favorite among East Bay locals looking for a quality pie in a low-key, family-friendly atmosphere.

Here you'll find exposed brick walls, laid-back service, and seats at a counter or bare tables that provide unassuming space for comforting Italian meals. Get your greens on in the form of tender asparagus with poached farm egg; then dig into signature seasonal pizzas topped with rapini and house-made fennel-pork sausage, or black olive and tomato with spicy arugula and shaved Grana Padano.

Bridges

International XX

44 Church St. (at Hartz Ave.), Danville

Lunch & dinner daily

Phone: 925-820-7200
Web: www.bridgesdanville.com
Prices: $$

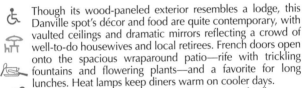

Though its wood-paneled exterior resembles a lodge, this Danville spot's décor and food are quite contemporary, with vaulted ceilings and dramatic mirrors reflecting a crowd of well-to-do housewives and local retirees. French doors open onto the spacious wraparound patio—rife with trickling fountains and flowering plants—and a favorite for long lunches. Heat lamps keep diners warm on cooler days.

Bridges' eclectic *carte du jour* spans a range of influences, from Thai-inspired chicken and prawn spring rolls with a sour-cherry dipping sauce, to Mexican-influenced swordfish accompanied with tangy salsa verde. Lunch favorites like salads and sandwiches are lighter but still very inventive. To fit in with the moneyed crowd, diners should dress to impress.

Brown Sugar Kitchen

American X

2534 Mandela Pkwy. (at 26th St.), Oakland

Lunch Tue – Sun

Phone: 510-839-7685
Web: www.brownsugarkitchen.com
Prices: $$

Southern folks looking for a taste of home will find it in an unlikely spot: the industrial park that Chef Tanya Holland calls "Sweet West Oakland." In her Brown Sugar Kitchen, the French-trained chef whips local, organic ingredients into down-home goodness—think buttermilk fried chicken atop cornmeal waffles with brown sugar butter and apple cider syrup.

Grab a counter seat overlooking the kitchen and let the hunger seep in. Soulful breakfasts include cheddar grits with poached eggs, while lunches offer fried oyster po'boys or baby back ribs glazed with brown sugar and pineapple. Wash it all down with a glass of wine from one of their many African-American producers. Don't miss the dessert counter brimming with snickerdoodle cookies and red velvet cake.

Café Colucci

B2

Ethiopian

6427 Telegraph Ave. (at 65th St.), Oakland

Phone: 510-601-7999

Web: www.cafecolucci.com

Prices:

Lunch & dinner daily

Looks can be deceiving and such is the case with Café Colucci, an Ethiopian eatery with an Italian name. First-timers will find another world where red wall coverings and colorful tables carry the fragrance of foreign spices, many blended in house. Novices need not fret: a friendly, all-Ethiopian staff has your back.

The menus also offer a glossary of sorts, chock-full of enticing delicacies: *shouro fitfit*, or shards of crêpe-like *injera* bread with tomato and jalapeño in olive oil and spicy dressing; *kitfo*, lean raw beef with cardamom in spicy *mitmita*; and *doro wat*, delicate chicken simmered in classic and delicious *berbere*. Vegetarians and meat lovers can put aside their differences: with no utensils to speak of, we're all in this together!

Camino

B3

Californian

3917 Grand Ave. (at Sunny Slope Ave.), Oakland

Phone: 510-547-5035

Web: www.caminorestaurant.com

Prices: $$

Lunch Sat – Sun
Wed – Mon dinner only

Escape from Oakland's Grand Avenue into Camino, a lofty Basque-style dining hall where pressed-tin ceilings and wrought-iron chandeliers hang above exposed brick and salvaged redwood communal tables lit by candles and lined with vintage church pews.

Mammoth bowls laden with fresh produce are a clue to what's on the menu: with 20-year Chez Panisse vet Russell Moore at the fire, you can count on perfectly rustic, seasonal fare. The menu is concise but has something for everyone. Watch from the butcher block counter as cooks in flannel shirts grill Dungeness crabs; bake Tomales Bay oysters in absinthe; and turn out juicy duck breast from the wood-fired oven. Finish with moist bread pudding crowned by huckleberries, almonds, and crème fraîche.

César

Spanish 🍴

B1

1515 Shattuck Ave. (bet. Cedar & Vine Sts.), Berkeley

Phone: 510-883-0222
Web: www.cesarberkeley.com
Prices: $$

Lunch & dinner daily

This tempting tapas bar applies a distinct Californian persuasion to the flavors of Iberia. That sense of "place" isn't surprising considering César was founded by a team of Chez Panisse alumni—the restaurant is located just next door.

Toy with any one of the menu's suggestions for a worthy culinary experience starting with a salt cod-and-potato *cazuela* presented piping-hot and served with a plate of croutons for slathering; transition to grilled *gambas* drenched with sweet yet spicy paprika oil; and conclude with *montadito* (an open-faced sandwich) layering slices of tender duck breast with orange-squeezed aïoli. An impressive beverage list complements the salient array with South American wines, Belgian draft beers, French ciders, and fruit sodas.

Champa Garden

Asian 🍴

C4

2102 8th Ave. (at 21st St.), Oakland

Phone: 510-238-8819
Web: N/A
Prices: ⬮⬮

Lunch & dinner daily

Attention Ivy Hill area residents: curious about the sumptuous scents wafting about the 'hood? Follow them straight to Champa Garden, where Thai, Vietnamese, and Laotian cuisines are served with authenticity. Inside, a small bar replete with an awning serves inexpensive beer and a full menu, while the deep rust dining room is equipped with a disco ball and TV monitor in the corner (karaoke anyone?).

Those overwhelmed by the options can begin with the fried rice ball salad—a tasty pile of crispy fried rice, crumbled pork, green onions, dried chilies, and lime juice, served with romaine lettuce, mint, and cilantro. Just wrap 'em up and enjoy the symphony of textures and flavors. Or rely on tasty dishes of old favorites like the classic pad Thai.

Chevalier

B1   French 🍴🍴

960 Moraga Rd. (at Moraga Blvd.), Lafayette

Phone: 925-385-0793   Dinner Tue – Sun
Web: www.chevalierrestaurant.com
Prices: **$$**

Chevalier radiates French charm from the flowers on its patio to the beautifully manicured hedges. Additionally, the dining room feels wonderfully European with chic inflections like drapes set across walls of windows. Adding to this lure is a cadre of friendly servers—even the chef circulates for a chat with guests, both old and new.

The three-course prix-fixe menu is the only way to go here. Par exemple, start with mixed greens topped with a warm, pastry-wrapped square of goat cheese sprinkled with *herbes de Provence* and a lemon-thyme vinaigrette. Next comes *poulet rôti fermier à la Tropézienne*, perfectly seasoned, crispy skinned chicken draped over a ragout of tomato, squash, olives, and rosemary. Finish with a luscious vanilla bean crème brûlée.

Chez Panisse

B1   Californian 🍴🍴

1517 Shattuck Ave. (bet. Cedar & Vine Sts.), Berkeley

Phone: 510-548-5525   Dinner Mon – Sat
Web: www.chezpanisse.com
Prices: **$$$$**

Much to the dismay of culinary luminaries, Alice Water's Chez Panisse recently suffered a devastating fire. But now there is only good news to report: this Berkeley institution has rebounded and despite some cosmetic boosts, the spirit of Chez Panisse is steadfast. A refreshed brick courtyard and redwood exterior greet the eternal stream of fans on pilgrimage here, even if it's just to glimpse the team at work in their inner sanctorum.

Speaking of which, the open kitchen allows for closer interaction with the brigade as they prepare the epitome of Californian cuisine as seen in a seafood salad of Monterey Bay squid and Tomales Bay clams; sorrel-and-spinach gnocchi with an heirloom tomato concassé; or grilled beef tenderloin with crispy corn fritters.

Chu

Chinese

5362 College Ave. (bet. Bryant & Manila Aves.), Oakland

Phone: 510-601-8818
Web: www.restaurantchu.com
Prices: $$

Lunch Mon – Sat
Dinner nightly

With black furnishings, a dramatic staircase leading to a second-level dining room, and modern Asian art creating a chic atmosphere, this is the rare Chinese restaurant that features a décor as contemporary as its menu. At lunch, the restaurant attracts a decent business crowd; come evening, find tony Rockridge couples sharing pots of fragrant jasmine green tea and refined renditions of Manchurian beef.

The menu combines bold flavors in such dishes as *mu shu bao bing* with tender, stir-fried strips of pork, earthy wood-ear mushrooms, and Chinese spinach ready for wrapping in delicate crêpes. Try the fresh and tasty combo *chow fun* noodles mingling garlic-soy sauce with fresh mussels, sliced calamari, plump prawns, and tender chicken morsels.

Comal

Mexican

2020 Shattuck Ave. (bet. Addison St. & University Ave.), Berkeley

Phone: 510-926-6300
Web: www.comalberkeley.com
Prices: $$

Dinner nightly

The word is out—Comal is excellent and everybody knows it! Jam-packed since day one, the hot spot on this (Berkeley) block serves delicious Mexican dishes in an industrial space fitted with soaring ceilings. Within this lofty lair, the dress is casual and the staff gracious.

The regional food (mostly small plates) is elevated by seasonal Californian ingredients and is great to share. The menu may change frequently, but flavors are consistently spectacular in fresh, tangy, and zesty halibut ceviche; tender corn tortillas filled with wood-grilled rock cod, spicy pickled cabbage, and avocado aïoli; or rich duck enchiladas smothered with delicious *mole coloradito*. Every item is made from scratch—from the griddled tortillas to the wonderful *moles* and salsas.

Commis ✦

Contemporary ✗✗

3859 Piedmont Ave. (at Rio Vista Ave.), Oakland

Phone: 510-653-3902

Dinner Wed – Sun

Web: www.commisrestaurant.com

Prices: $$$

Aaron Shienstra

James Syhabout continues to set the standard for Oakland culinary culture at his tasting menu-only restaurant, where innovative technique marries with pristine local ingredients. The narrow dining room is contemporary and very intimate with sleek unadorned white walls, gray tiles, and a central kitchen counter where the chef and his team carefully plate each dish.

Unusual wines pair wonderfully with the diverse food on offer, and a well-informed staff sets a perfect pace for the array of dishes. Syhabout himself may personally present some courses, offering thoughtful explanations of the technique—no wonder Commis is revered as welcoming without ever sacrificing style. Menus change regularly, but a sampling might include delights like a spoonful of Dungeness crab with quince "snow;" caramelized abalone with sea lettuce purée in a rich and well-seasoned jus; or aged, charcoal-roasted Sonoma duck set over a texturally exquisite walnut-potato mash. Every element of the meal is precise, from the tender house-made bread to the delicate mushroom tisane served between courses.

Desserts like a pistachio cake with diced Asian pear and chicory coffee *granita* deliver a refined finish.

Corso

Italian

B2

1788 Shattuck Ave. (bet. Delaware & Francisco Sts.), Berkeley

Phone: 510-704-8004   Dinner nightly
Web: www.trattoriacorso.com
Prices: $$

Wining and dining her way through Tuscany was hard work for Wendy Brucker, who now shows off the fruits of her labor at Corso in Berkeley. Mementos of her Florentine travels can be found in framed souvenir menus, an all-Italian wine list—poured by taste, glass, or carafe—and in the traditional *bistecca alla Fiorentina*, named for the Renaissance city's Trattoria Sostanza. Nosh on Dungeness crab toast; butternut squash and potato gnocchi; then perhaps panna cotta for dessert. Most menu items are under $20.

True to Tuscany, Corso's dining room is simply set. The best seats may be at the granite kitchen counter where meat lovers will enjoy the view of dangling, house-cured *salumi*. Movie buffs will dig the black-and-white Italian films screened over the bar.

Cosecha

Mexican

B4

907 Washington St. (at 9th St.), Oakland

Phone: 510-452-5900   Lunch & dinner Mon – Sat
Web: www.cosechacafe.com
Prices:

This Mexican café is housed in Old Oakland's historic Swan's Market, a great spot for die-hard food fans. Guests order at the counter and sit at one of the communal tables in the warehouse-like space. Note that they serve dinner but close early, so arrive in time to nibble your way through a menu featuring local ingredients infused into flavorsome Mexican fare.

Everything is homemade including the tortillas and *horchata*. Discover a quesadilla filled with sweet yam and Oaxaca cheese, served with a wonderfully zesty salsa verde. Both achiote-marinated chicken and braised pork tacos are explosively flavorful, topped with pickled onion and cilantro, but save room for *mole verde con pollo*—chicken breast steeped in a delish pumpkin seed-green chile *mole*.

Doña Tomás

 Mexican

5004 Telegraph Ave. (bet. 49th & 51st Sts.), Oakland

Phone: 510-450-0522
Web: www.donatomas.com
Prices: $$

Lunch Sat – Sun
Dinner Tue – Sat

Fresh, seasonal, organic ingredients from the Bay Area are fused with Mexican flavors and preparations resulting in a successful hybrid at Doña Tomás. The restaurant has two dining areas and a bar frequented by locals who come to chat with the friendly bartenders, mingle with friends, and dive into the flavorful Cal-Mex food.

Speaking of which, expect dishes like corn tortilla chips with well-seasoned guacamole; followed by slow-roasted pork layered in soft, delicate tacos and matched with *pico de gallo*, pinto beans, and red rice. Pan-fried petrale sole joined with luscious corn and zucchini pudding keeps fish fans elated.

The happy hour set return time and again for discounted drinks featuring a good selection of Mexican tequila, mezcal, and cerveza.

Dopo

 Italian

4293 Piedmont Ave. (at Echo Ave.), Oakland

Phone: 510-652-3676
Web: www.dopoadesso.com
Prices: $$

Lunch Mon – Fri
Dinner Mon – Sat

With California in the heart and Italy on the mind, Chef/owner Jon Smulewitz, a veteran of nearby mainstay Oliveto, relies on fresh ingredients grown close to home for simply satisfying spreads at Dopo. On sunny afternoons, if the sidewalk seating is full, rest assured that an ample skylight will illuminate the Mediterranean colors inside: mustard and terra-cotta coat the walls; azure tiles glint from the horseshoe bar; and tables are carved from platinum blonde pine.

Start a meal (the menu changes daily) with *crudi* like local halibut with favas and radish. Antipasti such as swordfish with pine nuts, currants, and lemon; or pastas including agnolotti stuffed with lamb and pecorino are not to be overlooked—even if you are a die-hard thin-crust fanatic.

Duende

Spanish XX

B4

468 19th St. (bet. Broadway & Telegraph Ave.), Oakland

Phone: 510-893-0174
Web: www.duendeoakland.com
Prices: $$$

Dinner Wed – Mon

East Bay

Savor the flavors and sounds of Spain at this novel restaurant in developing Uptown Oakland, where Chef Paul Canales turns out everything from *pintxos* to paella. The voluminous bi-level space set in the historic Floral Depot is packed with large windows, exposed brick, and colorful murals which contribute a fun vibe attracting groups of hip, urban types. The food is authentic with seasonal accents and has included rabbit and lobster sausage with blistered Padrón peppers; and seafood-studded *arroz negro*, thick with rockfish, scallops, cherry tomatoes, and garlic aïoli. The crowd is loud and festive, especially when one of the rotating local musicians hits the stage for a set. Like the food and ambience, the music lends Duende a casual, warm energy.

Encuentro

Vegetarian X

B4

202 2nd St. (at Jackson St.), Oakland

Phone: 510-832-9463
Web: www.encuentrooakland.com
Prices: ⊜

Dinner Tue – Sat

Schedule a happy encounter with local produce at Jack London Square's top vegan and vegetarian restaurant. The tiny, window-lined space is easy breezy and Asian-influenced with scattered bamboo tables and a conversation-worthy bar crafted from Japanese reeds. Whether it's gluten-free waffles at brunch or deviled eggs at happy hour, vegetarians and vegans flock here to savor their corner of haute cuisine in the Bay's meat-centric scene.
Inspired dishes include dates stuffed with macadamia-nut pâté, followed by eggs baked with cheddar and pumpkin-seed chili. Flavors are explosive and textures so ingenious that carnivores won't notice the absence of "animal" in seaweed cakes with tartar sauce, slaw, and chili jam, especially when finished with chocolate chip scones.

173

Esin

B5

Mediterranean ✗✗

750 Camino Ramon (at Sycamore Valley Rd.), Danville

Phone: 925-314-0974   Lunch & dinner daily
Web: www.esinrestaurant.com
Prices: $$

Esin brings tasty Mediterranean and American inspiration to this boutique-filled Danville shopping complex. The spacious restaurant outfitted with a front bar combines several dining areas trimmed in dark wood, nicely contrasted with soft beige walls and bright windows. Lunchtime service efficiently accommodates groups of area business people, while evenings draw locals who soak in the ambience.

Meals here might begin with a hearty Tuscan-style kale and white bean soup flavored with oregano and garlic, liberally sprinkled with Parmesan cheese. Then, sample the tender pot roast in reduced jus over a generous mound of garlicky mashed potatoes and roasted root vegetables. Homemade dessert specials are sure to beckon, as in the warm fig and almond galette.

FIVE

B2

American ✗✗

2086 Allston Way (at Shattuck Ave.), Berkeley

Phone: 510-225-6055   Lunch & dinner daily
Web: www.five-berkeley.com
Prices: $$

Set on the main level of the Shattuck Plaza, FIVE caters to hotel guests and stylish suits. Yet, it is an equally cherished destination among locals and families too. The boldly patterned walls and massive chandelier lend a sense of drama, while service is welcoming and friendly.

The menu of well-prepared American fare is as wonderful as the décor itself. Expect items where every element oozes deliciousness as in rich duck confit enchiladas crowned with tangy salsa verde, avocado purée, lime crème fraîche, and *queso fresco*. Add to it an elegant side of "mac" and cheese (piping-hot orzo with smoked Gouda and tangy organic tomato jam), and finish with an excellent butterscotch pudding with peanut brittle and whipped cream that simply must *not* be missed.

Gather

B2

2200 Oxford St. (at Allston Way.), Berkeley

Phone:	510-809-0400	Lunch & dinner daily
Web:	www.gatherrestaurant.com	
Prices:	$$	

For organic omnivorous fare and biodynamic wines, set off to Gather, just a stone fruit's throw from UC Berkeley. From the open kitchen, skilled cooks boldly master the humble vegetable with a dexterity that can make even the most self-assured carnivore begin to question himself. These conversions begin with the vegan charcuterie platter (served at dinner only).

This is campus territory where a festive collegiate vibe rules and the cocktails flow freely. Herbivores might opt for roasted brassicas with chanterelles, artichokes, Red Flint polenta, and hazelnut breadcrumbs; while meat lovers relish golden-seared diver scallops atop tender shredded oxtail. The fig cake may be a crowd-pleaser, but the Redwood Hill Farms goat milk semifreddo is a revelation.

Grand Avenue Thai

B4

384 Grand Ave. (bet. Perkins St. & Staten Ave.), Oakland

Phone:	510-444-1507	Lunch Mon – Sat
Web:	www.grandavethai.net	Dinner nightly
Prices:		

Thanks to its charming décor, friendly service, and flavorful cuisine, Grand Avenue Thai is a winning standout—just one block from picturesque Lake Merritt. The space is small with bright walls, fresh flowers, and colorful local artwork. Service is prompt even with a steady to-go business.

Be sure to try one of the house favorites like the sweet and fragrant coconut curry with chunks of pumpkin, eggplant, broccoli, and string beans. The summer rolls neatly wrap up fresh veggies and garlicky rice noodles for a dip in peanut-chili sauce. The ever-popular pad Thai combines plump prawns stir-fried with egg, bean sprouts, scallions, and peanuts in a tasty tamarind-Thai fish sauce. Spice can be tame, but the kitchen is happy to indulge the fire fiends.

Hamro Aangan

A1

Nepali

856 San Pablo Ave. (bet. Solano & Washington Aves.), Albany

Phone: 510-524-2220 Lunch & dinner daily
Web: www.hamroaangan.com
Prices:

 Hamro Aangan is not your routine Indian spot with Nepali accents thrown in for good measure. Instead, this trinket parades an excellent mix of Indian and Nepali dishes that are as spicy as they are addictive. Housed within a spacious room, pretty peach tones contrast rather lyrically with a brick wall canvassed in scenes of Nepal and Tibet.

Matching its fiery flavor-profile, tabletops are also dressed in bright woven fabrics. Add this to the lure of Indian hospitality, and it's no wonder Hamro is so adored for its substantial portions of chicken *momo*, steamed chicken dumplings splashed with mint chutney; *khashi ko masu*, goat curry infused with smoky *garam masala*; and a delightfully crispy *masala dosa* served with creamy coconut chutney.

Haven

B4

Contemporary

44 Webster St. (at Jack London Sq.), Oakland

Phone: 510-663-4440 Lunch Sun
Web: www.havenoakland.com Dinner nightly
Prices: $$$

 Daniel Patterson of Coi fame is responsible for this wonderful arrival in Jack London Square. Haven's ample space, with its floor-to-ceiling windows and harbor-facing views, has an airy feel, and is styled in warm woods, shiny steel, and pristine white tiles.

The best seats in the house reside at the kitchen-facing counter, so snag one and get things started with smoked pasta—ribbons of al dente goodness bursting with pancetta and cracked black pepper in a decadent cream sauce. Next, try the tender lamb braised in coffee liqueur and paired with carrots, onions, and shallots. Pan-roasted Brussels sprouts tossed with mint and lime juice are bound to elevate any experience, thrillingly chased by baked California, an almond cookie topped with yuzu sorbet.

Hawker Fare

A s i a n

2300 Webster St. (at 23rd St.), Oakland

Phone:	510-832-8896
Web:	www.hawkerfare.com
Prices:	

Lunch Mon – Fri
Dinner Tue – Sat

Street carts often dole out some of the tastiest food you can find, but who wants to stand on a street corner as you nibble and nosh? Salvation can be found at Hawker Fare. This Oakland newcomer brings the flavors of Southeast Asian street carts inside to a funky, but friendly, space filled with graffiti-decorated walls and stained concrete floors.

Mostly Thai in influence, the inexpensive menu features appetizers and main course rice bowls topped with everything from lemongrass chicken and pork belly to *Issan* sausage and beef short ribs. Tasty salads like the *larb* with grilled beef and fish sauce-lime vinaigrette; and the Hawker *affogato*, made with condensed milk-flavored soft-serve ice cream and a shot of Thai coffee, are especially refreshing.

Hong Kong East Ocean

C h i n e s e

3199 Powell St. (at Emeryville Marina), Emeryville

Phone:	510-655-3388
Web:	www.hkeo.us
Prices:	

Lunch & dinner daily

Primo panoramic views of the Bay Bridge and cityscape give this two-story favorite well-deserved attention. The spacious dining rooms may appear slightly dated, but who cares, given the stunning waterfront scene?

Lunchtime here at Hong Kong East Ocean is a dim sum affair. The place is packed with business folks savoring their *xiao long bao* (ground pork soup dumplings with fragrant, ginger-infused pork broth); fluffy pork buns; delicious sticky-rice-noodle crêpes filled with garlicky beef and cilantro; or steamed vegetable rolls, stuffed with sautéed mushrooms and wrapped in tofu. Nights draw a large crowd of local families who show up for seafood offerings such as wok-fried Dungeness crab with spicy herbs, or rock cod with ginger and scallions.

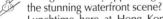

Ikaros

 B4

Greek 🍴🍴

3268 Grand Ave. (bet. Mandana Blvd. & Santa Clara Ave.), Oakland

Phone: 510-899-4400   Lunch & dinner daily
Web: www.ikarosgr.com
Prices: 💰💰

♿ While there are no white, sandy beaches here, the soothing Grecian vibe, Greek patrons, and scrumptious bites will take you at least part of the way to the Aegean Islands. Inside, Mediterranean blues and whites color the high-arched ceiling, where a long skylight evokes that sublime island feel; framed photos of the coast, white stone sculptures, and authentic music seal the deal.

Sit down to an order of tangy *dolmades* stuffed with rice and fresh herbs, served with a thick yogurt sauce. Next sink your teeth into a gyros stacker—chunks of well-seasoned lamb and chicken, served with pita, thick steak fries, sliced red onion, tomato, and *tzatziki*. The classic spanakopita filled with spinach, dill, and feta is crispy and very delicious.

Ippuku

B2

Japanese 🍴

2130 Center St. (bet. Oxford St. & Shattuck Ave.), Berkeley

Phone: 510-665-1969   Lunch Fri – Sat
Web: www.ippukuberkeley.com   Dinner nightly
Prices: $$

♿ Ippuku is not just tasty but a wholly fun experience. The hidden gem, just steps from UC Berkley, thrives in a strip of restaurants and bars. Its traditional entrance leads to the slim room outfitted with low tables over floor cut-outs, booths, and a dining counter situated before a grill in the back. However, the front is really where the chefs meticulously work their magic.

The décor is a stunning display of urban Japan with wood and cement accents. Ippuku is also an ace date place, secreted away from the bustle outside even though it sees a routine roster of students and locals. Lit sake bottles cast a gentle glow upon plates of yuba dolloped with wasabi; *tsukune* with yakitori sauce; and skewered Brussels sprouts with *shichimi*-Kewpie mayo.

Kamdesh

Afghan ✕

B4

346 14th St. (at Webster St.), Oakland

Phone:	510-286-1900
Web:	N/A
Prices:	💰

Lunch & dinner daily

Cheerfully perched on a commercial corner in downtown Oakland, Kamdesh's sunny yellow façade is a welcome sight. Expect to find business folks at lunch, locals at dinner, and a take-out clientele all day long.

Afghan *kababs* are all the rage here—perfectly seasoned, marinated, charbroiled, and absolutely mouthwatering. Try the lamb *tikka kabab*, moist and smoky with cumin, piled over fluffy *pallow* (brown basmati rice) infused with lamb jus and completed with a spicy cilantro chutney and salad. Other delicious options include tender *mantoo* dumplings stuffed with seasoned ground beef and onions, then drizzled with tangy yogurt sauce; or the flavorful charbroiled chicken wrap with yogurt, cucumber, tomato, mint, and red onion in a chewy, thick *nan*.

Kirala

Japanese ✕

B2

2100 Ward St. (at Shattuck Ave.), Berkeley

Phone:	510-549-3486
Web:	www.kiralaberkeley.com
Prices:	💰

Lunch Mon – Fri
Dinner nightly

This Berkeley corner locale is completely casual and packed at prime times. Though its retro Formica-topped look is rather dated, nobody seems to mind. Kirala is a great stop for Japanese chow, no matter what you crave. Purists beware: the crowd-pleasing menu spans the cuisine, from *robata*-grilled specialties to sushi and noodle dishes.

Meals may start with crisp-fried *gyoza* stuffed with pork, scallion, and ginger served with a salty-tangy ponzu dipping sauce. If you're not going the sushi route, salmon teriyaki is a delicious choice—the moist, flaky fish with nicely balanced sauce is served with a mixed green salad and roasted, glazed sweet potato.

Food arrives quickly, though *robata* and sushi dishes take a bit more time and care during the rush.

Marzano

C4

Pizza

4214 Park Blvd. (at Glenfield Ave.), Oakland

Phone: 510-531-4500
Web: www.marzanorestaurant.com
Prices: $$

Lunch Sat – Sun
Dinner nightly

This Oakland eatery takes its name from the town located on the volcanic slopes that produce the world's best tomatoes, and Marzano strives to honor this legacy. Gothic chandeliers and hand-blown glass wine casks illuminate the timber beams and brick walls, while an 800-degree fire in the wood-burning pizza oven casts a glow on the kitchen. Tip your hat to the *pizzaiolo*: his blood and sweat are your tears of joy.

Charred and chewy Neapolitan pies are pure perfection whether you choose the simple Margherita or a specialty topped with calamari, pecorino, and spicy tomato. Begin with *gnocchi alla Romana* set on goat cheese and wilted spinach or fire-roasted winter squash with *burrata* and marjoram. The close-knit bar is ideal for an antipasto and *vino*.

Metro Lafayette

B1

Californian

3524 Mt. Diablo Blvd. (bet. 1st St. & Oak Hill Rd.), Lafayette

Phone: 925-284-4422
Web: www.metrolafayette.com
Prices: $$

Lunch & dinner daily

The signs and framed vintage map hint of the Paris Metro, but this longtime hot spot could be renamed "The Patio." Both cuisine and dining are decidedly Californian and that means enjoying this flavor-packed fare out on the patio or inside the sophisticated space fitted with a bar and sunroom overlooking local scenesters dining alfresco.

The oft-changing menu embraces global flavors, so a meal might start with a surprisingly light and complex rendition of onion soup that is perfectly seasoned, silky from a dash of cream, and presented with Parmesan toast. Follow this with two tacos loaded with tender grilled fish, salsa verde, avocado, drizzles of lime *crema*, and fresh tomato salsa. Seasonal desserts may reveal a warm organic plum crisp.

Miss Ollie's

Caribbean ✗

901 Washington St. (at 9th St.), Oakland

Phone: 510-285-6188   Lunch & dinner Tue – Sat
Web: www.missolliesoakland.com
Prices: $$

Raised in Barbados, Chef/owner Sarah Kirnon brings a taste of the Caribbean to her novel home in Old Oakland. Named after her grandmother, Miss Ollie's features an utilitarian-chic space, enlivened by corner windows, cheerful paintings, and deep orange bottles of house-made habanero sauce. Watch out—it rings with spice and packs a punch.

Callaloo, *ackee*, *chow chow*, and *giromon* may not be words in the average foodie's vernacular, but Chef Kirnon presents them here, as part of a pleasing roster of dishes like *phulourie*—crisp *garam masala*-tinged split-pea fritters, served with *shado beni* or tamarind chutney—washed down with sorrel, a sweet hibiscus punch. But, it's that familiar moist, crispy fried chicken that takes the crown, so grab it if available.

Mount Everest

Nepali ✗✗

2598 Telegraph Ave. (at Parker St.), Berkeley

Phone: 510-843-3951   Lunch & dinner daily
Web: www.themounteverestrestaurant.com
Prices: ⊜

Lured by the wafting scents of spices just a few blocks south of UC Berkeley's campus, students, professors, and local business people flock to Mount Everest. The corner spot has plenty of light, cheery yellow walls, friendly service, and a relaxed atmosphere. Overflow crowds settle on the balcony.

The menu offers Indian cuisine, but specializes in traditional Nepalese dishes like steamed *momos* filled with minced cabbage, carrot, and onion, with a deeply spiced dipping sauce of sesame, turmeric, and ginger. The earthy *channa masala* or chickpea stew with distinct seasoning; and chicken *tikka masala* featuring creamy tomato sauce infused with pungent spices, both beg to be sopped up with naan and rice. Students appreciate the inexpensive *thali* at lunch.

East Bay

East Bay

900 Grayson

American

900 Grayson St. (at 7th St.), Berkeley

Phone: 510-704-9900
Web: www.900grayson.com
Prices:

Lunch Mon – Sat

On the corner of a commercial stretch of Berkeley is a colorful cottage with decorative tile trim that practically shouts, "chicken and waffles." Good thing, too, since 900 Grayson is only open for breakfast, lunch, and weekend brunch. But the little spot has a dedicated following of regulars who don't mind waiting for a table during the busy brunch time.

See what the fuss is about with a Caesar salad of gem lettuce and rustic croutons showered with *manchego* and tossed in classic dressing with a hint of anchovy; or a "piggy" sandwich of milk-braised pulled pork shoulder slathered onto an Acme bun with barbecue sauce, caramelized onions, and tangy red cabbage slaw, served with herb-dusted fries. Top it off with an artisanal root beer float. Ah, weekends.

Ohgane

Korean

3915 Broadway (bet. 38th & 40th Sts.), Oakland

Phone: 510-594-8300
Web: www.ohgane.com
Prices:

Lunch & dinner daily

Ohgane still beats out the local Korean competition thanks to its delicious food, contemporary dining rooms, and private parking lot (huge bonus in this area!). Business crowds appreciate the all-you-can-eat lunch buffet. At night, Korean families gather beneath the ventilation hoods for tabletop mesquite grilling (*soot-bool*)—a specialty that is absolutely the way to go for dinner. During lunch, have the kitchen grill it for you and still enjoy the likes of smoky and tender *galbee*—beef short ribs marinated for 72 hours in garlic, soy, and sesame oil.

First, meals here start with an assortment of *banchan*—sixteen small bites including spicy kimchi, glazed sweet yam, and mild egg cake. Other kitchen-prepared dishes include *mandoo* and *dolsot bibimbap*.

Oliveto

Italian

B3

5655 College Ave. (at Shafter Ave.), Oakland

Phone: 510-547-5356

Web: www.oliveto.com

Prices: $$$

Lunch Mon – Fri

Dinner nightly

Sandwiched between a gourmet market and bud-sized flower shop in impossibly charming Rockridge, Oliveto is just the sort of secluded spot that's perfect for a mid-afternoon glass of *vino*. The café downstairs serves a mean oven-grilled pizza, but for real culinary action, wind your way up the spiral staircase and into the well-loved dining room.

Here, guests have reserved early for tables by large windows overlooking College Avenue; gastronomes prefer the view of the central wood-burning oven that's fired up to turn out pan-roasted pigeon with meaty porcini mushrooms. A shaved root vegetable salad with almond pesto provides just the right amount of crunch before a hearty plate of saffron-infused *chitarra* with Monterey squid ragù redolent of hot peppers.

Phnom Penh House

Cambodian

B4

251 8th St. (bet. Alice & Harrison Sts.), Oakland

Phone: 510-893-3825

Web: www.phnompenhhouse.com

Prices:

Lunch & dinner Mon – Sat

Devotees in the know pray to the parking gods and push through Oakland's Chinatown crowds to get to one of the best Cambodian restaurants in the Bay Area. While the outside appears unassuming, the interior is a calm respite with colorful, native artwork and temple tiles. Expect a warm welcome from the family who runs this simple but pleasant place.

The menu is full of flavorful, fragrant, and fresh dishes such as a vibrant salad of shredded green papaya, carrots, and delicious herbs tossed in a garlicky house-made vinaigrette. The spicy flavors of lemongrass permeate tofu cubes sautéed with onion, button mushrooms, and red bell pepper; and infuse the *sach chhrouk ann kreun*—charbroiled and glazed pork with crunchy, tangy pickled vegetables.

Picán

Southern XXX

2295 Broadway (at 23rd St.), Oakland

Phone: 510-834-1000

Lunch & dinner daily

Web: www.picanrestaurant.com

Prices: $$

Picán is all business in Oakland—jamming with a corporate set at lunch and after-work cocktail clusters at dusk. The large space flaunts a bar and lounge (where you can order off the menu), and elegant dining areas with soaring ceilings and stately columns. The team of servers are friendly if a bit scattered during busy meal times.

While the chef change may have at times brought a few bumps in the road, the dishes turned out by the kitchen now are smoothing out nicely. Look for braised pork belly with buttery white beans and thick toast; the signature buttermilk fried chicken with decadent smoked Gouda mac 'n cheese and a side of cabbage- and pickled red onion-slaw; or hushpuppies with mustard dipping sauce. Don't miss their fantastic Bourbon selection.

Pizzaiolo

Pizza X

5008 Telegraph Ave. (bet. 49th & 51st Sts.), Oakland

Phone: 510-652-4888

Dinner Mon – Sat

Web: www.pizzaiolooakland.com

Prices: $$

Lines are still a given at Temescal's pizza palace. In fact, find eager patrons arriving before the doors even open. A smattering of entrées and hearty plates like king salmon baked on a fig leaf with asparagus and mint yogurt evoke spring on a plate. But, crowds are here for their pies, crisp from the wood-burning oven and topped with the finest and freshest of ingredients like tangy tomato sauce, house-made sausage, and decadent *panna*.

The large dining room with handsome plank floors and dark wood tables centers around the exhibition kitchen lined with bowls of pristine local produce. Couples and groups gather at tables or pack the polished wood bar; add on a rich caramel *pot de crème* and the endless queues will start to make sense.

Plum

Contemporary ✗✗

B4

2214 Broadway (at 22nd St.), Oakland

Phone: 510-444-7586   Dinner nightly
Web: www.plumoakland.com
Prices: $$

Gourmands in the know congregate for a casual meal and cocktails at this discreet spot in Uptown, marked only by a crown of lights. Inside, like its namesake fruit, the dining room is shaded a rich purple and pivots around a sleek counter with a view into the gleaming, open kitchen. The boxy wood stools are more comfortable than they look, as are the chunky communal tables.

Seasonality rules the changing menu, which may open with a fragrant green garlic- roasted leeks- and potato-chowder; segue into homemade duck pastrami over strawberries and fried *farro*; and close with white chocolate cheesecake crested with grapefruit gelée. Along the way, feel free to quiz the eager cooks on their job and ask for a wine recommendation from the all-Californian list.

Prima

Italian ✗✗

C1

1522 N. Main St. (bet. Bonanza St. & Lincoln Ave.), Walnut Creek

Phone: 925-935-7780   Lunch Mon – Sat
Web: www.primawine.com   Dinner nightly
Prices: $$$

With a premier location amid high-end boutiques, this contemporary Italian Romeo is a draw for business folk and local shoppers alike. The spacious interior wears a contemporary style accentuated by smart tables.

There are three distinct seating areas: a glass-enclosed porch framed in dark wood, a front room with views of the wood-fired oven, and another dining haven just past the bar with a fireplace and vaulted ceilings. The food is authentically Italian, from a refreshing panzanella salad tossed with sweet basil and ripe heirloom tomatoes; to al dente *tagliatelle* swirled with a meaty ragù. Considering the hefty prices, service may be lacking. But, all blemishes quickly fade away thanks to their distinguished atmosphere and notable food.

Ramen Shop

Japanese

B2

5812 College Ave. (bet. Chabot Rd. & Oak Grove Ave.), Oakland

Phone: 510-788-6370   Dinner Wed – Mon
Web: www.ramenshop.com
Prices:

A trio of Chez Panisse buddies have brought their innovative take on ramen to this quaint stretch of Rockridge. The slender shop has been a winner since day one and seats local residents plus visitors at a Douglas fir counter. Beyond, find the talented brigade hard at work in the steaming kitchen accented with jade green tiles. Tables are a more child-friendly seating option.

Ingredient-driven goodness is revealed in each bowl. Take for example the *shoyu* Meyer lemon ramen with its amber, pork-infused broth afloat with droplets of melted fat, plunged with distinctly straight, thin, house-made noodles and luscious *chasu* bobbing with a soft-boiled egg and chewy Mendocino nori. A swipe of fragrant citrus zest offers that oh-so-Californian flourish.

Riva Cucina

Italian

A2

800 Heinz Ave. (at 7th St.), Berkeley

Phone: 510-841-7482   Lunch Tue – Fri
Web: www.rivacucina.com   Dinner Tue – Sat
Prices: $$

Riva Cucina has all of the charm you'd expect from a restaurant specializing in what is ostensibly, Italy's culinary soul—Emilia Romagna, where Chef Massimiliano Boldrini hails from. Most of the kitchen action is on view from the tables or bar in the airy room, but for a private repast make your way behind those red velvet panels. The walls are bare, but the colors are deep and warm.

Locals are lucky to partake of their regional cooking. From a small but appealing menu, pick an artichoke soup before moving on to cloud-light knobs of gnocchi in a creamy sauce of smoked salmon; and finish with an excellent pork loin scaloppini trickled with capers and verdant spinach. With just one bite of the *torta della nonna* you'll notice the kitchen's attention to detail.

Rivoli

Californian XX

 A1

1539 Solano Ave. (bet. Neilson St. & Peralta Ave.), Berkeley

Phone: 510-526-2542   Dinner nightly
Web: www.rivolirestaurant.com
Prices: $$

 Northern Californian cooking with a trace of Italian flavor is the main draw at this lush charmer on the Albany-Berkeley border, serving up delectable and seasonal dishes. Rivoli is always popular and a winner among its patrons, who come here to savor undeniably excellent items like a crisp endive salad tossing peppery arugula, sweet plums, and blue cheese. Tender braised lamb-stuffed ravioli topped with tomato sauce, spiced chickpeas, and garlic-mint yogurt is another jewel.

Set in an adorable cottage, the dining room also features enormous picture windows overlooking a verdant "secret" garden blooming with tender fronds and climbing ivy. The greenery is a stunning contrast to the crisp, white-linen tables, smartly serviced by an engaging waitstaff.

Sahn Maru

Korean X

B3

4315 Telegraph Ave. (bet. 43rd & 44th Sts.), Oakland

Phone: 510-653-3366   Lunch & dinner Wed – Mon
Web: www.sahnmarukoreanbbq.com
Prices: $$

 As one of East Bay's top Korean restaurants, Sahn Maru's name (which translates as "top of the mountain") is perfectly fitting. Its casual vibe, large size, and friendly service makes it a good choice for groups. Never mind the wainscoting and country-quaint chairs that juxtapose walls covered with pictures of Korean dishes—this is a place for authentic food. Meals start with barley tea and tasty *banchan* like daikon kimchi, bean sprout salad in sesame oil, and fish cakes, alongside a bowl of delicately flavored kelp and daikon soup. Lunchtime might feature a deliciously unexpected combination of beef *bulgogi* stir-fried with *jap chae*. While the spot earns raves for Korean barbecue, the kitchen prepares it for you, as there are no tabletop grills.

Sasa

C1

Japanese 𝕏𝕏

1432 N. Main St. (bet. Cypress St. & Lincoln Ave.), Walnut Creek

Phone: 925-210-0188   Lunch & dinner daily
Web: www.sasawc.com
Prices: $$

For a stylish, contemporary Japanese retreat in the heart of Walnut Creek, Sasa is a true find. Sleek furnishings, stone accents, water streams, and a lovely garden patio give this respite its flair and feel. Not to be outdone, the crowd here is as chic as the space itself and gathers for delicious sake sips alongside small plates of modern Japanese fare.

While avid Japanophiles and purists might cry foul, the rest of us can enjoy the creative interpretations of traditional ingredients and flavors, evident in such sushi and *makimono* as the N. Main filled with tuna, crab, and a spicy aïoli. Other dishes might include smoky kalbi beef lettuce wraps crested with *sukemono* or fluffy popcorn chicken *kara-age* finished with sea salt and lemon juice.

Sidebar

B4

Gastropub 𝕏

542 Grand Ave. (bet. Euclid Ave. & MacArthur Blvd.), Oakland

Phone: 510-452-9500   Lunch Mon – Fri
Web: www.sidebar-oaktown.com   Dinner Mon – Sat
Prices: $$

Waft into Sidebar along with the breeze from Lake Merritt for artisanal cocktails (need a Corpse Reviver?) and Mediterranean-inspired gastropub dining in a quirky space. Photographs of life on the road add character to the pumpkin-spiced interior, anchored by a U-shaped copper bar. Go with friends and belly up to the communal table or score a seat at the dining counter with views of the open kitchen.

Lunchtime focuses on sandwiches, such as a meaty Cuban with roast pork, Gruyère, and jalapeño relish; or the Monte Cristo *panino* with lighter options including a smoked trout salad. Dinners are hearty and wholesome, featuring the likes of baked pasta dishes or a Basque seafood stew. Wine lovers will find varietals from California, France, and Spain.

Slow

Californian

B2

1966 University Ave. (bet. Martin Luther King Jr. Way & Milvia St.), Berkeley

Phone: 510-647-3663   Lunch Mon – Sat
Web: www.slowberkeley.com   Dinner Tue – Sat
Prices:

Slow lives up to its credo of presenting gourmet food crafted from local ingredients at judicious prices. Once inside this slightly sized refuge, place your order at the counter, and then take a seat among a handful of tables in the jovial, yellow-walled front area featuring an open kitchen. Note—for those looking to linger, dine out back in the pretty rose garden.

The roster of Californian dishes spins to the season and expectedly gushes with flavor. While some may start with a chilled beet and savoy salad tossed with tangy goat cheese and a refreshing Meyer lemon *citronette*; others may opt to dive straight into meaty ox tail braised until falling off the bone and coupled with caramelized pieces of sunchoke, heirloom carrots, and cauliflower.

Tacubaya

Mexican

A2

1788 4th St. (bet. Hearst Ave. & Virginia St.), Berkeley

Phone: 510-525-5160   Lunch & dinner daily
Web: www.tacubaya.net
Prices:

Don't let the crowded patio and long line deter you from this Fourth Street neighborhood favorite: good frijoles come to those who wait. But truly, once you reach the register at this go-to Mexican, your order will arrive faster than you can correctly pronounce Tacubaya.

Sister to Oakland's Doña Tomas, Tacubaya has all the trimmings of a beloved taqueria—festive color scheme, wrought-iron chandeliers, and a communal vibe. But the vibrant chalkboard is the object of everyone's focus. Here, find the likes of *tacos al pastor*; seasonal *chile rellenos*; and mushroom quesadillas. Open at 10:00 A.M. for *desayuno*, arrive here early for the *revueltos Norteños*, or scrambled eggs with *nopales*, tomatoes, and black beans. Wash it down with a blood orange *aqua fresca*.

Tamarindo

B4

Mexican

468 8th St. (at Broadway), Oakland

Phone: 510-444-1944   Lunch & dinner Mon – Sat
Web: www.tamarindoantojeria.com
Prices: ⊜⊜

Gather a gang of amigos and pop into this sunny spot for a banquet of mouthwatering *antojitos*—small plates, or "little whims." These sharable bites may be small, but they're big on flavor, so park it on the wooden communal table and prepare for a feast. Munch on the likes of *tamales de Oaxaca* steamed in banana leaves; smoky chipotle meatballs; crispy shrimp tacos; or *torta Poblana*, a pile of grilled chicken, melted cheese, avocado, and roasted poblano in a fresh torpedo roll spread with black beans and aïoli.

In a space styled in whitewashed walls and tin ceilings, the Miel tequila bar pours a wealth of *coctels* made with the beloved liquor. Hospitality is first-rate, thanks to Gloria Dominguez and her family, who run the place with heart.

Thai House

B5

Thai

254 Rose Ave. (bet. Diablo Rd. & Linda Mesa Ave.), Danville

Phone: 925-820-0635   Lunch Mon – Fri
Web: www.thaihousedanville.net   Dinner nightly
Prices: ⊜⊜

On a quiet, tree-lined street just off of the main road, flower beds and large umbrellas surround this charming bungalow. Inside, cozy nooks accommodate work lunches or families dining amid ornate Thai art, carvings, and tapestries. Embroidered fabrics cover the tables and complement the pretty blue-and-white pottery.

The menu is just as impressive, offering authentic dishes made from fresh ingredients with explosive flavor (heat levels are adjusted per your request). The red curry with moist, tender chicken, perfectly cooked vegetables, and basil served with jasmine rice has a delectable balance of creaminess, sweetness, spiciness, and tanginess. Silky yet crisp cubes of tofu *pad kra-prow* infused with fantastic red-chili heat are sure to delight.

The Peasant & The Pear

B5

267 Hartz Ave. (at Linda Mesa Ave.), Danville

Phone: 925-820-6611   Lunch & dinner Tue – Sun
Web: www.thepeasantandthepear.com
Prices: $$

East Bay

Peasants are hard to come by at this upscale Danville bistro, which draws ladies who lunch for leisurely meals in its cozy environs. But despite its wealthy clientele, this spot isn't the least bit stuffy, thanks to a friendly staff in the dining room and a relaxed California spirit in the kitchen.

Named for a nearby pear orchard that was once the world's largest, this restaurant features numerous pear dishes, like a grilled double-cut Sonoma pork chop with sweet potato-and-pear gratin. Chef/owner Rodney Worth, who trained under Loretta Keller, offers a playful and eclectic menu, from creamy *burrata* in a toasted baguette sandwich with pear-honey compote to Kentucky Bourbon crème fraîche atop a velvety butternut squash soup.

Tribune Tavern

B4

401 13th St. (at Franklin St.), Oakland

Phone: 510-452-8742   Lunch & dinner daily
Web: www.tribunetavern.com
Prices: $$

The team behind foodie-mobbed Chop Bar resurrected an Oakland landmark for their latest project: the former newsroom of the iconic *Tribune* building. And baby boy is quite the looker, featuring luxe leather sofas, wine barrels, and stained glass casting an elegant light onto the horseshoe-shaped bar.

Corporate types pack the bar for hearty, English-inspired items like a whole rabbit cooked down and presented as a jar of spreadable delight; Shepherd's pie bubbling with ground meat and topped with Parmesan-potato mash; and a strawberry trifle sundae. Groups can go whole hog with a $75 sausage platter which includes sides and a pitcher of beer from the well-curated selection. Cocktails are stellar, while teetotalers are kept happy with house-made sodas.

Uzen

B3

 Japanese

5415 College Ave. (bet. Hudson St. & Kales Ave.), Oakland

Phone: 510-654-7753
Web: N/A
Prices: $$

Lunch Mon – Fri
Dinner Mon – Sat

Small Uzen may have a blink-and-you-missed-it façade, but really, you wouldn't want to pass up this popular sushi restaurant. There isn't much in terms of décor, but the space gets flooded with natural light from a front wall of windows. The best seats in the house are at the sushi bar where you can chat with the friendly chefs who will share their recommendations.

The à la carte menu is ideal for less exploratory palates, but the best way to enjoy Uzen is via their list of fresh nigiri personally handled by the *itamae*. Traditional flavors come alive in a crispy vegetable roll with toasted nori; firm slices of albacore tuna, rich silky slivers of mackerel, and tender fresh water eel, each presented over neat mounds of sushi rice. It's all so *oishi-so*!

Va de Vi

C1

Fusion

1511 Mt. Diablo Blvd. (near Main St.), Walnut Creek

Phone: 925-979-0100
Web: www.vadevi.com
Prices: $$

Lunch & dinner daily

"Va de vi" is a Catalan phrase that roughly means "It's all about wine." Here you'll find no dissent from the moneyed locals who gather for flights with such cheeky names as "There's No Place Like Rhone." The fountain-enhanced, bucolic patio is a treasured sipping destination, as is the L-shaped counter with a view of the open kitchen set amid rich polished woods.

Good wine demands good food, and the global menu offered here entices with ultra-fresh choices like ahi tuna tartare topped with wasabi tobiko; or roasted asparagus in romesco, crowned with baked prosciutto chips. Asian influences abound particularly in soy-glazed black cod; or pork belly with sticky rice and a chili glaze. Add on a sweet staff and easy vibe—no wonder it's such a hit.

Vanessa's Bistro

Vietnamese

A1

1715 Solano Ave. (at Tulare Ave.), Berkeley

Phone: 510-525-8300   Dinner Wed – Mon
Web: www.vanessasbistro.com
Prices: $$

There may be no sexier pairing of words than French-Vietnamese, the culinary temptress behind wonders like duck strudel with wild mushrooms and basil risotto. For this tasty fix, head to Vanessa's Bistro, the packed Berkeley spot, run by Chef Vanessa Dang, and begin the night with wicked specialty cocktails at the bamboo-topped bar.

Creative types are wise to listen for the specials; or, go all the way with a four-course tasting menu for parties of 7 or more. Of course, ordering à la carte does have its perks—small plates are perfectly suited for sharing. Tease your palate with crispy salt-and-pepper prawns with chili-lime dipping sauce, green papaya salad, and banana-raisin-peach bread pudding for dessert. Also look for Vanessa's Bistro in Walnut Creek.

Walnut Creek Yacht Club

Seafood

C1

1555 Bonanza St. (at Locust St.), Walnut Creek

Phone: 925-944-3474   Lunch & dinner Mon – Sat
Web: www.wcyc.net
Prices: $$

Keys to a yacht are not required at this marine-themed restaurant in Walnut Creek, with mahogany and teak fixtures and a boatload of sailing tchotchkes. America's Cup pennants and an authentic jib add to the nautical vibe; if that's not enough, grab a seat at the raw bar for a lesson in oyster shucking.

Chef/owner Kevin Weinberg takes seafood seriously—as did the Mako shark now hanging over the bar. Fish is fresh, never frozen, with nearly a dozen daily selections ready to be grilled and served with simple sides. Other aquatic fare may include seafood cocktails; lobster macaroni and cheese gratin; mahi mahi tacos; or an Idaho trout BLT on ciabatta. Few can resist the Commodore's sundae or warm triple chocolate brownie with vanilla bean ice cream.

Wood Tavern

Californian

6317 College Ave. (bet. Alcatraz Ave. & 63rd St.), Oakland

Phone: 510-654-6607
Web: www.woodtavern.net
Prices: $$

Lunch Mon – Sat
Dinner nightly

 Wood Tavern borders Oakland and Berkeley on a stretch of College Avenue full of little shops and cafés. Surrounded by pale green walls, wood joists, and wine racks, locals gather at the happening bar or catch up with friends over a meal. It's the idyllic, casual, neighborhood spot.

The butcher-block charcuterie and cheese board selections are popular starts. Then, move on to the black mission fig tart on puff pastry with onion jam and blue cheese foam, served with a watercress salad with prosciutto. Linger over perfectly seasoned burgers topped with oozing cheddar and homemade pickles on crusty baguettes, served with mounds of crisp shoestring fries. Save room for the chocolate brownie in a pool of salted caramel with a scoop of malt ice cream.

Zachary's Chicago Pizza

Pizza

5801 College Ave. (at Oak Grove Ave.), Oakland

Phone: 510-655-6385
Web: www.zacharys.com
Prices:

Lunch & dinner daily

 Zachary's is an institution. Established thirty years ago, the company is now 100% employee-owned and has four locations in the East Bay, all specializing in Chicago-style stuffed pizza. They also bake a more traditional pie, which may be thin on crust, but is always thick on flavor, as in the Mediterranean with zesty tomato sauce, olives, artichoke, feta, and oozing jack cheese. Going for a Zachary's special means you will be stuffed with a classic combination of Italian sausage, peppers, onions, and mushrooms, layered with cheese and tomato. Expect to take home a delicious doggie bag to enjoy later.

With basic service and a casual vibe, this pizzeria is good for families or to just enjoy a slice. Avoid the lines by calling ahead with your order.

Zut!

Mediterranean XX

A2

1820 4th St. (bet. Hearst Ave & Virginia St.), Berkeley

Phone: 510-644-0444 Lunch & dinner daily
Web: www.zutonfourth.com
Prices: $$

For ladies looking for a light lunch that won't bog them down while shopping in Berkeley's Fourth Street district, Zut! answers the call with tuna Niçoise salads, sandwiches, and wraps. But the warm, cherry and pine wood interior sates heartier palates too, serving oven-baked flatbreads and artisanal pizzas all day—try the cremini mushroom pie with bits of Brie and thyme.

Short for *zut alors*, or "shucks" in French slang, Zut! is a cozy little spot with copper mirrors, billowing textiles, and a backlit bar. At dinner, the Mediterranean café resembles its mural of a bustling restaurant scene as tables are loaded with the likes of lamb meatballs in tangy tomato sauce; falafel with red pepper and yogurt; and chèvre cheesecake on a gingersnap cookie crust.

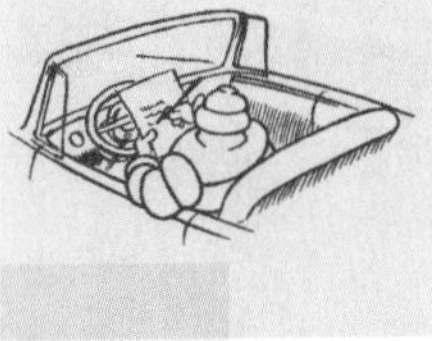

Avoid the search for parking. Look for .

Marin

Marin

Journey north of the Golden Gate Bridge and entrée sprawling Marin County. Draped along the breathtaking Highway 1, coastal climates hallow this region with abounding agricultural advantages. Snake your way through this gorgeous, meandering county, and find that the food oases are spread out. But, when fortunate to "catch" them, expect fresh and luscious seafood, oysters, and cold beer…slurp! Farm-to-table cuisine is the par in North Bay and they boast an avalanche of local food purveyors.

Begin with the prodigious cheese chronicles by visiting the quaint and rustic **Cowgirl Creamery** where "cowgirls" make delicious, distinctive, and hand-crafted cheeses. As a result of focusing and producing only farmstead cheese, they help refine and define artisan cheesemaking—respect! The cheese conte continues at **Point Reyes Farmstead Cheese Co.** For a more lush and heady blue cheese, dive into their decadent "Original Blue." These driving and enterprising cheesemakers live by terroir. Restaurants here follow the European standard and offer cheese before, or in lieu of a dessert course. The ideal is simply magical, end of story. Not sweet enough? Get your candy fix on at **Munchies** of Sausalito; or you can opt for a more sinful (read: creamy) affair at **Noci**'s gelato. From tales of cheese to ranch romances, **Marin Sun Farms** is at the crest. A magnified butcher shop, their

heart, hub, and soul lies in the production of local and natural-fed livestock for a sweeping nexus of establishments—from farmers and grocery stores, to a plethora of restaurants. Speaking of marvelous meats, a visit to **Mill Valley Market** is also a must for their dazzling selection of high-quality gourmet foods, deli items, and other organic produce.

For those ravenous after hours of scenic driving and the ocean waft, sojourn at **The Pelican Inn**. Their hearty stew of English country cooking and wide brew of the classic "bar" will leave you yearning for more of the bucolic. Carry on your hiatus and stroll into foodie paradise, otherwise known as **Spanish Table**. Settled in Mill Valley, gourmand's revel in their range of Spanish cookbooks, cookware, specialty foods, and rare, palate-pleasing wines. Like most thirsty travelers, let your desire lead the way to **Three Twins Ice Cream**. A lick of their organically produced creamy goodness is bound to bring heaven to earth.

Waters off the coast here provide divers with exceptional hunting ground, and restaurants across the country seek the same including fresh oysters, fleshy clams, and mussels. The difficulty in obtaining a hunting permit, as well as the inability to retrieve these large savory mollusks, makes red abalone a treasured species, especially in the surrounding Asian restaurants. Yet, despite such hurdles, seafood is the accepted norm and form at most respites in Marin County. One such gem is **Sam's Anchor Cafe** known for their glorious views and fresh, well-prepared seafood. Then, turn the leaf to oceanic haven, also known as **Western Boat & Tackle**. Admired greatly by the fishing community, this San Rafael seafood market is outfitted with all things maritime including a diverse menu and marine supply store. Not feeling fishy? Entice your taste buds with authentic Puerto Rican flavors and extraordinary *especiales* at

Sol Food. Finally, the county is also known for its local and organic ingredients carried in the numerous farmers' markets. This marriage of food and wine is best expressed at Sausalito's own Marin County Tomato Festival. Magnificent Marin, with its panoramic vistas, is one of the most sought after localities and celebrities abound. Naturally, some diners may bear a touristy mien. However, it is undeniable that restaurants and chefs here are blessed with easy access to the choicest food, produce, and local food agents.

Arti

A1

Indian ✗

7282 Sir Francis Drake Blvd. (at Cintura Ave.), Lagunitas

Phone: 415-488-4700
Web: www.articafe.com
Prices: ✑

Lunch & dinner daily

If Indian cuisine is about aromas, flavors, and textures, then Arti is an idyllic incarnation. Settled in a surreptitious shopping center in sleepy 'lil Lagunitas, this *desi* den is all charm and cheer—a yellow dining room is propitiously chaperoned by vases of fresh flowers. Befitting its delicate disposition, a handful of tables spaced along wood benches are embellished with colorful fabric pillows.

Arti tantalizes all callers with her inventive food. Tour your way through the fiery south with tangy Goan shrimp *vindaloo*. Then journey north for a beautifully spiced and creamy chicken *tikka masala*. If fish and fowl don't fit the bill, tender lamb cubes in a rich cashew-coconut *korma* served with fragrant basmati rice are bound to hit the spot.

Arun

B1

Thai ✗

385 Bel Marin Keys Blvd. (near Hamilton Dr.), Novato

Phone: 415-883-8017
Web: www.arunnovato.com
Prices: ✑

Lunch Mon – Fri
Dinner Mon – Sat

Nestled in an area void of Thai treats, Arun's is a fresh little find in meandering Marin. This neighborhood dwelling is beloved by businessmen, software suits, and local families alike who can't help but smile at the sight of such large portions of boldly flavored, well-prepared Thai food.

It may reside in a commercial park, but Arun's handsome floors and furnishings, vibrant accents, intricate Thai relics, and friendly staff oozes warmth. Strutting a variety of dishes, the menu might also unveil tasty Thai finds like *larb gai*, that tasty plate of ground chicken spiked with fish sauce, lime juice, and chilies; or pumpkin curry luscious with prawns, potatoes, and coconut milk. The ginger ice cream is spicy, but a perfect palate-cleanser.

Bar Bocce

 A3

Pizza   ✗

1250 Bridgeway (bet. Pine & Turney Sts.), Sausalito

Lunch & dinner daily

Phone: 415-331-0555
Web: www.barbocce.com
Prices: $$

The only view in Sausalito to rival Bar Bocce's boat-dotted harbor vista is that of its own wood-burning pizza ovens in the exhibition kitchen. Locals and tourists are happy to wait for a seat at the simple wooden table, particularly on weekends, for a taste of the artisanal pies.

Bar Bocce finds inspiration both here and there: while a turn at the bocce court is a tribute to Italy, Dungeness crab and Meyer lemon piled atop an avocado and crème fraîche pizza tastes distinctly like California. Additional pies include calamari and clam sprinkled with spicy chili oil, or pork sausage with fennel pollen and onion. Light salads of artichoke, fennel, celery, and pecorino; roasted chicken with lemon and herbs; and sweet fudgesicles complete the menu.

Barrel House Tavern

A3

Californian   ✗✗

660 Bridgeway (at Princess St.), Sausalito

Dinner nightly

Phone: 415-729-9593
Web: www.barrelhousetavern.com
Prices: $$

The former San Francisco-Sausalito ferry terminal has found new life as this lovely Californian restaurant, which gets its name from its barrel-like arched wood ceiling. A front lounge with a crackling fireplace and well-stocked bar is popular with locals, while tourists can't resist the expansive dining room and back deck, which boasts spectacular views of the Bay.

The cocktail and wine offerings are strong, as is the house-made soda program which produces intriguing, never-too-sweet combinations like yellow peach, basil, and ginger. These pair beautifully with meaty Dungeness crab sliders coupled with watermelon-jicama slaw; though they might be too tasty to keep around by the time grilled swordfish and pork belly with white beans hit the table.

Brick & Bottle 😊

C2

55 Tamal Vista Blvd. (bet. Madera Blvd. & Wornum Dr.), Corte Madera

Phone: 415-924-3366   Dinner nightly
Web: www.brickandbottle.com
Prices: $$

Discover a world of comfort going on behind the door to Brick & Bottle. This may seem like just a marketplace bar with happy hour from 4:00-7:00 P.M. every day and TV's screening football, but in the back, diners are snuggled into their booths tucking into American classics with a distinct Californian twist.

The pizzas and sandwiches take center stage, as in a pulled pork sandwich with cider-vinegar barbecue sauce. Dinners may include Maine diver scallops with herb-flecked risotto, or Petrale sole with Dungeness crab and Yukon potato purée. Don't miss the noteworthy side of orzo mac and local goat cheese with tomato jam, or grandmother's lovely recipe for butterscotch pudding. It may not seem the trendiest spot, but the food here is all-American good.

Buckeye Roadhouse

A2

15 Shoreline Hwy. (west of Hwy. 101), Mill Valley

Phone: 415-331-2600   Lunch & dinner daily
Web: www.buckeyeroadhouse.com
Prices: $$

Buckeye Roadhouse is a Marin classic. And while it may be a flap to get here—the Roadhouse sits on the edge of a highway, off a ramp to the same—once inside this lodge with vaulted ceilings, warm wood paneling, and oversized windows, you will be thoroughly enamored. This isn't a haven for the hip, but that seems just fine with the loyal patrons who are smitten by their massive roster of hearty dishes.

Kick things off with salmon tartare or "oysters bingo" topped with garlic aïoli and cheese, broiled until caramelized. Entrées may unveil a robust filet mignon with green peppercorn sauce; or pork shoulder with mustard greens and sweet butternut squash. A warm s'more pie piled high with temptingly sweet meringue is the only way to finish this feast.

Bungalow 44

American 🍴🍴

B2

44 E. Blithedale Ave. (at Sunnyside Ave.), Mill Valley

Phone: 415-381-2500
Web: www.bungalow44.com
Prices: $$

Dinner nightly

Nestled amid the fancy stores of quaint Mill Valley, vibrant Bungalow 44 draws a varied crew to its casual, contemporary environs. It's always busy at the bustling bar and more subdued dining room, so for some peace and quiet, retire to the tented outer room with its glowing fireplace. Some prefer the counter to soak up the sizzle from the open kitchen.

Playful American cuisine is their dictum which shines through in tuna carpaccio—an homage to Italian small bites—here starring tissue-thin slices of tuna served with citrusy *mizuna* and creamy mustard sauce. The whiff of cayenne from kickin' fried chicken is as tempting as the juicy meat—add the rich mashed potatoes. Local draft wines paired with pillowy-soft beignets make for a rewarding finish.

Copita

Mexican 🍴🍴

A3

739 Bridgeway (at Anchor St.), Sausalito

Phone: 415-331-7400
Web: www.copitarestaurant.com
Prices: $$

Lunch & dinner daily

One of Sausalito's newest additions is this easy breezy Bridgeway bar and kitchen owned by cookbook author Joanne Weir. The congenially attended room is a lovely spot to while away a lazy afternoon amidst sienna-glazed walls and vivid tile accents. A wall of tequila bottles behind the bar and a prominently positioned wood-burning rotisserie arouse the desire to drink, eat, and relax.

Copita's expert kitchen produces sumptous south-of-the-border fare dressed with a distinctly Californian sensibility. Munch on crisp jicama batons sprinkled with chile, lime, and salt before delving into a bowlful of tart halibut ceviche studded with bits of ripe mango; or house-made tortillas stuffed with plump shrimp, strips of roasted poblano, and early corn.

El Huarache Loco

C2

1803 Larkspur Landing Circle, Larkspur

Phone: 415-925-1403
Web: www.huaracheloco.com
Prices:

Lunch & dinner daily

What started as a food truck now occupies a spot in the Marin County Mart. But it's a far cry from an urban taqueria as denizens peck away on laptops after ordering at the counter. Inside, bright natural light flows through and framed photos provide a crash course on important terminology pertaining to organic and sustainable permaculture.

Here, atop a decorative tiled floor, patrons peruse a menu focused on the delicious street fare of Mexico City. Start with crispy fried chicken *taquitos* topped with guacamole and *queso fresco*, or mini *sopes* overflowing with potatoes and chorizo. Try a *huarache* in one of eight versions—perhaps steak or smoky chorizo–crowned with salsas (from a station that covers every level of heat) and nirvana will follow.

El Paseo

B2

17 Throckmorton Ave. (at Blithedale Ave.), Mill Valley

Phone: 415-388-0741
Web: www.elpaseomillvalley.com
Prices: $$$

Dinner nightly

"Rockstar chef" is a term that often gets tossed around, but it's all too true at this rustic steakhouse, co-owned by celebrity toque Tyler Florence and rocker Sammy Hagar. Hidden down an alley off the shopping arcade of Mill Valley, El Paseo reeks of old-world charm with rustic wood-beamed ceilings and brick walls. Adding a dose of romance are cool high-backed leather chairs warmed up by a live fireplace.

Once seated, the tuxedoed staff will present a cast iron tray of roasted bone marrow topped with a mild horseradish crust and turnip marmalade. Heritage pork chop is grilled to smoky perfection and coddled with pea purée; while the béarnaise burger makes for a primally satisfying meal, especially if paired with a Napa red from the cavernous cellar.

Farmshop

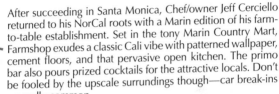

Californian 🍴🍴

 C2

2233 Larkspur Landing Cir., Larkspur

Phone: 415-755-6700
Web: N/A
Prices: $$$

Lunch Sat – Sun
Dinner nightly

After succeeding in Santa Monica, Chef/owner Jeff Cerciello returned to his NorCal roots with a Marin edition of his farm-to-table establishment. Set in the tony Marin Country Mart, Farmshop exudes a classic Cali vibe with patterned wallpaper, cement floors, and that pervasive open kitchen. The primo bar also pours prized cocktails for the attractive locals. Don't be fooled by the upscale surrundings though—car break-ins are sadly common.

Begin with shared plates like fried smelts over mustardy potatoes or crispy artichokes topped with rich *burrata*. Draft rosé whets the appetite for olive-crusted rock cod with artichoke-studded Israeli couscous; and Telecherry peppercorn meringue filled with custard wins over even this glam, health-conscious set.

Fish

Seafood 🍴

 A3

350 Harbor Dr. (off Bridgeway), Sausalito

Phone: 415-331-3474
Web: www.331fish.com
Prices: $$

Lunch & dinner daily

Casual and family-friendly, this Sausalito seafood spot offers diners the choice of a bright and airy dining room with simple wood furnishings or an alfresco picnic table, both with great views of the harbor. If you dine outdoors, watch out for the local seagulls and crows, who are always ready to snag a snack from your plate (but provide great entertainment for the younger set).

The cooking is fresh and flavorful, from a Dungeness crab roll with butter and chives to crisp Anchor Steam-battered halibut served with house-made wedge fries and tartar sauce. Check the chalkboard for the latest specials, like mussels with chorizo and fennel or grilled Monterey sardines. After dining, visit the raw seafood counter for a selection of items to cook at home.

Frantoio

Italian ✗✗

152 Shoreline Hwy. (Stinson Beach exit off Hwy. 101), Mill Valley

Phone: 415-289-5777
Web: www.frantoio.com
Prices: $$

Dinner nightly

Named after the olive press used in olive oil production throughout Italy, Frantoio is distinguished by its own house-made olive oil, cold-pressed in a hefty granite contraption displayed just off the dining room. Bottled and sold on-site, this stellar product beams atop shavings of *Prosciutto di Parma* with arugula and *mozzarella di Bufala*. Baked sea bass fillets are spread with an herbaceous horseradish crust—big on flavor but gentle on garnishes like chive-infused olive oil. Though its proximity to Highway 101 and the Holiday Inn Express isn't pleasant, an orange-and-charcoal color scheme and lofty ceilings ensures that the surrounds become a quickly fading memory. Also of assistance: perfectly crisp Neapolitan pizzas, quenched by some fine wines.

Insalata's 😊

Mediterranean ✗✗

120 Sir Francis Drake Blvd. (at Barber Ave.), San Anselmo

Phone: 415-457-7700
Web: www.insalatas.com
Prices: $$

Lunch & dinner daily

In Italy, cooking is a family affair. And so it is at Insalata's, the charming Sausalito hangout named for Chef/owner Heidi Krahling's late father, Italo Insalata. Today, Krahling pays homage to her beloved *babbo* by mixing tender loving care with Mediterranean fare and local, seasonal ingredients.
Insalata's dining room is spacious and perpetually packed yet somehow remains snug with wood furnishings and art that depicts nature's bounty. Expect Middle Eastern specialties and meze plates of eggplant fries with *tzatziki*, crispy spanakopita, and duck confit cigars; or heartier dishes like roasted honey- and pomegranate-glazed duck breast with couscous and Moroccan tomato jam. In the spotlight every Tuesday to Thursday night is a prix-fixe for under $30.

Left Bank

French 🍴🍴

B2

507 Magnolia Ave. (at Ward St.), Larkspur

Phone: 415-927-3331
Web: www.leftbank.com
Prices: $$

Lunch & dinner daily

Next time you're in Larkspur, wing over to Left Bank where pressed-tin ceilings, wood accents, a slender bar, and a wraparound dining porch are clues that this is no typical chain restaurant. Tucked inside the historic Blue Rock Inn, this authentic French brasserie is one of three Bay Area locations. Following the Inn's pleasant and calm vibe, Left Bank is a low-key spot to enjoy French comfort foods. On chilly days, the rich onion soup with Emmental gratinée is a must, perhaps paired with a *salade Lyonnaise* tossing frisée, bacon, and a warm poached egg. Fish fans die over *truite Grenobloise*, roasted trout with brown butter, lemon, and capers; while *magret de canard* with spätzle, Brussels sprouts, and huckleberry-Port jus will sate fowl fiends.

Le Garage

French 🍴

A3

85 Liberty Ship Way, Ste.109 (off Marinship Way), Sausalito

Phone: 415-332-5625
Web: www.legaragebistrosausalito.com
Prices: $$

Lunch daily
Dinner Mon – Sat

There may be no other picturesque (and tough to find) place for a Gallic lunch than Le Garage, the Sausalito restaurant at the tip of Liberty Ship Way with a bay breeze and view of bobbing yachts and dinghies. Housed in, yes, a real converted garage, the stark and stylish space features crimson retractable doors thrown open to the waterfront air, making it a serene spot for an aperitif and light lunch.

Servers keep with the service station theme in classic mechanics' uniforms, though the accent is French—of both the staff and food. Pull up a wooden bistro chair and order such delights as shrimp Napoleon with avocado mousse and lobster oil, or Tasmanian pepper-crusted steak with house-cut frites. French and Californian wines make for perfect pairing.

Marché aux Fleurs

Mediterranean ✗✗

B2

23 Ross Common (off Lagunitas Rd.), Ross

Phone: 415-925-9200

Web: www.marcheauxfleursrestaurant.com

Prices: $$

Dinner Tue – Sat

Its dark wood dining room is charming, but Marché aux Fleurs truly comes alive on warm spring and summer evenings, when Marin residents flock to the picturesque hamlet of Ross to enjoy a meal on its front patio. Mediterranean-inspired eats with a California twist is what these patrons are after—imagine soft gnocchi with corn and chanterelles or squash blossom tempura with fresh ricotta and you will start to grasp the picture.

Local couples love it here and though many are regulars, even first-timers receive a friendly welcome from the engaging staff. Groups are everywhere and their smiles omniscient as they savor bacon-wrapped king salmon over sweet corn and green garbanzo succotash; or split bites of warm chocolate cake with vanilla bean ice cream.

Marinitas 😊

Latin American ✗✗

B2

218 Sir Francis Drake Blvd. (at Bank St.), San Anselmo

Phone: 415-454-8900

Web: www.marinitas.net

Prices: $$

Lunch & dinner daily

Nothing is free in the posh enclave of Marin. Well, except for those delicious and warm homemade tortilla chips with peppery red and green salsas at Marinitas, Heidi Krahling's local tribute to Mexican and Latin American culinary traditions. The lofty cantina makes everyone feel at home with sports streamed on the big screen and a stone fireplace to keep the taxidermy warm.

Fresh-squeezed juices and sweet-and-sour mixes made in-house highlight the focus on bright flavors and complement a major tequila selection. Sip one of Marinita's killer margaritas and relax while perusing the menu. With options like grilled Atlantic cod tacos, *chiles rellenos* stuffed with butternut squash, and daily specials like savory slow-braised carnitas, choosing can be brutal.

Murray Circle

Californian   ✗✗

A3

601 Murray Circle (at Fort Baker), Sausalito

Phone: 415-339-4750   Lunch & dinner daily
Web: www.murraycircle.com
Prices: $$

Winding headlands lead to Murray Circle—the restaurant at Fort Baker's Cavallo Point, also a lodge with dramatic views of the city and Golden Gate Bridge. A nostalgic sense of history flows through this charming arena with its pressed-tin ceilings, wagon wheel light fixtures, and front porch dotted with rocking chairs—Murray Circle's colonial spirit entertains guests as well as the general public.

A meal here features crispy squid mixed with fried jalapeños; then parcels of Parmesan *gnocchetti* blended with asparagus, fava beans, and hearts of palm. You must not pass up on an excellent torte layering lemon chiffon and key lime curd, garnished with a mango and mint brunoise.

During the week, a reasonable lunch prix-fixe lures folks from far and wide.

Nick's Cove

American   ✗✗

A1

23240 Hwy. 1, Marshall

Phone: 415-663-1033   Lunch & dinner daily
Web: www.nickscove.com
Prices: $$

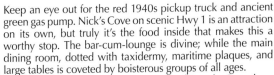

Keep an eye out for the red 1940s pickup truck and ancient green gas pump. Nick's Cove on scenic Hwy 1 is an attraction on its own, but truly it's the food inside that makes this a worthy stop. The bar-cum-lounge is divine; while the main dining room, dotted with taxidermy, maritime plaques, and large tables is coveted by boisterous groups of all ages.

An enclosed patio offers stunning views of Tomales Bay where noisy clusters can be seen enjoying a Dungeness crab Louis laden with cucumber, avocado, and a perfect pink "Louis" dressing; or "Nick-erfellers," grilled oysters topped with butter and tarragon-Pernod sauce. Juicy meatballs enhanced with Rossotti Ranch goat cheese are not-to-be-missed, as is the warm gingerbread with Comice pears and sabayon.

Osteria Stellina

A1

Italian

11285 Hwy. 1 (at 3rd St.), Point Reyes Station

Phone: 415-663-9988
Web: www.osteriastellina.com
Prices: $$$

Lunch & dinner daily

Point Reyes Station feels like a mythical Western town with barns, weathered clapboards, and the wholesomeness of an area dominated by cheese-making farms. It's all very restful and sitting on a prominent corner is Stellina. This "little star" sports a lively room within which easygoing patrons enjoy wonderful artwork and tables graced with tiny vases of fresh flowers.

The menu is impressively listed with places from where ingredients are derived, and expectedly all the items are bursting with flavor. Let the informed staff guide you toward an enjoyable penne with cannellini beans and braised greens, or delicate petrale sole laced with fingerling potatoes and baby carrots. Seal this unforgettable meal with a velvety milk chocolate panna cotta.

Picco

B2

Italian

320 Magnolia Ave. (at King St.), Larkspur

Phone: 415-924-0300
Web: www.restaurantpicco.com
Prices: $$

Dinner nightly

If sharing is caring, then Larkspur's Picco is a thoughtful spot indeed. Bruce Hill's popular Italian eatery delivers each small plate right to the center of the table, as friends help themselves, then others, to the likes of local halibut crudo plated with fennel, blood orange, and jalapeño. Those craving comfort food will relish cauliflower gratin with cheddar cheese and breadcrumbs; or ever-changing *risotti* made from scratch each half hour.

Exposed brick, dim lighting, and redwood accents make this a romantic date-night spot. Before heading home, cap the meal with a selection of artisanal cheeses. Locals love Marin Mondays, which showcase the best of North Bay produce.

City dwellers can get a taste of Picco at Hill's SoMa outpost, Zero Zero.

Pizzalina

Pizza

B2

914 Sir Francis Drake Blvd. (at Sunny Hills Dr.), San Anselmo

Phone: 415-256-9780
Web: www.pizzalina.com
Prices: $$

Lunch & dinner daily

Buried in a corner of the Red Hill Shopping Center, this rustic, casual, yet very comfy pizzeria oozes *molto* charm via distressed wood walls and a marble dining counter. An open kitchen keeps all eyes at the hopping communal tables focused on the eye-catching wood-burning oven. The nose will follow once it catches a whiff of pies, spread with mozzarella, olive oil, meats, and vegetables from local producers, and named after old Marin railroad stops—who wants the Baltimore Park?

A versatile wine medley, much of it on tap, arrives in cute glass beakers, adding to the warm, classy vibe. For extra bliss, pair this with a roasted pear, *burrata*, and arugula salad; then dive into a seasonal pizza; and finish with rich, hearty, and house-made meatballs.

Poggio

Italian

A3

777 Bridgeway (at Bay St.), Sausalito

Phone: 415-332-7771
Web: www.poggiotrattoria.com
Prices: $$

Lunch & dinner daily

Situated along Sausalito's main drag at the base of the Casa Madrona hotel, Poggio will be celebrating over a decade in business; and yet its wide-ranging Italian menu is far from tired. The dining room is plush with mahogany-lined archways and lavish booths, but the most desirable seats are on the front terrace, with views of the quaint harbor and yacht club. Sunny by day and heated at night, it's a great place to savor a crisp pizza, bottle of wine, and watch the world go by.

A meal at this upscale trattoria might include sautéed day boat scallops with sunchoke purée and salty pancetta; trailed by braised veal tortellini in a nutty *Parmigiano* broth; or roasted halibut with seared artichokes—likely sourced from the restaurant's own hillside garden.

R'Noh Thai

B2

Thai ✗✗

1000 Magnolia Ave. (bet. Frances & Murray Aves.), Larkspur

Phone: 415-925-0599
Web: www.rnohthai.com
Prices:

Lunch Mon – Sat
Dinner nightly

A tranquil setting (envision a back deck overlooking marshland and a creek), an easy mien, and attentive service make up the allure of this Thai pet. Its name means "rising sun," and the cuisine—marked by uplifting, robust, and satiating flavors—follows suit. The bi-level space radiates character from rich red walls and a toasty fireplace, to billowing white fabric under a sunny skylight.

On a balmy day, kick things off with a creamy Thai iced coffee which magnificently quenches the heat from a spicy prawn salad infused with chili and lime. The jaunty journey turns serious with the arrival of house specials like stir-fried eggplant with garlic and basil; or a beautifully barbecued chicken marinated in spices and finished with zesty plum sauce.

Sana Marin 😳

B2

Mediterranean ✗✗

2200 4th St. (at W. Crescent Dr.), San Rafael

Phone: 415-457-4164
Web: www.sanamarin.com
Prices: **$$**

Lunch & dinner Tue – Sun

This unique sib of L.A.'s A Votre Sante is a rare beacon of healthy food in the pleasure-oriented NorCal dining world, but with less attitude than predecessor Café Gratitude. Soothing and sleek, the neutral dining room orbits around an oval banquette and chic dark wood tables. Yes, the food is healthy, but never joyless. Add on a vast drinks program or desserts like caramelized pear *crostata* and you have a smash-hit on your hands. Vegans, vegetarians, and raw-foodists will of course find much to love here, but so will their carnivore chums.

Begin with pita bread and herbaceous *za'atar* oil, before moving on to flavorful chicken soup with quinoa and garbanzo beans. Sesame-crusted salmon over a ponzu-tinged vegetable stir-fry is a fave for good reason.

Sir and Star

American ✗✗

A1

10000 Sir Francis Drake Blvd. (at Hwy. 1), Olema

Phone: 415-663-1034   Dinner Wed – Sun
Web: www.sirandstar.com
Prices: **$$**

The dynamic duo of Chef/owners Daniel DeLong and Margaret Gradé have been missed in Marin's culinary scene since their previous restaurant, Manka's Inverness Lodge, was destroyed in a fire. Now, they're cooking again in this quaint yet quirky dining room, this time situated in the historic Olema Inn. It's a roadhouse, but a very quiet one—so don't bring your rowdy pals.

Simplicity and hyper-local fare are the focus here with dishes like Tomales Bay oyster shooters with wee ribbons of kohlrabi; spring onion soup with *gougères*; or luscious pork meatballs with "Jessie's Chinese speaking broccoli." A medieval fireplace (in winter) or tree-shaded patio (in summer) provides a romantic setting to unplug and relax over a wine list dominated by Marin grapes.

Sushi Ran

Japanese ✗✗

A3

107 Caledonia St. (bet. Pine & Turney Sts.), Sausalito

Phone: 415-332-3620   Lunch Mon – Fri
Web: www.sushiran.com   Dinner nightly
Prices: **$$**

Sushi fans have long flocked to Sausalito to dine at this pleasant, if sparsely appointed, Japanese room armed with genuine warmth. A mixed crowd fills the packed-together tables, murmuring gently over sips of green tea in ceramic mugs or the impressive variety of sake and wine. Despite a prime location on Caledonia, the city's main shopping street, the vibe here is quiet and never boisterous.

At Sushi Ran, the fish is as pristine as the execution which may reveal smoked trout salad, sweet with carrots yet punchy with yuzu and miso. Prices are elevated but so is the freshness in sushi like *ana ebi*, *kani*, and crab; or hamachi and *maguro* sashimi. In light of *aji nori* potatoes hit perfectly with salt and truffle oil, the inept service is pardoned.

Tavern at Lark Creek

234 Magnolia Ave. (at Madrone Ave.), Larkspur

Phone: 415-924-7766
Web: www.tavernatlarkcreek.com
Prices: $$

Lunch Sun
Dinner nightly

At Tavern at Lark Creek, a lone dartboard (tucked behind flowers) carries the flag for more traditional taverns inside this redwood-shaded Victorian home with a somewhat misleading name. Valet your wheels and roll up to the spacious bar where wine, not beer, awaits on tap. Order by the glass, half, or full bottle, and congratulate yourself on money well saved.

Another bargain may be found in the fab three-course prix-fixe menu, which changes according to the season. Look for delights such as blue cheese soufflé with arugula, walnuts, and grapes; panko-crusted macaroni and cheese croquettes; and lemon cheesecake brûlée. On Sunday, commence your morning with brunch at the communal table beneath a massive skylight, or imbibe creative cocktails at dusk.

tavola

5800 Nave Dr. (near Roblar Dr.), Novato

Phone: 415-883-6686
Web: www.tavolaitaliankitchen.com
Prices: $$

Lunch & dinner daily

This *osteria* in Novato has welcoming service, a casual atmosphere, and streams of light (envision large arched windows) that families will enjoy. Located merely steps from the Hamilton Marketplace shopping center, tavola offers an attractive respite to weary shoppers amidst its stylish space featuring a gleaming exhibition kitchen, concrete floors, and soaring ceilings.

This is the place to refresh with a starter of über creamy *burrata* served with thinly sliced rustic toast spread with a tangy tomato-herb-garlic jam. Refuel with a thin-crust *aglio verde* pizza topped with tender shaved asparagus, melted Asiago, and aromatic speck, before splurging on a decadent and rich chocolate ganache tart in an olive oil shell sprinkled with *fleur de sel*.

Terrapin Crossroads

American   XX

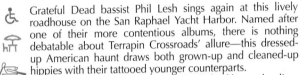

C2

100 Yacht Club Dr. (at Francisco Blvd. E.), San Rafael

Phone: 415-524-2773
Web: www.terrapincrossroads.net
Prices: $$

Lunch Sat – Sun
Dinner Tue – Sun

Grateful Dead bassist Phil Lesh sings again at this lively roadhouse on the San Raphael Yacht Harbor. Named after one of their more contentious albums, there is nothing debatable about Terrapin Crossroads' allure—this dressed-up American haunt draws both grown-up and cleaned-up hippies with their tattooed younger counterparts.

The diverse crowd tucks in to global delights like smoky slices of cured salmon fanned around lightly dressed arugula; or pork *chilaquiles* blending crispy tortilla chips, black beans, and *pico de gallo*. Musicians regularly regale the space, with Lesh himself dropping in to jam in the main dining room. Weekend brunch may turn into a fête with fans swarming the bar—it's a ton of fun, unless you wish to actually hold a conversation.

The sun is out – let's eat alfresco! Look for 🍴.

Jay Graham

Peninsula

The Peninsula may not be internationally heralded for its celebrity chefs and groundbreaking Californian cooking, but with such a diverse population rich in Asian cultures, the area is laden with neighborhood eateries and bountiful markets that appeal to locals craving authentic cuisines. Those seeking a taste of the East should scoop up inexpensive seafood (and links of *longaniza*) alongside the Filipino population at Daly City's **Manila Oriental Market** as well as at **Kukje Super Market**, replete with prepared Korean food. If not, they can practice the art of chopstick wielding at one of the many Japanese sushi bars, ramen houses, and *izakayas*. Chinese food fiends may tickle their fancy with traditional sweets such as assorted mooncakes and yolk pastries at San Mateo's cash-only **Sheng Kee Bakery**; while sugar junkies of the western variety can chow on faithful Danish pastries at Burlingame's **Copenhagen Bakery**, also lauded for its special occasion cakes.

In addition to harboring some of the Bay Area's most impressive and enticing Cantonese and dim sum houses, Millbrae is a lovely spot to raise one last toast to summer. The Millbrae Art & Wine Festival is a cornucopia of wicked fairground eats— think of gooey cheesesteak, Cajun-style corndogs, and fennel-scented sausages. Wash this down with a glass of wine or cold microbrew, and kick up your heels to the tune of a local cover band. Speaking of which, **Back A Yard** (in Menlo Park) may be a total dive, but it offers some über flavorful Caribbean food. And if it is cooking classes that you require, head to **Draeger's Market** in San Mateo and sign up for a variety of classes from basic to specialty subjects. While here, you can also sample artisan and specialty goods (maybe at **Suruki Japanese Market**?), or pick up some wine and cheese to-go.

In keeping with the take-home tone, Half Moon Bay is beloved for fresh and seasonal produce. Make sure you load up on gorgeous fruits and vegetables at the many roadside stands on Route 92; and don't miss the town's **Coastside Farmer's Market** where you'll find such local bounty as **Harley Farms** goat cheese (from Pescadero), and organic eggs from **Green Oaks Creek Farm** up in the Santa Cruz Mountains. Seafood more your speed? **Barbara's Fish Trap**, just north in Princeton by the Sea, serves fish 'n chips by the harbor. Pork ribs are in order after all things piscine, so join the locals at **Gorilla Barbeque** for meaty combos and tasty sides, served out of an orange railroad car on Cabrillo Highway in Pacifica.

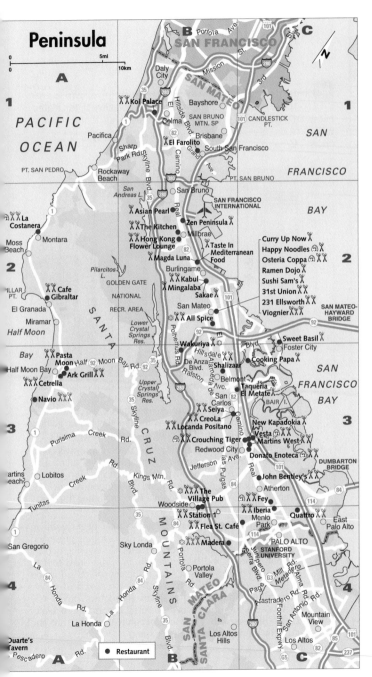

Peninsula

0   5mi
0   10km

A

PACIFIC OCEAN

Daly City

Portola Ave.
B   **C**
SAN FRANCISCO

SAN MATEO

1

⨉⨉ **Koi Palace**

Bayshore

SAN BRUNO
MTN. SP

CANDLESTICK PT.

Colma

Pacifica

⨉ **El Farolito**

Brisbane

South San Francisco

SAN FRANCISCO

PT. SAN PEDRO

Rockaway Beach

Sharp Park Rd.

PT. SAN BRUNO

BAY

San Andreas L.

San Bruno

SAN FRANCISCO INTERNATIONAL

⨉⨉ **La Costanera**

⨉ **Asian Pearl**

Zen Peninsula ⨉

Montara

Moss Beach

⨉⨉ **The Kitchen**

⨉⨉ **Hong Kong Flower Lounge**

Millbrae

⨉ **Taste In Mediterranean Food**

Curry Up Now ⨉

Happy Noodles ⨉

Osteria Coppa ⨉⨉

Ramen Dojo ⨉

Sushi Sam's ⨉

31st Union ⨉⨉

231 Ellsworth ⨉

Viognier ⨉⨉⨉

2

ILLAR PT.

⨉⨉ **Cafe Gibraltar**

⨉ **Magda Luna**

Burlingame

⨉⨉ **Kabul**

⨉ **Mingalaba**

Sakae ⨉

El Granada

Miramar

Half Moon

Pilarcitos L.

GOLDEN GATE

NATIONAL

San Mateo

⨉⨉⨉ **All Spice**

SAN MATEO-HAYWARD BRIDGE

Bay

Lower Crystal Springs Res.

⨉⨉ **Pasta Moon**

Half Moon Bay

RECR. AREA

Wakuriya ⨉

Sweet Basil ⨉

Foster City

Half Moon Bay

Half Moon Bay Rd.

⨉⨉ **Ark Grill**

De Anza Blvd.

Shalizaar ⨉

Cooking Papa ⨉

SAN FRANCISCO

⨉⨉⨉ **Cetrella**

Upper Crystal Springs Res.

Ralston

Belmont

Taqueria El Metate ⨉

⨉ **Navio**

San Carlos

⨉⨉ **Seiya**

BAIR I.

BAY

3

Purisima Creek

⨉⨉ **CreoLa**

⨉⨉ **Locanda Positano**

⨉⨉ **Crouching Tiger**

Redwood City

New Kapadokia ⨉

Vesta ⨉⨉⨉

Martins West ⨉⨉

artins each

Lobitos

Creek

Kings Mtn. Rd.

Jefferson

Donato Enoteca ⨉⨉⨉

DUMBARTON BRIDGE

Tunitas

⨉⨉⨉ **The Village Pub**

Woodside

⨉⨉ **Station 1**

John Bentley's ⨉⨉

Atherton

⨉⨉ **Fey**

San Gregorio

⨉⨉ **Flea St. Café**

Menlo Park

⨉ **Iberia**

Quattro ⨉⨉

East Palo Alto

⨉⨉⨉ **Madera**

4

Sky Londa

Portola Valley

PALO ALTO

STANFORD UNIVERSITY

La Honda

La Honda

San Mateo

SANTA CLARA

Los Altos Hills

Mountain View

Duarte's Tavern

Pescadero

● **Restaurant**

Los Altos

219

All Spice ⌘

Indian 🍴🍴

1602 El Camino Real (bet. Barneson & Borel Aves.), San Mateo

Phone: 650-627-4303
Web: www.allspicerestaurant.com
Prices: $$

Dinner Tue – Sat

Hardy Wilson

Pay attention or fly right by this radiant wooden house, set back off El Camino Real. Convenient on-site parking alleviates any trouble (if at all) getting here. An elegantly dressed *patronne* (the chef's wife in fact) offers a warm greeting before guiding you to a table in one of the snug interconnecting rooms.

Wooden floors, a rustling fireplace, and vibrant walls with heavy window dressings help create a warm yet sultry aura. In turn, these bright rooms bestow a soft glow upon large tables accoutered in full linen and contemporary crockery. Everything here evinces California love, including the chatty but very courteous waitstaff.

The California-centric Indian cuisine may begin with an "Ode to my Wife, Part II" which is a chef's tribute presented as a crunchy, decadent savory cheesecake layering ricotta-almond mousse and beet mirepoix in a sun-dried tomato crust. Lemon verbena sea bass rustically served on a bed of sweet corn and charred potatoes is cooked to pearly perfection with a dusting of spices and dab of lemon jelly that boosts, but never overpowers. The rich chocolate-coffee mousse with a quenelle of lightly minted cream and crunchy meringues is utterly pleasing.

Ark Grill

Indian ✗✗

724 Main St. (bet. Correas & Filbert St.), Half Moon Bay

Phone: 650-560-8152
Web: www.arkgrill.com
Prices: $$

Lunch & dinner Tue – Sun

This North Indian spot offers a lunch buffet and à la carte dinner experience that is worth the trek to Half Moon Bay. Set in a converted old house that has a front bay window and small porch, Ark Grill is flooded with natural light and exudes a homey ambience.

In fact, you may as well be sitting in your *nani*'s kitchen with their roster of boldly spiced and flavored fare. Begin with tasty and crispy-fried samosas stuffed with spiced potatoes and peas, before moving on to entrées like plump, succulent prawns and potatoes stewed in a well-spiced *vindaloo*; or tender chunks of marinated chicken in a creamy *tikka masala*—both the perfect foil for a charred and chewy garlic-cilantro *naan*. Need to turn the heat down? Check in with the obliging staff.

Asian Pearl

 Chinese ✗

1671 El Camino Real (at Park Pl.), Millbrae

Phone: 650-616-8288
Web: N/A
Prices:

Lunch & dinner daily

Asian Pearl is lauded for its dim sum, but the dinner menu of mostly Cantonese-style dishes is really where the restaurant shines. The large banquet style tables are perfect for groups, while smaller rooms can be portioned off for private parties. The staff is curt, but the food is worth it. A back wall lined with tanks full of crustaceans, fish, and mollusks will get your appetite going.

Start with a superbly crisp and crackly-skinned duck that was brined before roasting; then a clay pot filled with tender slices of braised beef in a thick soy- and oyster-sauce—enoki mushrooms are tossed in tableside as if to further tease your taste buds. Can't move? Tender pieces of pumpkin and taro root simmered in creamy coconut milk are also served over the burner.

Cafe Gibraltar

A2

Mediterranean

425 Avenue Alhambra (at Palma St.), El Granada

Phone: 650-560-9039
Web: www.cafegibraltar.com
Prices: $$$

Lunch Sun
Dinner Tue – Sun

The world is small and delicious at Cafe Gibraltar, the coastal San Mateo county kitchen that melds French, Italian, Persian, and Moroccan flavors all in one big pot—plus a dash of Turkey, Greece, and Spain. Watch the cuisine come to life over the wood-fired oven in the open kitchen, or sink into a floor cushion beneath a tented table tucked away for a sexy North African vibe.

Wherever you sit, prepare to be charmed. Sunny hues and Moorish accents set the scene for Chef/owner Jose Luis Ugalde's aromatic Mediterranean fare. Begin with an ample meze platter laden with flatbread, roasted garlic, olives, and spreads; then meander on to a slow braised lamb shank in harissa-date-red wine broth. For dessert, indulge in a velvety lavender crème brûlée.

Cetrella

A3

Mediterranean

845 Main St. (at Spruce St.), Half Moon Bay

Phone: 650-726-4090
Web: www.cetrella.com
Prices: $$$

Lunch Sun
Dinner Tue – Sun

In the beach town of Half Moon Bay lives stylish and sophisticated Cetrella. Decorated like a Mediterranean villa with stucco walls and vaulted ceilings, there is even a temperature-controlled cheese room to gratify those dairy fanatics. The best seats in the house are those in the private wine cellar or around the roaring fireplace in the main dining room, making this a beloved destination for celebrations, groups, and date-night.

The enticing *carte du jour* is produced with skill, and may reveal such delights as a velvety green garlic soup, enriched with cream and delicately garnished with a prosciutto chip; or a braised lamb shank with tender root vegetables. Cardamom panna cotta with strawberry salad is the best way to seal this lovely meal.

Cooking Papa

Chinese ⅄

C3

949 Edgewater Blvd., Ste. A (at Beach Park Blvd.), Foster City

Phone: 650-577-1830
Web: www.mycookingpapa.com
Prices:

Lunch & dinner daily

Cantonese and Hong Kong-style dishes draw weekend crowds to the sleek and minimally adorned Cooking Papa, set back in a shopping center alongside one of the Foster City canals. Inside, find expats clustered around faux-granite tables armed with dark wood chairs and framed by a wall of windows running the length of the space—every seat has a glorious water view.

A vast menu features all types of dishes, from simple yet heart-warming *congee* and soft tofu braised with vegetables, to sweet and salty barbecued pork—honey glazed and intensely moist. Americanized standards like hot-and-sour soup may disappoint, so it's best to think outside the box and get the crispy, beignet-like egg puffs for dessert: they're perfect with strong black tea.

CreoLa

Southern ⅄⅄

B3

344 El Camino Real (bet. Bush & Oak Sts.), San Carlos

Phone: 650-654-0882
Web: www.creolabistro.com
Prices: $$

Lunch Fri
Dinner Tue – Sun

Cravin' Cajun? Head on down to this San Carlos favorite for a taste of New Orleans-style heaven where authentic, hearty dishes are fired up with a whole lotta love. Jazz tunes pep up the space, decked in brick and yellow walls, funky art prints, and white wood-planked ceilings.

Loyal locals pack the place, as does a business crowd at lunchtime. Start the feast with delectable crawfish hushpuppies, perfectly spiced and cooked to a tender crunch, served with tasty remoulade sauces for dipping. The Cajun jambalaya is a sure bet comprised of spiced rice chock-full of sliced andouille, plump prawns, shredded chicken, and scallions, served with a quarter of smoky chicken, and grilled slices of sausage and tasso ham. Service is relaxed but responsive.

Crouching Tiger

Chinese 🍴🍴

2644 Broadway St. (bet. El Camino Real & Perry St.), Redwood City

Phone: 650-298-8881   Lunch & dinner daily
Web: www.crouchingtigerrestaurant.com
Prices:

A word of warning to the chili-intolerant: this fiery cat will pounce. These Sichuan and Hunan signature dishes ain't for the faint, humming with chilies, chili oil, chili paste, fearlessly kicking up that painful-but-heavenly heat (though tamer options do exist). A popular spot for inexpensive business lunches and family-style dinners, the inviting space sports dark wood furnishings, vibrant touches, and large round tables with lazy Susans.

Get your spice on with a number of delicious goodies like silky *mapo* tofu with ginger and garlic; flaky white fish fillets with sautéed zucchini, carrot, and bamboo shoots braised in red chili sauce; succulent Sichuan prawns; and tender wok-fried Mongolian beef with caramelized onions and oyster sauce.

Curry Up Now

Indian 🍴

129 S. B St. (bet. 1st & 2nd Aves.), San Mateo

Phone: 650-316-8648   Lunch & dinner daily
Web: www.curryupnow.com
Prices:

Curry Up Now has settled into its brick and mortar house, though the food truck itself continues to turn its wheels. Having mastered operations, this Indian jewel now handles its lunchtime rush with ease. Inside, the colorful chalkboard menu presides by listing the exotic preparations of the day.

Place your order, pay at the counter, get a number, and wait among a troop of young professionals. Curry Up Now keeps Indian street food (delivered in biodegradable disposable dishes) inspired with combo *thali* platters featuring items like tofu *tikka masala*, *aloo gobi*, pork belly, and flaky *paratha*; or an open-faced "Naughty Naan" topped with greens, shaved jalapeño, and seasoned lamb.

Outposts in the city and Palo Alto have been drawing a crowd.

Donato Enoteca 😋

Italian 🍴🍴

C3

1041 Middlefield Rd. (bet. Jefferson Ave. & Main St.), Redwood City

Phone: 650-701-1000

Lunch & dinner daily

Web: www.donatoenoteca.com

Prices: $$

Donato Enoteca, settled in the heart of Redwood City and just steps away from City Hall, oozes with rustic northern ambience, from its wood-beamed dining room to the counter facing the busy open kitchen. The latter is perfect for solo diners or those who wish to watch the cooks up close.

The seasonally inspired menu might begin with such wonderfully simple pasta courses as *spaghetti alle vongole* tossed with spicy Calabrian chilies. Expect mains like *controfiletto scalogno*—tender sirloin steak served with roasted scallions and fresh rosemary—and sides of organic *fagiolini* flavored with caramelized *guanciale*. Tiramisu layered with espresso-soaked ladyfingers makes for a luscious finale; and the wine list features a good selection of Italian varietals.

Duarte's Tavern

American 🍴

A4

202 Stage Rd. (at Pescadero Creek Rd.), Pescadero

Phone: 650-879-0464

Lunch & dinner daily

Web: www.duartestavern.com

Prices: $$

Duarte's is a longtime favorite of the food media who are perpetually extolling the virtues of this old-time place with amazing American staples. Naturally, die-hard foodies and tourists pack the 115-year-old family-run tavern, but pulling up to its Pescadero locale, it's easy to wonder if you're in the wrong place: Duarte's surrounds resemble the Wild West, and that's part of the charm.

The legendary duo of artichoke and green chile soups (that locals like to mix) is worth all the hype, but instead of a slice of the overrated olallieberry pie, focus on the simply prepared seafood and specials. Coastal proximity means superior swimmers so don't miss outstanding baked oysters, pan-seared abalone, lightly fried calamari, or an aromatic bowl of cioppino.

El Farolito

394 Grand Ave. (at Maple Ave.), South San Francisco

Phone: 650-737-0138   Lunch & dinner daily
Web: www.elfarolitoinc.com
Prices:

This is *the* taqueria—just ask the Spanish-speaking families, day laborers, and young foodies lining up to order at the self-serve counter. Sure, the basic décor consists of molded pink benches, well-worn checkerboard floors, and tables topped with disposable utensils. Yet inside those retro plastic dining baskets are some of the area's best tacos and burritos.

Sample à la carte tacos served on corn tortillas, topped with cilantro and chopped onion, stuffed with a range of meats like tender, juicy chicken or the wonderfully caramelized and smoky *carne asada*. No matter your filling, no taco is complete without a trip to the fresh salsa bar and exploring its array of salsa verde, red chili varieties, *pico de gallo,* and pickled jalapeños.

Fey

1368 El Camino Real (bet. Glenwood & Oak Grove Aves.), Menlo Park

Phone: 650-324-8888   Lunch & dinner Tue – Sun
Web: www.feyrestaurant.com
Prices: $$

30 Rock comediennes are nowhere to be found at this elegant, upscale Chinese restaurant, but you'll grin all the same once you taste their outstanding tea-smoked duck, roasted to order with meltingly tender meat and shatteringly crisp skin. It's the first of many Sichuan delights to be had, from fiery *mapo* tofu to whole fish piled with hot peppers, numbing peppercorns, and fragrant chili oil. For the best in food, stick to the Sichuan menu; Americanized orders can be met with indifference.

The contemporary dining room features chrome orb lights, cushioned booths, and large tables with built-in heating elements for their signature hot pot offerings. A private room lures Silicon Valley businessmen and big tables in the back cradle families and groups.

Flea St. Café

Californian

3607 Alameda de las Pulgas (at Avy Ave.), Menlo Park

Phone: 650-854-1226   Dinner Tue – Sun
Web: www.cooleatz.com
Prices: $$$

Beloved Flea St. Café in Menlo Park fills up early and stays packed until closing time with professor-types and well-to-do couples dressed up for date-night. Located on a sloping hill, the homey bungalow features tiered dining areas, pastel walls, white moldings, and cozy candlelit tables. One of the few bar tables may be open, but reservations are necessary for the dining room.

Flea St. delivers in-season, local, and sustainable ingredients, as in a smooth and earthy roasted pumpkin soup topped with pork belly. Expect the professional service staff to bring the likes of Dungeness crab and sweet potato cake; pan-roasted black cod with nutty wild rice, butternut squash, and crispy leeks; or honey-sweet and gently floral lavender panna cotta.

Happy Noodles

Chinese

153 S. B St. (bet. 1st & 2nd Aves.), San Mateo

Phone: 650-342-5330   Lunch & dinner Tue – Sun
Web: N/A
Prices:

This San Mateo newbie has been known to sate many a fiery palate with the spicy dishes of Chengdu, Chongqing, and Sichuan featuring pickled chilies, chili oil, and other pungent ingredients. Keep in mind that almost everything here is spicy, so if you don't enjoy the heat, take a pass. *Hui guo rou*, pork with smoked tofu in a zesty soy-and-oyster sauce provides a pleasing burn, while hand-cut *dan dan* noodles with minced garlic and chilies are intense, but supremely delicious.

The décor is unassuming with wood fittings and pendant lights. Families with children make up much of the clientele, and thankfully so, as Happy Noodles is small and large groups are best avoided. Basic but adept servers allow diners to keep their focus on sweating out the spice.

Hong Kong Flower Lounge

B2

Chinese 🍴🍴

51 Millbrae Ave. (at El Camino Real), Millbrae

Phone: 650-692-6666   Lunch & dinner daily
Web: www.mayflower-seafood.com
Prices: $$

When in Millbrae, do as the local Chinese do and go directly for dim sum at Hong Kong Flower Lounge. No need to look hard—its dramatic, multi-level, pagoda-style façade is immediately recognizable. On weekends, bring your morning paper and wait among the crowds craving sticky rice noodle rolls with tender beef and scallions; smoky-salty-sweet sliced barbecue pork; and Wushi–style spareribs infused with rice wine, soy, and ginger.

Luckily, 400 seats give Hong Kong Flower Lounge the upper hand; like the namesake city itself, it is a veritable mob scene. Look for the servers in pink jackets if you don't speak Cantonese. Crowds aren't your thing? Forgo the whirling rolling carts at lunch and come for seafood and traditional à la carte fare at dinner.

Iberia

C4

Spanish 🍴🍴

1026 Alma St. (at Ravenswood Ave.), Menlo Park

Phone: 650-325-8981   Lunch Mon – Sat
Web: www.iberiarestaurant.com   Dinner nightly
Prices: $$

Spain has landed in Menlo Park, in the form of a fetching brick bungalow on Alma Street. It's a bonanza of bona fide Spanish heart and soul here at Iberia, where traditional tapas, a homey interior, and adjacent food and import shop delight in all things *España*. Seating options range from a gorgeous garden patio; sun-drenched dining room decked in artwork and linen-topped tables; or the impossibly adorable bar set atop hard wood floors.

Beneath the glow of an intricate wine cellar (that hangs overhead), tables are awash with the likes of *tortilla de patatas*, mini pan-fried potato "omelets;" crispy-fried Dungeness crab fritters; or smoky-sweet chorizo-stuffed dates wrapped in bacon.

Not feeling the tapas? Order the seafood and chicken paella.

John Bentley's

Contemporary ✗✗

2915 El Camino Real (bet. Berkshire Ave. & E. Selby Ln.), Redwood City

Phone: 650-365-7777
Web: www.johnbentleys.com
Prices: $$

Lunch Mon – Fri
Dinner Mon – Sat

Peninsula

Set on a quiet stretch of El Camino Real, a vine-covered trellis walkway leads to the stately John Bentley's. A squad of date-night duos and locals from around the way seeking contemporary American cooking have found a fine refuge in this quaint, very classic tavern, whose dark wood wainscoting and oil paintings recall an earlier era of power-lunching. But now along with those wealthy retirees, lunching ladies and even families with well-behaved children come to savor simple, well-executed dishes like flaky broiled Loch Duart salmon set over sautéed spinach drizzled with basil oil.

Arched banquettes make for the best seats in the house and are ideal for savoring each bite of the grilled watermelon Napoleon, sandwiched with Dungeness crab and avocado.

Kabul

Afghan ✗✗

1101 Burlingame Ave. (at California Dr.), Burlingame

Phone: 650-343-2075
Web: www.kabulcuisine.com
Prices: $$

Lunch & dinner daily

Though it's settled on a hopping corner in Burlingame's main shopping district and steps from the Caltrain station, this bright, light-filled spot transports diners to Afghanistan with tasty and unique offerings. Hearty *sambosa-e-goushti* (fried dough pockets filled with lamb and chickpeas); *kabab-e-murgh* (tender-charred chicken skewers atop *pallaw*); or sautéed pumpkin with a rich yogurt sauce draws business types at lunch and local families for dinner.

But irrespective of time, service is always casual, despite the white tablecloths. Diners must exercise care not to load up on the fluffy flatbread with a green chili-and-herb chutney that's served at first, lest they miss out on a final course of syrup-soaked baklava studded with chopped walnuts.

The Kitchen

B2

279 El Camino Real (at La Cruz Ave.), Millbrae

Phone: 650-692-9688   Lunch & dinner daily
Web: www.thekitchenmillbrae.com
Prices: ☜☜

Brimming with Chinese diners and clans of corporate types, this chic Millbrae joint entices those hankering for tasty and heart-warming dim sum. While the décor may boast only a few frills (banquet-style tables, bright lights, and white walls with grey wainscoting), the menu is replete with specialties starring fresh seafood—note the wall of fish and crustacean tanks.

Once inside the airy space, start demolishing sure bets like caramelized, crispy roasted duck folded into steamed *bao* with hoisin; or spareribs glazed in a Sichuan chili sauce. But we suggest taking a hint from the crowd and digging into some dim sum. Try the cold jelly fish and seaweed salad tossed in a rice wine dressing; or go for golden perfection in crispy pork dumplings.

Koi Palace

B1

365 Gellert Blvd. (bet. Hickey & Serramonte Blvds.), Daly City

Phone: 650-992-9000   Lunch & dinner daily
Web: www.koipalace.com
Prices: $$

One of the Bay Area's premier dim sum spots, this Daly City destination is perpetually packed with a heavily Chinese clientele feasting on delicacies like moist barbecue pork buns, flavorful Shanghai soup dumplings, and rich roasted duck with a crisp, salty-sweet glazed skin.

With food this good, you can expect a wait in the parking lot and at the host stand, especially during the day and on weekends. Try to angle for a seat in the main dining room, which boasts high ceilings and shallow koi ponds encircling the tables. Service is efficient and prompt, though getting a clear English explanation of unusual dishes can be challenging. With a booming banquet and wedding business, it is more upmarket than most other Chinese restaurants.

La Costanera

Peruvian ✗✗

A2

8150 Cabrillo Hwy. (bet. 1st & 2nd Sts.), Montara

Phone: 650-728-1600   Dinner Tue – Sun
Web: www.lacostanerarestaurant.com
Prices: $$$

A stunning location with breathtaking views are the chief draw at this seaside Peruvian bungalow, perched on a bluff over the Pacific. Time your visit correctly, and you may be able to witness a perfect sunset or pod of migrating whales swimming by—even if you don't, the fire pits and crashing waves are postcard-worthy. Inside, seashell lights and sails add to the oceanic flavor.

The kitchen churns out savory, spicy, yet refined riffs on Peru's culinary hallmarks including ultra-fresh snapper ceviche in *aji rocoto*-infused *leche de tigre*; potato chip-crusted Dungeness crab cakes with sweet *rocoto*-pimento sauce; and salty, crispy chicken thigh *chicharrónes*. Argentine and Spanish wines complement the varied crowd who can be found savoring the vista.

Locanda Positano

Italian ✗✗

B3

617 Laurel St. (bet. Cherry St. & San Carlos Ave.), San Carlos

Phone: 650-591-5700   Lunch & dinner daily
Web: www.locanda-positano.com
Prices: $$

San Carlos foodies have good reason to toast this wood-burning pizza oven, imported directly from Italy, at Laurel Street's Locanda Positano. Fired up and ready to lick thin Neapolitan-style crusts, the oven churns out fragrant, delicious pies such as the Sofia Loren—a signature topped with buffalo mozzarella, prosciutto, peppery arugula, eggplant, artichoke, and zucchini.

The selection of pizzas, salads, and a menu for *bambini* make this a go-to fave for local families. Amid the chic dining room, find a host of friendly servers buzzing around. Tasty salads like grilled artichokes with arugula in tangy citronette make way for the star of this show, best viewed from a seat at the counter facing the pizza oven.

Visit sister restaurant Limone next door.

Madera

B4

Contemporary

2825 Sand Hill Rd. (at I-280), Menlo Park

Phone:	650-561-1540
Web:	www.maderasandhill.com
Prices:	$$$$

Lunch & dinner daily

Rosewood Hotels & Resorts

Power lunches and corporate dinners are the norm at Madera, the restaurant settled inside the tony Rosewood Sand Hill hotel. Though it's just a mile from the highway through Silicon Valley's heart, it feels worlds apart. This is largely due to the glorious views over the Santa Cruz mountains and vaulted wood ceilings that give it the vibe of a contemporary lodge (not to mention the entrancing stone fireplace).

Lunches here are simple with soups, sandwiches, and a few mains, while dinner takes on a more elevated, contemporary feel. Meals may begin with a delicate salad like frisée and mustard greens with *burrata*, persimmon, pomegranate, and Marcona almonds; then transition to rustic chicken roasted in the wood-fired hearth, with smoky skin and juicy flesh perfectly accented by caramelized Brussels sprouts, soft cippolini onions, and tender pork belly lardons.

As befits an affluent haunt, the wine list here is extensive and excellent. Equally enticing are a mélange of delightful desserts like sweet potato custard with dark chocolate and maple sugar foam. Be sure to wear your smartest attire if you want to fit in with the chic crowd of affluent locals and jet-setting business types.

Magda Luna

B2

✗

1199 Broadway, Ste. 2 (bet. Chula Vista & Laguna Aves.), Burlingame

Phone: 650-393-4207   Lunch & dinner Tue – Sun
Web: www.magdalunacafe.com
Prices: 💰

"Mexican food with a conscience" is on the menu at this new café in Burlingame, which prides itself on vegetable-heavy, oil-light dishes made with hormone-free, sustainably raised meats. Located on the busy main drag, the restaurant is full of vibrant color and authentic details like decorative murals of Dia de los Muertos-style skulls.

Though healthy, the food here doesn't skimp on flavor. Start with a bowl of warm tortilla chips and a duo of salsas, then dive into a selection of tacos, burritos, and quesadillas. Entrées include *enchiladas Michoacanas* in a spicy-smoky *guajillo* chile sauce, which pair nicely with a fruity house-made *agua fresca*. A welcoming staff and a special menu for *niños* also make it a great choice for families.

Martins West

C3

✗✗

831 Main St. (bet. Broadway & Stambaugh St.), Redwood City

Phone: 650-366-4366   Lunch & dinner Mon – Sat
Web: www.martinswestgp.com
Prices: $$

This gastropub brings old-world charm to Redwood City with a rich wood bar, wax-dripped candelabras, and exposed brick walls. Yet it shines with new-world edge through brushed aluminum chairs, exposed steel beams, and reclaimed materials.

This is all reflected in a kitchen dedicated to contemporary interpretations of pub classics—think golden-fried Scotch quail eggs, their velvety yolks infused with garlic, fennel, and a touch of pepper. Served with updated farm-to-table fashion, "rarebit" becomes thick slices of toasted artisanal bread with savory fenugreek béchamel and tomato-mozzarella salad.

A subdued lunch crowd walks in from the nearby courthouse and city offices. Cocktail hour and dinner have that deliciously rambunctious vibe, befitting a pub.

Mingalaba

B2

Asian

1213 Burlingame Ave. (bet. Lorton Ave. & Park Rd.), Burlingame

Phone: 650-343-3228 Lunch & dinner daily
Web: www.mingalabarestaurant.com
Prices: $$

With a guaranteed crowd at prime hours, a meal at this Burmese gem in downtown Burlingame almost always means a wait. It's worth it, though, even if it's just to sample such authentic dishes as Burmese-style curry beef with tender potatoes and hints of cumin; pork sautéed with peppers and fragrant basil; or pan-fried string beans flavored with dried shrimp and red chili-garlic sauce. The token Chinese dishes are best avoided.

Mingalaba attracts corporates and families with children in tow—many of whom begin their meals with fresh coconut water. Tables are set against colorful rose-and-gold walls, which teem with urns and other native ephemera. Though service is rushed, unique and pleasing dishes provide an oasis of flavor amid the hustle and bustle.

Navio

A3

Californian

1 Miramontes Point Rd. (at Hwy. 1), Half Moon Bay

Phone: 650-712-7040 Lunch Sat – Sun
Web: www.ritzcarlton.com Dinner nightly
Prices: $$$$

Fresh off a million-dollar renovation, the dining room of the Ritz-Carlton Half Moon Bay is utterly grand, with sweeping views of the Pacific Ocean and golf course. Hotel guests and golfers can be seen dining beneath the boat-like wood walls, while friendly and efficient waiters bustle to and fro from the open kitchen.

Seafood is the focus here, with dishes like seared scallops over sweet pea risotto and morel mushrooms, Mt. Lassen trout fillet with curry-leek fondue and fingerling potatoes, and classic *baba au rhum* with Chantilly cream. The wine list offers a rich, extensive selection of both American and French bottles; and even if prices are quite high, the crowd has no problem shelling out for a chance to gaze out on the extraordinary view.

Osteria Coppa 😊

B2

Italian ✗✗

139 S. B St. (bet. 1st & 2nd Aves.), San Mateo

Phone: 650-579-6021
Web: www.osteriacoppa.com
Prices: $$

Lunch & dinner daily

Osteria Coppa may not literally mean "pasta," but this house-made specialty is on everyone's mind upon entering. The spacious dining room is rustic, contemporary, and relaxed—though hungry hearts are known to skip a beat upon glimpsing those racks of fresh, drying pasta in the kitchen. If available, the *scialatielli* is a rare treat: thicker than spaghetti, it has an alluring texture, perhaps served here in tomato sauce with roasted eggplant and shaved *ricotta salata*.

Whether seated beneath those lofty ceilings or enjoying the windowed tables overlooking B Street, the service is friendly. And if you don't feel like pasta, the thin-crust pizza topped with sausage crumbles, speck, tender cremini mushrooms, and spicy Calabrian chilies is simply delicious.

Pasta Moon

A3

Italian ✗✗

315 Main St. (at Mill St.), Half Moon Bay

Phone: 650-726-5125
Web: www.pastamoon.com
Prices: $$

Lunch & dinner daily

It's definitely *amore* when this (Pasta) moon hits your eye. Located on the main drag in charming Half Moon Bay, Pasta Moon is a sure bet for yup, you guessed it, pasta!

Its design can feel like a haphazard and half-finished mix of spaces that afford views of pasta-making during trips to the restrooms; but after a few bites, you won't care that the owner needs to find an architect—stat. Dreamy pastas along with homemade pizzas and breads are divine. You can't go wrong with anything on this Californian-Italian menu. The lasagna strays from grandma's standard with impressive results and is packed with rich, creamy flavor; while crispy *fritto misto* and a Brussels sprout salad tossed with pancetta and cannellini beans are beloved at all times.

Quattro

C4 Italian

2050 University Ave. (at I-101), East Palo Alto

Phone: 650-470-2889   Lunch & dinner daily
Web: www.quattrorestaurant.com
Prices: $$$

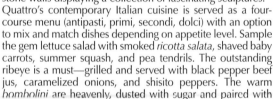

Whether or not you're staying at the Four Seasons, swing by this swanky lair, just off of the hotel's lobby. Its airy atmosphere is marked by a sleek design, natural light, and stone walls displaying a collection of fascinating sculptures.

Quattro's contemporary Italian cuisine is served as a four-course menu (antipasti, primi, secondi, dolci) with an option to mix and match dishes depending on appetite level. Sample the gem lettuce salad with smoked *ricotta salata*, shaved baby carrots, summer squash, and pea tendrils. The outstanding ribeye is a must—grilled and served with black pepper beef jus, caramelized onions, and shisito peppers. The warm *bomboloni* are heavenly, dusted with sugar and paired with chocolate-Guinness and salted caramel sauces.

Ramen Dojo

Japanese

B2

805 S. B St. (bet. 8th & 9th Aves.), San Mateo

Phone: 650-401-6568   Lunch & dinner Wed – Mon
Web: N/A
Prices:

Busy office types find plenty of time to catch up on the morning paper while in line for lunch at Ramen Dojo, the popular San Mateo Japanese noodle house that often comes with a half hour wait. Add your name to the clipboard at the door and ponder your soup of choice.

The dining room isn't much to look at, and service is quick and minimal, but everyone is here for the hearty, steaming bowls of ramen. Soups are available with three base options (soy sauce, garlic pork, and soy bean) and three degrees of heat (mild, regular, and extra spicy). All orders come heaped with roasted pork, fried garlic, *kikurage* mushrooms, scallions, and hard-boiled quail egg, but a list of extra toppings also includes Napa cabbage, shiitakes, and Kurobuta pork.

Sakae

Japanese ✕

B2

243 California Dr. (at Highland Ave.), Burlingame

Phone: 650-348-4064   Lunch Mon – Sat
Web: www.sakaesushi.com   Dinner nightly
Prices: $$

Peninsula

Downtown Burlingame may be the last place one would expect to find authentic sushi, but Sakae hits the spot with fish flown in daily from Tokyo's Tsukiji Market. While it may be surprising, this stylish eatery is certainly no secret—at lunch, the blonde wood sushi bar and tables are crammed with local business suits.

For those on the go, affordable combinations are an easy treat; but those with time to savor a meal should first check out the boards listing the daily specials. Sample a nigiri plate of albacore and bluefin tuna, kanpachi, and mackerel; or warm up with a bowl of udon noodle soup with seaweed and spicy *togarashi*.

Weekends feature sake flights and live karaoke for all. Also try Yuzu, their sister restaurant in San Mateo.

Seiya

Japanese ✕✕

B3

741 Laurel St. (bet. Cherry & Olive Sts.), San Carlos

Phone: 650-508-8888   Lunch Tue – Fri
Web: www.seiyasushi.com   Dinner Tue – Sun
Prices: $$

Sleepy San Carlos has awoken to find this mod Japanese respite, Seiya, in its midst. Inside, find an urbane Asian aesthetic in dark wood furnishings, stone accent walls, low lights, and a long sushi bar. Lunch is quiet, but come dinnertime, the handful of tables and sushi counter fill up with locals eager to sample and share the small plates.

And this is what sets Seiya apart: a full range menu revealing small plates, *robata*, sushi, sashimi, and maki, that has a little something for everyone. Try beef *tataki* (seared filet mignon with garlic *tataki* sauce); *ankimo* (monkfish liver with garlic ponzu); or Great Balls of Fire (deep-fried, panko-crusted, spicy tuna roll with spicy mayo). Savor sesame and green tea ice cream on the sidewalk patio on warm days.

237

Shalizaar

Persian ✕✕

300 El Camino Real (bet. Anita & Belmont Aves.), Belmont

Phone: 650-596-9000   Lunch & dinner daily
Web: www.shalizaar.com
Prices: $$

For a taste of Persia on this side of the pond, head to Shalizaar—a large restaurant sleekly attired in wood floors, walls of windows, and French doors that flood the room with light. A central chandelier adorned with leaves sparkles above beautiful wood-wainscoting and a communal table packed with regulars and visitors alike.

An open wood-fired oven in the back is used for baking warm flatbread paired with feta, walnuts, and fresh mint. Served with every meal, this may be chased by ample portions of *tah dig*, crisped rice topped with *gheymeh* (a flavorful stew of ground beef, chickpeas, and Persian spices); *soltani* mingling *barg* and *koobideh* (beef) kabobs with saffron-tinged white rice; and flaky *baghlava* redolent of walnuts and cinnamon.

Station 1

Californian ✕✕

2991 Woodside Rd. (bet. Mountain Home & Whiskey Hill Rds.), Woodside

Phone: 650-851-4988   Dinner Tue – Sat
Web: www.station1restaurant.com
Prices: $$$

Station 1 is a quaint Californian eatery tucked into picturesque Woodside. The restaurant feels homey and familiar, furnished with repurposed barn wood tables, a cozy fireplace, and covered back porch. In other words, head this way with your date for a quiet and intimate feast.

The menu spins to highlight local and seasonal ingredients, but a set tasting deal could reveal butter bean and prosciutto soup; a poached farm egg atop buttery black rice garnished with enoki mushrooms and shisito peppers; or tender "pork squared," named for the braised pork shoulder as well as the loin, cooked with black tea and served over a sweet roasted plum purée and pickled cabbage salad. To conclude, savor a sweet absinthe lemon bar with a torched juniper marshmallow.

Sushi Sam's

B2

Japanese

218 E. 3rd Ave. (bet. B St. & Ellsworth Ave.), San Mateo

Phone: 650-344-0888
Web: www.sushisams.com
Prices: $$

Lunch & dinner Tue – Sat

Fresh sushi in San Mateo means a trip to Sushi Sam's, which is no secret among connoisseurs and neighbornood folk who regularly flock here the moment it opens to avoid a wait. Service is fast and efficient, though stark white walls, Formica tables, and simple wood chairs do little for the no-frills décor. Check the daily specials on the board for the best and freshest fish, which are mostly from Japan. Selections might include silky salmon placed atop neat mounds of rice with a light grating of wasabi; rich, firm mackerel brushed with a dab of ponzu; and buttery toro lightly seared and unembellished to enhance the delicate flavor. The spicy pickled ginger is house-made. For those who don't feel like choosing, order one of the chef's menus.

Sweet Basil

C2

Thai

1473 Beach Park Blvd. (at Marlin Ave.), Foster City

Phone: 650-212-5788
Web: www.sweetbasilfoster.com
Prices: $$

Lunch & dinner daily

 It's no wonder this Thai fave (and Thai Idea, its vegetarian baby sis a few doors down) is forever-packed. Superb ingredients whipped up into irresistible plates of sumptuousness keep folks coming back every time. Chillin' in a shopping center in Foster City, Sweet Basil's casual vibe and chic décor is marked by modern light fixtures, multi-hued wood floors, and black-lacquered chairs.

Atop bamboo tabletops, feast on such delectable offerings as red coconut curry overflowing with juicy prawns, pumpkin, carrots, bamboo shoots, and basil; or *pad see-ew*, wide stir-fried noodles tossed with cabbage, broccoli, egg, and tender slices of beef. The sweet basil chicken speckled with chilies, onions, and crunchy bell peppers is a classic that never fails to sate.

Taqueria El Metate

✗

120 Harbor Blvd. (at Hwy. 101), Belmont

Phone: 650-595-1110
Web: N/A
Prices: 🫘

Lunch & dinner daily

Taqueria El Metate will become a personal favorite as soon as you've discovered it. Most everybody here seems well acquainted with this classic hangout and its long lines out the door. From the Harbor Blvd. exit off Highway 101 south, make a sharp right to arrive at their parking lot. Inside, El Metate is roomy with rows of hand-painted local furniture; the wood tables and chairs depict colorful scenes of Mexican food and art.

Long tables laden with chips and salsa feel communal; plan to share these during peak hours. The delicious scent of a pork chili verde burrito filled with rice, beans, and *queso fresco*; and the salty and pineapple-sweet, caramelized *al pastor* "super" taco topped with chopped onion and cilantro have everyone clamoring for more.

Taste In Mediterranean Food

✗

1199 Broadway, Ste. 1 (bet. Chula Vista & Laguna Aves.), Burlingame

Phone: 650-348-3097
Web: www.tasteinbroadway.com
Prices: 🫘

Lunch & dinner daily

Taste In Mediterranean Food could easily get lost along Broadway's blocks of cafés and boutiques, but this tiny restaurant is truly not to be missed. Beyond the deli cases of baklava and salads, find the open kitchen where rotating lamb, chicken, and beef slowly turn and roast to become gyros, shawarma platters, and wraps.

About half of the guests grab take out; the others sit in the small dining room to enjoy the likes of combo platters spanning the Mediterranean from Greece to Lebanon. Chewy pita bread scoops up nutty hummus, smoky-garlicky baba ghanoush, and herbaceous Moroccan eggplant salad. Or try thin slices of lamb shawarma in a pita wrap with homemade garlic sauce, cabbage, and fried potatoes. Don't forget the baklava from the counter.

31st Union

Californian   ✗✗

B2

5 S. Ellsworth Ave. (at Baldwin Ave.), San Mateo

Phone: 650-458-0049
Web: www.31stunion.com
Prices: $$

Lunch Wed – Fri
Dinner Tue – Sun

California may have been the 31st state in the union, but it's #1 at this temple of locally sourced fare, where every bite and sip can trace its origins to the Golden State. The rustic-chic décor, with wood sawhorse tables, concrete floors, and soaring ceilings, can get noisy, but the yupster crowd is undeterred, and the friendly servers and casual atmosphere keep things lively.

While the menu is large and eclectic with dishes like oxtail tacos, IPA-battered fish and chips, and grilled lamb flatbread; the small portions quickly elevate the bill, making 31st Union a better choice for drinks and nibbles with a group than a full meal. Those who do stay for an entrée should check out the nightly specials, like duck confit and house-made pasta.

231 Ellsworth

Contemporary   ✗✗

B2

231 S. Ellsworth Ave. (bet. 2nd & 3rd Aves.), San Mateo

Phone: 650-347-7231
Web: www.231ellsworth.com
Prices: $$$

Lunch Tue – Fri
Dinner Mon – Sat

231 Ellsworth is one of the most popular picks for company junkets in San Mateo. Businessmen adore this contemporary pearl for its reliably good American food served in a classically elegant setting. For those ever-important deals, find refuge in one of many private dining areas. Otherwise, the main room with mauve walls, metallic accents, and a dramatic blue barrel ceiling offers a pretty perspective.

The finest seats in the house are at the cushioned banquettes, but a wine cellar up front is ace for a casual repast that may unveil the likes of roasted vegetables smothered in a rich buttery-cheesy sauce; fresh, seared and flaky king salmon paired with Italian butter beans; and a decadent Valrhona chocolate lava cake crowned with *feuilletine*.

Vesta

Peninsula

C3 — Pizza ✕✕

2022 Broadway St. (bet. Jefferson Ave. & Main St.), Redwood City

Phone: 650-362-5052   Lunch & dinner Tue – Sat
Web: www.vestarwc.com
Prices: $$

In the minds of locals and foodies in-the-know, this outstanding pizzeria in downtown Redwood City serves *the* best pizza south of San Francisco. It draws business lunchers and residents for their smoky, chewy, and blistered wood-fired pies spread with tomato, *burrata*, and peppery arugula; or potato, rosemary, and caramelized bacon—the latter crowned with a fresh farm egg. Additionally, a handful of small plates like pork meatballs, seasonal salads, and grilled carrots round out the cheesy roster.

The high-ceilinged space with mosaic-tiled floors is especially lovely on warm days, when diners can sit in front of wide-open French doors and linger over creamy gelato. Given their quality of food, waits are inevitable, so do consider making a reservation.

Viognier

B2 — — — — — — — — — — — — — — — — Contemporary ✕✕✕

222 E. 4th Ave. (at B St.), San Mateo

Phone: 650-685-3727   Dinner Mon – Sat
Web: www.viognierrestaurant.com
Prices: $$$

Get gussied up and make your way to this elegant spot, nestled atop Draeger's Market in San Mateo. Spend an afternoon browsing the aisles of the gourmet grocery below, or sneak a peek at the cooking class taught in the kitchen upstairs. It's a full day of foodie heaven! Finally, snag a cushioned banquette next to the fireplace and let the feasting begin.

The menu divides into three- four- or five-course fixed price meals where the following may be featured: a salad of heirloom tomatoes with mozzarella, basil, black olive tapenade, and toasted slices of levain bread; chased down by cuttlefish slices with grilled shrimp posed atop white peaches. Pleasing palates for its unique flavors is grilled Hawaiian walu laid over a square of *pommes fondant*.

The Village Pub ❀

B3

Gastropub XXX

2967 Woodside Rd. (off Whiskey Hill Rd.), Woodside

Phone: 650-851-9888
Web: www.thevillagepub.net
Prices: $$$

Lunch Sun – Fri
Dinner nightly

Ed Anderson

Part relaxed pub, part fine dining destination, The Village Pub blends both identities seamlessly, which may explain why it's such a solid fixture in the tiny town of Woodside. While most guests order small bites at the bar and select from a more refined menu in the elegant, white-tablecloth dining room, there's no rule against doing the opposite. Plus, the friendly staff is happy to accommodate.

Those opting to go more upscale are in for a treat, as the well-dressed local couples out with friends for a night on the town are wholly aware. The short menu spins to the season, but might begin with a crisp, golden brown *arancino* and peppery pesto; then transition to butter-poached abalone and a slow-cooked farm egg over silky roasted parsnip purée. The roast chicken, with its crisp skin and accompaniment of roasted beets and tender huckleberry financier, is another favorite.

Beverages are just as notable with immense offerings on the wine, beer, and spirits fronts. Suits may relax over a Burgundy, best savored with the dining room's delectable chocolate soufflé poured with a dab of Earl Grey crème anglaise. Either way, a nightcap in front of the roaring wood fireplace is de rigueur.

Wakuriya ✿

B3

Japanese 🍴

115 De Anza Blvd. (at Parrot Dr.), San Mateo

Phone: 650-286-0410   Dinner Wed – Sun
Web: www.wakuriya.com
Prices: $$$$

Wakuriya

Located in a popular shopping plaza, Wakuriya's dining room may first seem dark and rather nondescript. On further inspection, it becomes serene with thick curtains to keep away the outside world and a line of tables that seem to point to the chefs and open kitchen—offering a bit of dinner theater. Delighted diners do much to make the vibe more celebratory. Service is knowledgeable to the point of enlightening on the finer points and flavors of a new dish.

The fixed menu may change price and content frequently, but the cuisine is always elaborate, stunning, and filled with seasonal beauty. After a refreshing cup of sake with a hint of lemon, dip into a lacquer bowl brimming with *somen* and slices of tender duck in delicate and smoky dashi spiced with *shimichi*. Move on to a cool appetizer trio of caviar-topped shrimp in egg-yolk sauce and crunchy snow peas; *madai* snapper and salmon roe dressed in mustard greens; and tofu-pockets of *inari* stuffed with Alaskan snow crab. Depending on availability, a sashimi course may present excellent fatty tuna, amberjack, and monkfish liver set atop shiso and paper-thin radish with bonito soy sauce.

Accompany any meal here with a flight of dry sake.

Zen Peninsula

Chinese ✗

1180 El Camino Real (at Center St.), Millbrae

Phone: 650-616-9388
Web: www.zenpeninsula.com
Prices: $$

Lunch & dinner daily

It's a dim sum extravaganza here at Zen Peninsula where delicious, steaming hot bites served out of traditional rolling carts keep the crowds a coming. Special event menus and à la carte seafood specialties are also on offer, but that's not why you're here. Tightly positioned, banquet-style round tables fill up with large groups devouring the likes of *har gow*—sticky wrappers stuffed with shrimp, ginger, garlic, and sesame oil; or roasted suckling pig in a smoky-sweet five spice glaze.

Be prepared to wait for a table during peak hours or on weekends. Clearly the never-ending crowds can't get enough of lip-smacking ground beef crêpes drizzled with soy and sprinkled with slices of scallion; or fluffy egg custard buns flavored with a hint of coconut.

Red=Particularly Pleasant.
Look for the red ✗ and 🏠
symbols.

Peter L. Wrenn/MICHELIN

South Bay

South Bay

Tech geeks around the world know the way to San Jose, but foodies typically will get lost in San Francisco. It's a shame really as tech money plus an international population equals a dynamic and superb culinary scene. Not to mention the rich wine culture descending from the Santa Cruz Mountains, where a burgeoning vintner community takes great pride in its work. In May, you can sample over 70 area wines at the **Santa Cruz Mountains Wine Express**, at Roaring Camp Railroad in Felton.

Festive Foods

The Valley may have a nerdy reputation, but South Bay locals definitely know how to party. In San Jose, the festival season kicks off in May with music, dancing, drinks, and eats at the wildly adored Greek Festival. Then in June, buckets of cornhusks wait to be stuffed and sold at the Story Road Tamale Festival, held within the orchards of Emma Prusch Farm Park. In July, Japantown comes alive for the two-day Obon/Bazaar and, in August, the Italian-American Heritage Foundation celebrates its yearly Family Festa. **Santana Row** also keeps the party going year-round: this sleek shopping village is home to numerous upscale restaurants, and its very own farmer's market. Opened in August 2010, San Jose's newest and noted foodie destination is **San Pedro Square Market**, which houses artisan merchants at the historic Peralta Adobe downtown. Farmers and specialty markets are a way of life for South Bay locals and each city has at least one or more throughout the week.

A Morsel of Vietnam

San Jose is also a melting pot for global culinary influences. Neighborhood *pho* shops and *bánh mì* delis sate the growing Vietnamese community, that also frequents **Grand Century Mall** for a host of hard-to-find, authentic snacks. Meanwhile, the intersection of King and Tully streets is home to some of the area's best Vietnamese flavors: try **Huong Lan** for its delicious *bánh mì* sandwiches; cream puffs at **Hong-Van Bakery**; and crispy green waffles flavored with *pandan* paste at **Century Bakery**, just a few blocks away. And that's not all: **Lion Plaza** is another such hub for Vietnamese bakeries, markets, and canteens. If Cambodian noodle soup is more your cup of tea, look no further than **Nam Vang Restaurant** or **F&D Yummy**. The large and lofty **Dynasty Chinese Seafood Restaurant** on Story Road is popular for big parties and is also a local favorite for dim sum. In keeping with the Asian vein, **Nijiya Market** is a Japanese jewel in Mountain View, coveted for its specialty goods, fabulous ingredients, and all things Far East. Long before it was trendy to be organic in America, Nijiya's mission was to bring the taste of Japan in the form of high-quality, seasonal, and local ingredients to the California crowd. Stop by this tantalizing sanctum for fresh seafood, meat, veggies, and fruit, as well as an array of sushi and bento boxes. Also available on their website are a spectrum of sumptuous recipes that range from faithful noodle and rice preparations, to ethnic delicacies. Moving from Asia to South America, devotees of Mexican cuisine are smitten by the fresh and still-warm tortillas at **Tropicana**, or the surprisingly good tacos from one of the area's many **Mi Pueblo Food Centers**.

A Spread for Students

And yet there is more to the South Bay than just San Jose. Los Gatos is home to the sweet patisserie **Fleur de Cocoa** as well as **Testarossa Winery**, the Bay Area's oldest, continually operating winery. Meanwhile, Palo Alto is a casual home base for the countless students and faculty of reputed Stanford University. Here, locals line up for organic and artisanal yogurts (both fresh and frozen) at **Fraîche**; or delish double-decker sandwiches at **Village Cheese House**—perhaps the vegetarian-friendly Italian Veggie-Ball spread with tofu, marinara, and mozzarella? If you're dreaming about Korean food, then make your way to Santa Clara where the Korean community enjoys a range of authentic nibbles and tasty spreads at **Lawrence Plaza** food court. But, if in urgent need of groceries, shopping along El Camino Real near the Lawrence Expressway intersection is a feast for the senses. Local foodies favor the caramelized and roasted sweet potatoes at **Sweet Potato Stall**, just outside the Galleria, and **SGD Tofu House** for *bibimbop* or *soondubu jjigae*. Despite the fast pace of technology in Silicon Valley, Slow Food—the grassroots movement dedicated to local food traditions—has a thriving South Bay chapter.

Even Google, in Mountain View, feeds its large staff three organic square meals a day. For a selection of delicacies, South Bay's eateries and stores dish up gourmet goods and ethnic eats. The rest of us can visit nearby **Milk Pail Market**, known for more than 300 varieties of cheese. Have your pick among such splendid choices as Camembert, Bleu d'Auvergne, Morbier, and Cabriquet. Another haunt popularized by meat-loving mortals is **Los Gatos Meats & Smokehouse**. This flesh food mecca has been serving the South Bay community for years via a plethora of poultry, fish, and freshly butchered meat sandwiches. Lauded for long now, this salty sanctum also quenches diners with such homey "specialties" as prime rib roasts, pork loin, beef jerky, sausages, corned beef, and of course, bacon: regular, pepper, country-style or Canadian anyone? Pair all these meat treats and cheese with a bottle from Mountain View's famous **Savvy Cellar Wine Bar & Wine Shop**—it's a picnic in the making!

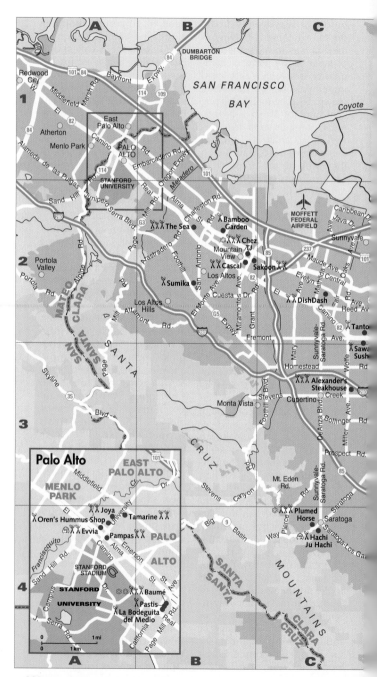

Palo Alto

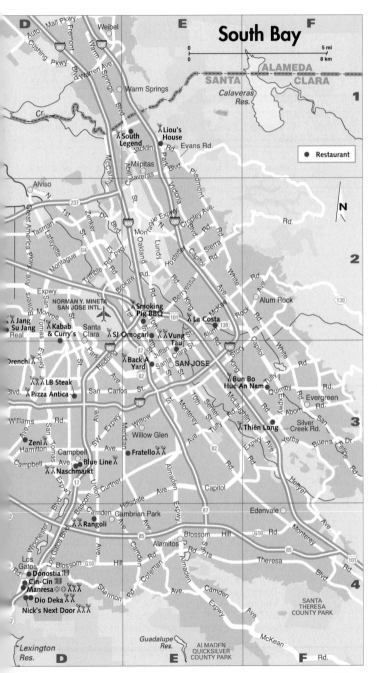

South Bay

D · E · F

Weibel
Auto Mall Pkwy.
Cushing Pkwy.
880
Fremont
Warren Springs
Blvd.
Warm Springs
Cr.

SANTA
Calaveras
Res.
ALAMEDA
CLARA

1

South Legend ✗
Liou's House ✗
Jacklin Rd.
Evans Rd.
Milpitas
Calaveras
Abel
Park
Victoria
Piedmont
● Restaurant

Alviso
237
1st St.
Zanker
Trimble Rd.
Brokaw Rd.
Montague Expwy.
Oakland Rd.
Lundy
Hostetter
Capitol
Sierra
Cropley Ave.
Berryessa
King
White Rd.
Rd.

N
N

Alum Rock
130

2

Great America Pkwy.
Bowers
Trasman
Lafayette
Monroe
Montague
880
Trimble Rd.
NORMAN Y. MINETA
SAN JOSE INTL.
Smoking Pig BBQ ✗
La Costa ✗
Rock Ave.
White
Capitol

Jang Su Jang ✗
Real
Kabab & Curry's ✗
Santa Clara
SJ Omogari ✗
Vung Tau ✗✗
SAN JOSE
Story Rd.
King
Rd.

Drenchi ✗
Park Ave.
Heading
Back A Yard ✗
Julian St.
Santa Clara St.
10th St.
Senter Rd.
McLaughlin
Bun Bo
Huc An Nam ●
Tully Rd.
Quimby
Rd.
Evergreen
Aborn
Rd.

LB Steak ✗✗✗
Pizza Antica ✗
San Carlos St.
280
Monterey
Rd.
Thiên Long ✗
Silver Creek Rd.
San
Buena
Yerba
Felipe Rd.

3

Williams Rd.
San Tomas
Zeni ✗
Hamilton
Campbell Ave.
Blue Line ✗
Naschmarkt ✗✗
17
Curtner
SW Expwy.
Willow
Willow Glen
Fratello ✗✗
Almaden
82
Capitol
Hellyer

Winchester Blvd.
Bascom
Camden
Cambrian Park
Rangoli ✗✗
85
Alamitos
Blossom Hill
Edenvale ○
G10 Rd.
Monterey
Ave.
101

4

Los Gatos
Blossom
G10
Hill
Donostia ▥
Cin-Cin ▥
Manresa ✗✗✗
Dio Deka ✗✗
Nick's Next Door ✗✗✗
Los Gatos Blvd.
Shannon
Coleman
Camden
Ave.
Almaden Expwy.
Theresa
85
Blvd.
SANTA THERESA COUNTY PARK

Lexington Res.
Guadalupe Res.
ALMADEN QUICKSILVER COUNTY PARK
McKean
F Rd.

0 ___ 5 mi
0 ___ 8 km

D · E · F

Alexander's Steakhouse

  Steakhouse

10330 N. Wolfe Rd. (at I-280), Cupertino

Phone:	408-446-2222	Lunch Tue – Fri
Web:	www.alexanderssteakhouse.com	Dinner nightly
Prices:	$$$$	

 Your mouth will begin to water the moment you stroll into this updated steakhouse, whose entry features an extensive display of T-bones, Porterhouses, Wagyu beef, and aged quarter-sections of prime cuts. They're all here for the delectation of the businessmen that are the backbone of Alexander's clientele, savoring bottles of expensive Napa cabs at spacious tables, on the company dime, of course.

While those beautifully marbled steaks are the obvious choice, the kitchen also displays talent with Asian-inflected seafood like perfectly seared Hokkaido scallops with sorrel coulis. Finish with a decadent slice of "24-karat" carrot cake, rich with cinnamon and frosted with coconut-saffron gel. Cityside deal-doers can visit a second location in SoMa.

Back A Yard

 Caribbean

80 N. Market St. (bet. Santa Clara & St. John Sts.), San Jose

Phone:	408-294-8626	Lunch & dinner Mon – Sat
Web:	www.backayard.net	
Prices:	🪙🪙	

Though this Caribbean spot is located in the heart of downtown San Jose, dining here feels like a vacation, thanks to cheerful murals, a lively soundtrack, and hospitable servers. Unlike its Menlo Park predecessor, which mainly does to-go orders, this location boasts a capacious brick dining room.

Back A Yard is a Jamaican term meaning "the way things are done back home," and the food doesn't disappoint on that count. Specialties include smoky, spicy, and tender jerk chicken, flavorful curry goat, and vinegar-marinated *escoveitch* fish fillets, all accompanied by coconut rice and red beans, a side salad, and caramelized fried plantains. Cool off your palate with a glass of coconut water, then order a slice of dense, flan-like sweet potato pudding.

Bamboo Garden

Chinese

B2

108 N. Rengstorff Ave. (at Central Expwy.), Mountain View

Phone: 650-967-7334
Web: N/A
Prices: 💳

Lunch & dinner daily

Don't let the fuss-free shopping center and well-worn interior deter you. This is the go-to place for real deal Shanghainese cuisine. Just follow the local Chinese residents, who can be found relishing in these fantastically authentic offerings. The menu provides some Americanized fare as well as some Mandarin options, but stay with their traditional items and you will be golden.

The sticky rice—served in a hollowed-out bamboo stalk and studded with tender-braised pork, fatty pork belly, and bamboo shoots—is an outstanding dish. Other notables feature rich and flavorful smoked duck; fresh fish fillets stewed in a thick rice wine sauce with wood ear mushrooms; or Shanghai greens—spinach shoots sautéed with broth, garlic, goji berries, and sesame oil.

Blue Line

Pizza

D3

415 E. Campbell Ave. (bet. Civic Center Dr. & Railway Ave.), Campbell

Phone: 408-378-2800
Web: www.bluelinepizza.com
Prices: $$

Lunch & dinner daily

Sibling to ever-popular Little Star pizza, Blue Line is a young recruit to the South Bay that is fast becoming a favorite. This large, casual dining room is mobbed by locals flanking its flat-screens, while families mill about amid exposed ductwork and blue-painted walls.

Named for the Chicago Blue Line, the cornmeal-crusted, deep-dish pizzas are sure to please—the veggie version comes with a thick tomato sauce topped with cheese and packed with zucchini, peppers, and mushrooms? For those who don't go deep, the thin-crust Italian combo offers a layer of sauce generously heaped with pepperoni, salami, and olives. Conveniently located on Campbell Avenue steps from the light rail tracks, you can also pick up baked or half-baked pizzas on your way home.

Baumé ✿ ✿

Contemporary 🍴🍴🍴

201 S. California Ave. (at Park Blvd.), Palo Alto

Phone: 650-328-8899
Web: www.baumerestaurant.com
Prices: $$$$

Lunch Fri – Sat
Dinner Wed – Sat

South Bay

Peter Giles

The fact that innovative Baumé is named for an 18th century French chemist hints at what to expect. Inside, the room has a polished look with large orange-striped curtains used as dividers, otherworldly music, and orchids. Conversations are kept to a library-like hush among gourmands basking in the glory of such sublime seasonality. Some tables are celebratory; others are corporate. Regardless, everyone here has a reason to splurge dearly. (The wine list is for Silicon Valley zillionaires.)

Service albeit inconsistent is a friendly and professional extension of the kitchen. The menu is presented as a list of ingredients that will be used to prepare your ambitious French meal, showcasing modernist techniques. Begin with the likes of cauliflower *espuma* topped with carrot cream and a plump mussel; or clean and salty-fresh caviar, its flavors heightened with a smear of rich parsnip purée, lemon zest, and brittle green shards of herbs. A beef fillet nearly melts in the mouth and is served with a range of ingredients at their peak, like baby leeks and rich celeriac purée.

Desserts may include a miso-accented vanilla *chiboust* with pistachio cake, fresh apricots, and raspberries.

Bun Bo Hue An Nam

F3

Vietnamese ✗

2060 Tully Rd. (at Quimby Rd.), San Jose

Phone: 408-270-7100
Web: N/A
Prices: 🍜

Lunch & dinner Thu – Tue

Take a hint from the local Vietnamese families and head into this second San Jose outpost, a slightly more contemporary version of the original. Inside, walls hang with flat screens showing Vietnamese TV, and wooden tables and chairs sit atop tiled floors.

As the name suggests, *bun bo hue* soup is the specialty here, though it may be a pleasure limited to intrepid diners. This spicy beef noodle soup blazes with chili oil, lemongrass, scallions, and cilantro, yet remains slightly gamey and rich with ample portions of tripe, tendon, and congealed pork blood. An array of *pho* is also a popular choice. Folks can be found slurping down *pho dac biet*, a fragrant star anise and lemongrass broth overflowing with meat, served with lime, basil, and chilies.

Cascal

B2

Latin American ✗✗

400 Castro St. (at California St.), Mountain View

Phone: 650-940-9500
Web: www.cascalrestaurant.com
Prices: $$

Lunch & dinner daily

Pan-Latin Cascal in Mountain View is the go-to spot for local tech types, who gather after work to sip mojitos, sangria, and margaritas. They can be seen sharing small plates like flaky wild mushroom empanadas oozing with *Manchego* and truffle oil; *albondigas*, lamb meatballs in a savory roasted piquillo pepper sauce; or a Cuban wrap packed with adobo-marinated pork.

The food is always top-notch, but the vibe remains casual, with families enjoying dinner and couples with dogs in tow benefitting from the spacious patio. Efficient servers bustle between tables inside the colorful room, flooded with light thanks to walls of windows. Sharing is the ethos here, so there's no shame in saving room for a *tres leches* cake to split between friends.

Chez TJ ✿

938 Villa St. (bet. Bryant & Franklin Sts.), Mountain View

Phone: 650-964-7466
Web: www.cheztj.com
Prices: $$$$

Dinner Tue – Sat

Mark Leet

Though it's housed in a charming Victorian that dates back to the 1890s, the food at Chez TJ is thoroughly modern, incorporating culinary innovation into its takes on classic French cuisine. The low lighting, quietly elegant décor, and professional service makes this *bijou* the perfect choice for a dose of romance.

Irrespective of the full dégustation menu or a slightly smaller prix-fixe, you will likely encounter novel ingredients and inventive techniques. Picture a rich yet very tender filet of antelope, or pine nut tuile and emulsified lobster stock garnishing a poached lobster tail and claw, only to find your palate utterly invigorated. That's not to say this fine *maison* can't handle the standards: duck breast is seared to a nice medium-rare and sided by tender confit, while tuna tartare gets a twist from wasabi, caviar, and arugula cream. The wine list is minimal, but a versed staff will happily educate diners on the perfect pairing.

Local couples celebrating milestones are visible throughout the dining room, warmed by the occasion into trading their last bites of devil's food cake with chocolate caramel sauce, or Greek yogurt panna cotta with strawberries and lavender.

Cin-Cin

International ▤

D4

368 Village Ln. (at Saratoga Los Gatos Rd.), Los Gatos

Phone: 408-354-8006
Web: www.cincinwinebar.com
Prices: $$

Dinner Mon – Sat

Sure, enjoy that well-priced Happy Hour (Monday-Saturday from 4:00-6:00 P.M.), but just make sure to stick around for the wonderfully diverse range of international small plates. Almost any craving can be quenched here, where Asian, American, Mexican, French, and Italian goodies are available for a sharing showdown.

The lively wine bar is styled in blonde woods, pale greens, and low lights, with two adjoining dining spaces and a primo lounge. To start, fill up on lettuce cups piled with cold soba noodles, shaved apple, fried shiitakes, and sauced with chipotle aïoli. Hamburger sliders on silver dollar rolls with grilled onion and aged cheddar fondue; or Korean tacos heaped with kimchi and shaved ribeye are a delightful balance of flavor and texture.

Dio Deka

Greek ☓☓

D4

210 E. Main St. (near Fiesta Way), Los Gatos

Phone: 408-354-7700
Web: www.diodeka.com
Prices: $$$

Dinner nightly

Whether closing a deal or savoring a night out, affluent Los Gatos locals flock to this wonderful Greek restaurant, housed in Hotel Los Gatos. Featuring a large, *taverna*-style dining room, Dio Deka isn't formal, but always seduces a stylish crowd by dint of a roaring fireplace, open exhibition kitchen, and exposed beams.

Savvy diners know that sharing appetizers is the way to go here and options include golden brown *haloumi* fritters; or fire-roasted Brussels sprouts drizzled with honey and topped with a soft-poached egg. Prime steaks get the mesquite treatment, while entrées like *arni kotsi* (braised lamb shank so tender that it falls apart in a pool of egg-lemon sauce) are wholly innovative. Finish with a homey pear rice pudding and fresh mint tea.

DishDash

Middle Eastern

C2

190 S. Murphy Ave. (bet. Evelyn & Washington Aves.), Sunnyvale

Phone: 408-774-1889
Web: www.dishdash.com
Prices: $$

Lunch & dinner Mon — Sat

This hoppin' South Bay spot is named after the traditional flowing garb worn by Middle Eastern men and captures just that kind of spirit. With notes of sumac and saffron drifting through the air, pendant lights, draped fabrics, and cultural knickknacks...is this the Arabic Peninsula?

Their dazzling menu is marked by bold flavors that are wonderfully conveyed in a lamb shawarma salad with marinated lamb, cucumber, tomatoes, and garlic yogurt atop romaine lettuce; or tasty *mashwi*—prawns and sea bass bathed in a superb lemon-cumin sauce, charbroiled, and then served with seasoned grilled vegetables and rice. The best way to get your sweet on is with the likes of *kenafeh* or shredded phyllo dough packed with sugared cheese, rosewater, and pistachios.

Donostia

D4

Basque

424 N. Santa Cruz Ave. (bet. Andrews St. & Saratoga Los Gatos Rd.), Los Gatos

Phone: 408-797-8688
Web: www.donostiapintxos.com
Prices: $$

Dinner Mon — Sat

Donostia is the Basque name for San Sebastián, and in the same vein, oodles of Basque flavor is on offer at this sister spot to popular Italian wine bar Enoteca la Storia. Even the walls, packed with glowing blue geode slices, suggest the color of the ocean. Whether they're sipping crisp Albariño or fruity sangria, a crew of chic locals pack the bar, sharing plates of *pintxos* like *patatas bravas* drizzled with spicy *crema* and eggy *tortilla de patata*.

Those seeking heartier fare have choices including slow-cooked beef cheeks over chickpea purée and romesco. Most opt to make a meal of tapas, sharing such tempting treats as spicy gazpacho and creamy, golden brown cod *croquetas*. The staff is always happy to suggest a wine from their carefully crafted list.

Evvia

Greek   XX

A4

420 Emerson St. (bet. Lytton & University Aves.), Palo Alto

Phone: 650-326-0983
Web: www.evvia.net
Prices: $$

Lunch Mon – Fri
Dinner nightly

As popular as ever, this downtown Palo Alto fixture draws a mix of suits by day and local couples by night, all of them bathed in the glow of the hearth that reflects off the hanging copper pans in the exhibition kitchen. This is an authentic Greek *estiatorio* experience, from the herbed feta that tops wood oven-baked *gigante* beans in tomato-leek sauce to the creamy tzatziki that enhances slices of tender roast lamb on house-made pita.

When it's warm in Palo Alto (as it often is), Evvia throws open its front glass doors, allowing the convivial staff to get a whiff of fresh air as they tend to a stream of regulars. At night, the experience is more intimate, providing a cozy environment for splitting a rich but devour-able olive oil-semolina cake.

Fratello

Italian   XX

E3

1712 Meridian Ave. (bet. Hamilton Ave. & Lenn Dr.), San Jose

Phone: 408-269-3801
Web: www.fratello-ristorante.com
Prices: $$

Lunch Tue – Fri
Dinner Tue – Sun

Fratello in San Jose might not be fancy-schmancy, but this quaint, casual, and family-friendly spot definitely has its own charm. Its theme is echoed in the terra-cotta-colored walls with paintings of the Italian countryside. The warm-spirited Italian family that runs the show welcomes you and yours with an array of authentic dishes that run the gamut from pastas and panini at lunch to more impressive seafood dishes in the evening.

Twist your fork around the homemade pappardelle topped with veal ragù or savor the charred taste of the tender grilled octopus, drizzled with fresh lemon, olive oil, and a sprinkling of fragrant Sicilian oregano. The crisp-skinned *salmone al brodo*, served in a roasted garlic and lemon broth, is delicious in its simplicity.

Hachi Ju Hachi 😊

Japanese ✗

14480 Big Basin Way (bet. Saratoga Los Gatos Rd. & 3rd St.), Saratoga

Phone: 408-647-2258
Web: www.hachijuhachi88.com
Prices: $$

Dinner Tue – Sun

Simple chairs and a blonde wood counter may not be much to look at, but the casual Saratoga interior manages to capture the serene essence of Japan. Wise visitors will take the straightforward space as a sign that Hachi Ju Hachi is focused on cuisine.

Delicate à la carte dishes may include cuttlefish with spicy cod roe and pork belly in white miso marinade, but the real adventure begins with a reservation. Folks with a bit of foresight and extra funds may pull up a chair for an elaborate *kaiseki* where the chef himself will comment on every course. Mouthwatering delights include the likes of kombu-burdock roll; hamachi skin and fragrant shiso; yellowtail sashimi with house-made sea salt; and miso-braised beef with blistered shisito peppers.

Jang Su Jang

Korean ✗✗

3561 El Camino Real, Ste.10 (bet. Flora Vista Ave. & Lawrence Expwy.), Santa Clara

Phone: 408-246-1212
Web: www.jangsujang.com
Prices: $$

Lunch & dinner daily

This stretch of El Camino may as well be renamed "Little Korea" as it teems with Korean diners and shops whose owners and families congregate at Jang Su Jang. A local stomping ground rife with authentic recipes, the bona fide beauté is far more chic than its companions with modern accents like cushioned banquettes and overhead ventilation hoods.

Screens offer some privacy between tables which are stocked with a good range of *banchan* and better kimchi. DIY-ers should request a grill table for succulent barbecue meats before delving into heftier items like old style *bulgogi*, marinated beef in a fragrant broth with clear noodles; *japchae*, stir-fried glass noodles with meat and veggies; or *yookgejang kalguksoo*, a spicy beef soup with hand-cut noodles.

Joya

A4

Latin American

339 University Ave. (at Florence St.), Palo Alto

Phone: 650-853-9800   Lunch & dinner daily
Web: www.joyarestaurant.com
Prices: $$

Come dressed to impress at Joya, the popular downtown Palo Alto hot spot for Latin tapas and sangria. Pose under oversized chandeliers in their stylish dark wood lounge area decorated with leather furnishings. Lunches are low-key, but the younger crowd kicks the volume up a notch over cocktail-fuelled evening meals.

Group dining is all the rage here, as the extensive menu of seasonal Latin tapas is ideal for sharing. Check out the fresh *masa sopes* made with tasty roasted chicken in a smoky chipotle sauce finished with pimento *crèma*; or the plump and sweet crab cakes, perfectly seasoned and drizzled with chipotle aïoli. Pair zesty dishes with refreshing tropical cocktails, such as the creamy-minty coconut mojito, for a mini-vacation.

Kabab & Curry's

D2

Indian

1498 Isabella St. (at Clay St.), Santa Clara

Phone: 408-247-0745   Lunch & dinner Tue – Sun
Web: www.kababcurrys.com
Prices:

The appeal is in the name at Kabab & Curry's, which has become a dining destination among Indian and Pakistani expats missing the comforts of home. On lunch breaks from the local tech giants, they pack the all-you-can-eat buffet, filling up their plates with fragrant chicken *boti kababs*, coupled with creamy *dal makhani* and slabs of charred naan for soaking up those savory sauces.

Set in a white house with simple tile floors and orange walls, Kabab & Curry's is more about food than service. But, that doesn't deter the crowd of local families from gushing in for dinner or to pick up take-out. With to-go bags laden with rich chicken *tikka masala* and pungent lamb *kadahi*, it's clear that everybody loves this *desi* diner's bold and authentic flavors.

La Bodeguita del Medio

B4

Cuban

463 S. California Ave. (bet. Ash St. & El Camino Real), Palo Alto

Phone: 650-326-7762

Web: www.labodeguita.com

Prices: $$

Lunch Mon – Fri
Dinner Mon – Sat

La Bodeguita del Medio is both a thriving Cuban restaurant and a separate tobacco shop, frequented by local businessmen at lunch and families for dinner. Welcoming you inside are clay tile floors, vibrant Cuban paintings, and amicable servers. Guests can sip cocktails at the bar and enjoy an authentic Cuban meal, before smoking those rare cigars in the back lounge.

The spread usually involves flaky, golden brown empanadas filled with shredded pork, spiced with chiles and pepper jack, and splashed with a delicious coconut-jalapeño sauce. *Tortillas con pescado* are filled with pan-seared salmon and topped with an herbaceous cilantro-avocado pesto flavored with lime and garlic. Couple that with buttery, caramelized sweet plantains for a *muy sabroso* finale.

La Costa

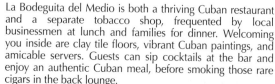

E2

Mexican

1805 Alum Rock Ave. (bet. Jackson Ave. & King Rd.), San Jose

Phone: 408-937-1010

Web: N/A

Prices:

Lunch & dinner daily

Authenticity is king at this casual San Jose taqueria, which draws a working crowd seeking a quick lunch and Hispanic families enjoying a casual outdoor dinner. Though it's housed in a dated building offering only counter service and a handful of patio tables, La Costa's repertoire of outstanding dishes more than make up for its lack of atmosphere.

The staff's English can be spotty at best, so you'll want to brush up on your high-school Spanish (or your pantomime skills) to order up tender *al pastor* tacos with marinated pork and caramelized pineapple or a hefty chicken burrito stuffed with rice, pinto beans, salsa, cilantro, cheese, and onion. Be sure to tack on an order of their famous ceviche, which you'll see on nearly every table.

LB Steak

Steakhouse ✗✗✗

D3

334 Santana Row, Ste. 1000 (bet. Olin Ave. & Stevens Creek Blvd.), San Jose

Phone: 408-244-1180
Lunch & dinner daily
Web: www.lbsteak.com
Prices: $$$

Roland Passot's French métier shines at LB Steak, from the opposite end of its tony Santana Row shopping center sister, Left Bank Brasserie. The vibe is upscale and cosmopolitan with high-backed banquettes and chandeliers in the elegant main room; chic, cabana-style front patio; and private dining room with fireplace perfect for celebrations. Behold the immaculate exhibition kitchen behind sleek, automatic glass doors.

The menu includes burgers and some seafood, but showcases a fine selection of juicy and well-marbled USDA prime steaks, including bone-in and dry-aged cuts, served flame-licked, tender, and perfectly caramelized. Complete a meal here with classic steakhouse sides and New York cheesecake with nectarine coulis to end on a sweet note.

Liou's House

Chinese ✗

E1

1245 Jacklin Rd. (at Park Victoria Dr.), Milpitas

Phone: 408-263-9888
Lunch & dinner Tue – Sun
Web: N/A
Prices: 💰💰

Trek out to this little restaurant in Milpitas to be rewarded with unique Hunan dishes not easily found elsewhere. Unassuming Liou's House is no-frills with tile floors and faux-granite tables. But note, lunches are filled with business people, and dinners are busy with families and groups, many of whom are Chinese; so rest assured, Liou's is very popular and very authentic.

The wise thing to do is order from the menu of chef's specialties, such as Hunan tofu infused with spicy garlic and fermented black bean sauce, served piping hot with mixed vegetables in a clay pot. Those in the know call ahead to pre-order from a separate listing of dishes needing extra time: honey ham with chestnuts; sea cucumber with ground pork; or spareribs in a kabocha squash.

Manresa ✿ ✿

D4

Contemporary XXX

320 Village Ln. (bet. Santa Cruz & University Aves.), Los Gatos

Phone: 408-354-4330
Web: www.manresarestaurant.com
Prices: $$$$

Dinner Wed – Sun

Michael David Rose

Manresa so clearly reflects Californian sensibilities that it seems doubtful that it could exist anywhere else. It is set in a little bungalow that manages to be charming yet contemporary and filled with character. Gray tones and uniquely crafted glass light fixtures carry through the two-room space, divided by a lounge and bar. Dining here is an easy and friendly experience with a distinct local elegance.

A sense of artistry, minimalism, and lightness pervades the seasonal menu. Dishes strive to highlight the best of seasonal ingredients, with results that are delicious and often healthful. A Japanese-inspired sea bream composition is lightly cured with salt and served with brilliant simplicity in micro-shreds of radish and olive oil. Harmony and creative flavor combinations are at the center of the Belon oyster with seaweed ice and *wekiwa tangelo*. A petite morsel of nut-crusted chicken breast is not only accompanied by roasted lettuce and kumquat compote, but also a separate bowl of "civet of leg" in a perfect reduction and juniper foam that is luxe and powerful.

Fascinating desserts include a chocolate pavé and frozen nougatine with caramel ice cream and marshmallow squiggles.

Naschmarkt

Austrian ✗✗

384 E. Campbell Ave. (bet. Central & Railway Aves.), Campbell

Phone: 408-378-0335
Web: www.naschmarkt-restaurant.com
Prices: $$

Dinner Tue – Sun

Named for the large produce market in Vienna known as the "city's stomach," this spot in Campbell is becoming a gastro-favorite. On weekends, find romantic couples savoring the contemporary space, boasting a wrap-around dining counter, open kitchen, exposed brick walls, and high ceilings.

The cuisine captures the true spirit of Austria by preparing its classics with modern style. Familiar traditions are found in Hungarian beef goulash braised in paprika with herbed spätzle; or classic wiener schnitzel with lingonberry sauce and potato salad. Innovations are clear in riesling-steamed black mussels with carrots and celery root. Stay for the sweet, as in a piping-hot and fluffy *salzburger nockerl* with tangy yogurt and stewed blueberry compote.

Nick's Next Door

American ✗✗✗

11 College Ave. (at Main St.), Los Gatos

Phone: 408-402-5053
Web: www.nicksnextdoor.com
Prices: $$

Lunch & dinner Tue – Sat

Though it originally opened as the sibling to Chef Difu's Nick's on Main, Nick's Next Door is now his sole restaurant—even more confusing given that it's actually across the street from his original spot. One fact is evident, though: the crowd here has ritzy tastes, often flocking in from the high-end cigar shop next door and Bentley dealership down the street.

Upscale American bistro cuisine is the focus with dishes like seared pepper-crusted ahi tuna, a veal rib chop with creamy Tuscan white beans, and meatloaf with potatoes and wild mushroom gravy. Whether you dine in the cozy yet elegant dining room with its black-and-gray motif or on the beautiful patio at the foot of a towering redwood, you'll receive a warm welcome, often from Nick himself.

South Bay

Orenchi

  Japanese   ✗

3540 Homestead Rd. (near Lawrence Expy.), Santa Clara

Phone: 408-246-2955

Lunch & dinner Tue – Sun

Web: www.orenchi-ramen.com

Prices:

 There are few bowls of soup worth a several-mile drive to a semi-defunct shopping center only to find a long line outside the door. However, if you are looking for such a soup, Orenchi serves ramen so authentic that Japanese expats come from all over for a piping-hot taste of home.

There is no need for décor in this faithful noodle house—you'll be too busy waiting in line and then slurping down soup to notice. Upon arrival, write your name on the clipboard and consider your options: Orenchi ramen has a *tonkotsu* base with chunks of pork, a tender soft-boiled chicken egg, and earthy enoki mushrooms; whereas Shio ramen comes brimming with seaweed, leeks, and yuzu zest. Additional menu items include braised pork belly and fish cake tempura.

Oren's Hummus Shop

  Middle Eastern   ✗

261 University Ave. (bet. Bryant & Ramona Sts.), Palo Alto

Phone: 650-752-6492

Lunch & dinner daily

Web: www.orenshummus.com

Prices:

 For a quick trip to Israel, head over to Oren's Hummus Shop in Palo Alto. It's a casual stop catering to tech-types, Stanford professors, and local families looking for very good and incomparable authentic Israeli food. Fresh and healthy is the name of the game here, where delicious bites are fired up with all natural ingredients and a lot of homemade love.

Try the salad trio of traditional Middle Eastern appetizers: smoky roasted eggplant baba ghanoush; *labane* (strained yogurt) topped with olive oil and spices; and crispy falafel balls served with tahini. Do not miss the signature hummus, drizzled with olive oil, paprika, and served with fluffy, warm pita bread. Or try the tender grilled chicken skewer, alongside salad and sweet potato fries.

Pampas

Brazilian ✗✗

A4

529 Alma St. (bet. Hamilton & University Aves.), Palo Alto

Phone: 650-327-1323
Web: www.pampaspaloalto.com
Prices: $$$

Lunch Mon – Fri
Dinner nightly

Pampas has a prime Palo Alto location across from the CalTrain, just steps from the shops on University Ave. The large brick façade is hard to miss, and judging by the half-off happy hour crowds, most yupsters don't. The voluminous, bi-level restaurant has the look of a sexy barn with dark masculine furnishings.

Pampas is a Brazilian *churrascaria* (carnivore heaven) where servers bring tender, well-seasoned, spit-roasted *rodizio* meat until you say "uncle." Standouts include the tenderloin filet seasoned with garlic and herbs; chicken legs marinated in garlic, chiles, and vinegar; and house-made chorizo with *harissa* and more chiles. In case this isn't enough, the sidebar buffet is unlimited. The slow-roasted pineapple makes an excellent finale.

Pastis

French ✗

B4

447 S. California Ave. (bet. Ash St. & El Camino Real), Palo Alto

Phone: 650-324-1355
Web: www.pastispaloalto.com
Prices: $$

Lunch Tue – Sun
Dinner Tue – Sat

Amid the cheerful yellow walls and vintage posters at Pastis, you may find yourself practicing your *français* with their French-speaking servers. New to Palo Alto, this cozy bistro has already begun attracting the local French expat community and is quite the brunch-time hit.

Of course, the menu of authentic bistro fare features the likes of *moules frites* and bœuf Bourguignon. Lunch may include a traditional and fresh *salade* Niçoise of mixed greens, tomato, red onion, anchovy, and hardboiled egg tossed in a light mustard dressing; or the ever-classic *croque madame* in a creamy Mornay sauce and topped with a perfectly fried egg. No matter what you order, a sweet sponge cake topped with juicy strawberries and whipped cream is always *très bon*!

Pizza Antica

D3

Pizza 🍴

334 Santana Row, Ste. 1065 (bet. Stevens Creek Blvd. & Tatum Ln.), San Jose

Phone: 408-557-8373
Web: www.pizzaantica.com
Prices: $$

Lunch & dinner daily

The name says it all: thin-crust pizza made in the Roman style. Since this outpost of Pizza Antica is situated in the Santana Row shopping mall, it attracts shoppers in need of refueling as well as families and small groups. This "pizzeria" has a vintage café feel with black-and-white tile floors, pressed-tin ceilings, and an exhibition kitchen pivoted around roaring pizza ovens.

The kitchen lists pizzas with the toppings decided (Our Pizza), or you can assemble your own (Your Pizza). Our Pizza might be covered with crumbled fennel-flavored pork sausage, meaty pieces of portobello, and caramelized roasted onion. Your Pizza might feature a flavorful tomato sauce, oozing slices of mozzarella, fresh basil leaves, and mildly spiced Calabrese sausage. *Buona*!

Rangoli

D4

Indian 🍴🍴

3695 Union Ave. (at Woodard Rd.), San Jose

Phone: 408-377-2222
Web: www.rangolica.com
Prices: $$

Lunch Sun – Fri
Dinner nightly

Located on the edge of San Jose, between Campbell and Los Gatos, Rangoli is a lovely and upscale Indian restaurant. Leagues ahead of its neighboring (read: pedestrian) *desi* diners, it is no wonder that elegant Rangoli is so popular among the local South Asians. The dining areas consist of half-partitions and little alcoves, and tabletops are adorned with pretty votive candles.

The restaurant offers a massive buffet, but the best option is to order à la carte. Try spice-sparked items like a tandoor-smoked eggplant appetizer blended with chilies; followed by lamb Madras—cubes of lamb stewed in a hearty red coconut curry; or juicy chicken in a nutty, creamy, and saffron-infused *korma*. As always, a chewy naan is the best way to sop up any leftover sauce.

Plumed Horse ✿

C4

Contemporary ✗✗✗

14555 Big Basin Way (bet. 4th & 5th Sts.), Saratoga

Phone: 408-867-4711
Web: www.plumedhorse.com
Prices: $$$$

Dinner Mon – Sat

James Fong

Set in picturesque, upscale Saratoga, this lovely restaurant draws couples seeking a quiet refuge in which to dine and celebrate special occasions. The attentive, suited staff gives them an unhurried space in which to relax. Overhead, contemporary LED chandeliers gently shift in color, illuminating the modern dining room and emphasize the depth of the arching barrel ceilings. Admittedly, it's hard not to feel celebratory after a first bite of silky, buttery goat-cheese tart topped with pickled beets and herbed olive oil, paired with a bottle from the dramatic, glass-enclosed wine cellar.

The ambitious food travels the globe, picking up Italian influences in a juicy roasted lamb loin over fluffy nettle gnocchi, then veering to Asia for a tamari-chili glazed abalone, crowned with a luscious slow-cooked egg. Though à la carte dining is available, diners going for the tasting menu will encounter special treats and surprises, from a truffled quail egg amuse-bouche to a chocolate-glazed cheesecake bonbon mignardise.

Some of the greatest pleasures here are more traditional, like a perfectly airy Meyer lemon-ricotta soufflé soaked in just the right amount of hazelnut créme anglaise.

Sakoon

B2

Indian ✗✗

357 Castro St. (bet. California & Dana Sts.), Mountain View

Phone: 650-965-2000
Web: www.sakoonrestaurant.com
Prices: **$$**

Lunch & dinner daily

For a sophisticated dose of cheer in Mountain View, make haste for Sakoon, a contemporary Indian restaurant dressed in a virtual riot of color and fun. Bright glass fixtures illuminate large mirrors and vibrant striped and polka-dotted furniture. The bar is backlit with neon hues; a fiber-optic light sculpture changes color every few seconds.

It may sound like a circus, but Sakoon is startlingly stylish and its cuisine is refined. Settle into a booth, order a pomegranate gin Kamasutra, and peruse the menu. Dishes include avocado *jhalmuri*, a fresh and flavorful layered salad; *murgh sakoonwala*, chicken curry stewed with Indian spices and bell pepper; and Punjabi black lentils simmered in a creamy sauce of tomatoes, ginger, and red chilies.

Sawa Sushi

C2

Japanese ✗

1042 E. El Camino Real (at Henderson Ave.), Sunnyvale

Phone: 408-241-7292
Web: www.sawasushi.net
Prices: **$$$$**

Dinner Mon – Sat

Paramount to enjoying a meal at this strip-mall sushi bar, where Chef Steve presides over a 12-seat counter and a handful of tables, is playing by the rules. Reservations are absolutely required; omakase is the only option; the price albeit high always varies depending on what you're served; and questions about the food are not welcomed. If those regulations don't scare you away, then get ready for a top-notch sashimi experience, with everything from buttery Hokkaido sea scallops to slices of toro topped with decadent uni. You can also expect a few cooked dishes like tender scallions wrapped with intricately marbled Wagyu beef.

Eavesdrop on the powerful clientele gabbing over big bottles of sake, and you just may hear a billion-dollar deal being done.

South Bay

The Sea

B2

4269 El Camino Real (at Dinah's Ct.), Palo Alto

Phone: 650-213-1111
Web: www.theseausa.com
Prices: $$$

Lunch Wed – Fri
Dinner nightly

Palo Alto's buzzy new arrival is brought to you by the folks behind Alexander's Steakhouse. Offering a sophisticated and capacious setting that boasts the finer touches and ample proportions, The Sea has already become a preferred destination for expense account meals and group dining.

The Sea's skilled chef and crew combine Asian accents, French technique, and Californian sensibility to produce a first-class roster of carefully sourced ingredients. Elegant appetizers include Dungeness crab salad with purple rice, blood orange, and ginger crème fraîche. Entrées may include fish like seared mero, caught off the coast of Hawaii, neatly trimmed, nicely seared, and plated with sweet potato purée, caramelized *cipollini* onions, and drizzle of Port.

SJ Omogari

E2

154 E. Jackson St. (at 4th St.), San Jose

Phone: 408-288-8134
Web: www.omogari.biz
Prices: ⊜⊛

Lunch & dinner Mon – Sat

SJ Omogari is a small, homespun, and unassuming Korean eatery in San Jose whose legit recipes can rival any and all of the cuisine's faithful go-to's in Santa Clara. Decked with just a few wooden tables and splashes of art, this family-owned jewel showcases some traditional *banchan*, but locals and foodies gather here mainly for their timely service and exquisitely flavorful tofu soups, grilled meats, and rice bowls. And while you won't find the ubiquitous grill-topped tables, discover the most memorable kimchi sizzling stone pot blending spicy pork, bean sprouts, and rice; marinated beef short rib *galbee*; and *meat-jun* or pan-fried beef in an egg batter. There is no another way to seal this meal than with a kiss of delectable green tea ice cream.

Smoking Pig BBQ

Barbecue ✗

1144 N. 4th St. (bet. Commercial St. & E. Younger Ave.), San Jose

Phone: 408-380-4784
Web: www.smokingpigbbq.net
Prices: 🥜

Lunch & dinner Tue – Sun

Leave your diet at home, ignore the neighborhood, and follow your snout to the waft of barbecue coming from the large, black smoker parked alongside the Smoking Pig BBQ. The old building has housed previous restaurants (the worn booths are telling). Still, aficionados run down here for heaping mounds of fingerlickin' good spare ribs and friendly down-home service.

The ribs and pulled pork are delectably, fall-off-the-bone delicious, especially when coupled with the cheekily named homemade sauces: Kansas City Hottie, California Honey, Carolina Sassy. Important points: food here is served on paper-lined aluminum trays with plastic cutlery; secondly, the wolf turds (smoky jalapenos stuffed with molten cheese) and peanut butter pie are not to be missed!

South Legend

Chinese ✗

1720 N. Milpitas Blvd. (bet. Dixon Landing Rd. & Sunnyhills Ct.), Milpitas

Phone: 408-934-3970
Web: www.southlegend.com
Prices: 🥜

Lunch & dinner daily

In the Sunnyhills strip mall, packed with Chinese restaurants and Asian markets, South Legend stands out for its fiery and lip-numbing interpretations of classic Sichuan cooking. Though Chengdu-style dim sum provides a brief respite on weekend mornings, it's all about the heat the rest of the week, in dishes like fried Chongqing chicken topped with piles of dried chilies.

Large and no-frills, South Legend is usually crammed with locals looking for an authentic taste of their Chinese childhoods, grungy dining room and dated décor be damned. They're too busy sweating out spicy pickled vegetables and enormous braised whole fish covered in still more chilies, then cooling off with some blander *dan dan* noodles and a pot of hot black tea.

Sumika

Japanese

B2

236 Plaza Central (bet. 2nd & 3rd Sts.), Los Altos

Phone: 650-917-1822
Web: www.sumikagrill.com
Prices: $$

Lunch Tue – Sat
Dinner Tue – Sun

Sumika is first and foremost an *izakaya*. There are just a handful of wood tables and the rest of the guests sit at a counter facing the kitchen, where they gaze longingly at the specialty—*kushiyaki,* skewers on a smoking grill set atop a charcoal fire. Lunch is a mellow meal frequented by local families. A noon spread likely includes fragrant miso soup, followed by a bowlful of white rice topped with crumbled chicken *tsukune* and a soft-cooked egg; or golden-fried chicken *katsu* matched with spicy Japanese mustard and smoky *tonkatsu* sauce.

At dinner, the place fills up with those seeking an easygoing vibe in which to enjoy beer and sake with their skewers of chicken heart or pork cheek. Small plates of deliciously crispy Japanese-style fried chicken anyone?

Tamarine

Vietnamese

A4

546 University Ave. (bet. Cowper & Webster Sts.), Palo Alto

Phone: 650-325-8500
Web: www.tamarinerestaurant.com
Prices: $$$

Lunch Mon – Fri
Dinner nightly

At Tamarine, contemporary Asian accents, low lighting, and walls showcasing works for sale by Vietnamese artists combine to fashion a swanky atmosphere that reflects the restaurant's modern take on Vietnamese cuisine.

All of this makes chic Tamarine a darling among Palo Alto's eclectic community. Corporate suits talk business in the large private dining room. Moneyed tech types fill up the front bar and share the likes of tender hoisin- garlic- and rosemary-glazed lamb chops, or *banh mi roti* with spicy coconut Penang curry sauce for dipping those puffy crêpes. There is a quieter nook in the back where one might find ladies who lunch and couples sharing the outstanding sticky toffee pudding oozing hot caramel, or sipping refreshing Kaffir lime cocktails.

Tanto

✗

C2

1063 E. El Camino Real (bet. Helen & Henderson Aves.), Sunnyvale

Phone: 408-244-7311   Lunch Tue – Fri
Web: N/A   Dinner Tue – Sun
Prices: $$

Lone rangers on tech-office lunch breaks pack this strip-mall Japanese spot, whose crowded parking lot belies its unimpressive façade. Waits are inevitable, but it's worth it to sit down to a steaming bowl of simple and flavorful udon. Indeed, all the standards are rendered beautifully here, from crisp vegetable tempura to tender, flaky grilled *unagi* set atop freshly steamed rice.

Tanto's menu expands a bit at dinner, bringing more grilled items and *izakaya*-style small plates. Pristine sushi and sashimi like albacore with ponzu are also a strong pick. You'll likely be seated at one of the closely-spaced dining room tables, but the occasional stroke of luck might land you in one of the curtained, semi-private alcoves popular with business diners.

Thiên Long

V i e t n a m e s e ✗

F3

3005 Silver Creek Rd., Ste.138 (bet. Aborn Rd. & Lexann Ave.), San Jose

Phone: 408-223-6188   Lunch & dinner daily
Web: www.thienlongrestaurant.com
Prices:

There are plenty of Vietnamese restaurants catering to the local expats in San Jose, but Thiên Long stands out for its pleasant dining room presenting delicious cooking—as the numerous families filling the large space will attest. Tile floors and rosewood-tinted chairs decorate the space, while walls hung with photos of Vietnamese dishes keep the focus on food.

Begin with sweet-salty barbecued prawns paired with smoky grilled pork and served atop rice noodles. But, it is really the *pho* with a broth of star anise, clove, and ginger, topped with perfectly rare beef that is a true gem—even the regular-sized portion is enormous. English is a challenge among the staff, but they are very friendly; plus the faithful flavors make up for any inadequacies.

Vung Tau

E3

Vietnamese ✕✕

535 E. Santa Clara St. (at 12th St.), San Jose

Phone: 408-288-9055   Lunch & dinner daily
Web: www.vungtaurestaurant.com
Prices: 💷

It's easy to see why Vung Tau is a longtime love and go-to favorite among South Bay locals: think elegant décor, hospitable service, massive menu, and tasty food. Inside, the large space combines several dining areas styled with soft beiges, wood accents, and pendant lights. Lunchtime draws in business crowds while dinner brings families, many of whom are of Vietnamese heritage.

Authenticity is paramount in such offerings as hearty *bun bo hue*—ask for Vietnamese (not American) style—which comes with sliced flank steak, beef tendons, and pork blood in a spicy, earthy broth, served with a side of fresh herbs, lime wedges, onion, and bean sprouts. Delicately sweet and creamy pleasures abound in the delightful coconut-prawn cups served with chili-fish sauce.

Zeni

D3

Ethiopian ✕

1320 Saratoga Ave. (at Payne Ave.), San Jose

Phone: 408-615-8282   Lunch & dinner Tue – Sun
Web: www.zenirestaurant.com
Prices: $$

Diners get to choose their own adventure at this Ethiopian standby located beside a shopping plaza. Zeni caters to expats as well as foodies of all stripes with traditional basket-like pedestals bounded by low stools. Regardless of your seat, you'll be served spongy, sour *injera* to scoop up delicious *yemisir wot* (red lentils with spicy *berbere*); *kik alitcha* (yellow peas tinged with garlic and ginger); or beef *kitfo* (available raw or cooked), tossed with *mitmita* (an aromatic spice blend) and crowned with crumbled *ayib* cheese. Here, *injera* is your utensil so no need to ask for one; there's a sink in the back to clean up after.

Sip cool, sweet honey wine to balance the spicy food, or opt for an after-dinner Ethiopian coffee.

Wine Country

Wine Country
Napa Valley & Sonoma County

Picnicking on artisan-made cheeses and fresh crusty bread amid acres of gnarled grapevines; sipping wine on a terrace above a hillside of silvery olive trees; touring caves heady with the sweet smell of fermenting grapes— this is northern California's wine country. Lying within an hour's drive north and northeast of San Francisco, the hills and vales of gorgeous Sonoma County and Napa Valley thrive on the abundant sunshine and fertile soil that produce grapes for some of North America's finest wines.

Fruit of the Vine

Cuttings of Criollas grapevines traveled north with Franciscan *padres* from the Baja Peninsula during the late 17th century. Wines made from these "mission" grapes were used primarily for trade and for sacramental purposes. In the early 1830s, a French immigrant propitiously named Jean-Louis Vignes (*vigne* is French for "vine") established a large vineyard near Los Angeles using cuttings of European grapevines *(Vitis vinifera)*, and by the mid-19th century, winemaking had become one of southern California's principal industries. In 1857, Hungarian immigrant Agoston Haraszthy purchased a 400-acre estate in Sonoma County, named it Buena Vista, and cultivated Tokaji vine cuttings imported from his homeland.

In 1861, bolstered by promises of state funding, Haraszthy went to Europe to gather assorted *vinifera* cuttings to plant them in California soil. Upon his return, however, the state legislature reneged on their commitment. Undeterred, Haraszthy forged ahead and continued to distribute (at his own expense) some 100,000 cuttings and testing varieties in different soil types. Successful application of his discoveries created a boom in the local wine industry in the late 19th century.

The Tide Turns

As the 1800s drew to a close, northern California grapevines fell prey to phylloxera, a root louse that attacks susceptible *vinifera* plants. Entire vineyards were decimated. Eventually researchers discovered they could combat phylloxera by replanting vineyards with disease-resistant wild grape rootstocks, onto which *vinifera* cuttings could be grafted. The wine industry had achieved a modicum of recovery by the early 20th century, only to be slapped with the 18th Amendment to the Constitution, prohibiting the manufacture, sale, importation, and transportation of intoxicating liquors in the United States. California's winemaking industry remained at a near-standstill until 1933, when Prohibition was repealed. The Great Depression slowed the reclamation of vineyards and it wasn't until the early 1970s that California's wine industry was fully re-established. In 1976, California wines took top honors in a blind taste testing by French judges in Paris. The results helped open up a whole new world of respectability for Californian vineyards.

Coming of Age

As Napa Valley and Sonoma County wines have established their reputations, the importance of individual growing regions has increased. Many sub-regions have sought and acquired Federal regulation of place names as American Viticultural Areas, or AVAs, in order to set the boundaries of wine-growing areas that are distinctive for their soil, microclimate, and wine styles. Although this system is subject to debate, there is no doubt that an AVA like Russian River Valley, Carneros, or Spring Mountain can be very meaningful. The precise location of a vineyard relative to the Pacific Ocean or San Pablo Bay; the elevation and slope of a vineyard; the soil type and moisture content; and even the proximity to a mountain gap can make essential differences.

Together, Sonoma and Napa have almost 30 registered appellations, which vary in size and sometimes overlap. Specific place names are becoming increasingly important as growers learn what to plant where and how to care for vines in each unique circumstance. The fact that more and more wines go to market with a specific AVA flies in the face of the worldwide trend to ever larger and less specific "branded" wines. Individual wineries and associations are working to promote the individuality of North Coast appellations and to preserve their integrity and viability as sustainable agriculture. In recent decades, the Napa Valley and Sonoma County have experienced tremendous levels of development. Besides significant increases in vineyard acreage, the late 20th century witnessed an explosion of small-scale operations, some housed in old wineries updated with state-of-the-art equipment.

Meanwhile, the Russian River Valley remains less developed, retaining its rural feel with country roads winding past picturesque wineries, rolling hills of grapevines, and stands of solid redwood trees. With such easy access to world-class wines, organic produce and cheeses from local farms, residents of northern California's wine country enjoy an enviable quality of life. Happily for the scores of visitors, those same products supply the area's burgeoning number of restaurants, creating a culture of gourmet dining that stretches from the city of Napa all the way north to Healdsburg and beyond.

Note that if you elect to bring your own wine, most restaurants charge a corkage fee (which can vary from $10 to as much as $50 per bottle). Many restaurants waive this fee on a particular day, or if you purchase an additional bottle from their list.

Which Food?	Which Wine?	Some Examples
Shellfish	Semi-dry White	Early harvest Riesling, Chenin Blanc, early harvest Gewürztraminer, Viognier
	Dry White	Lighter Chardonnay (less oak), Pinot Blanc, Sauvignon Blanc, dry Riesling, dry Chenin Blanc
	Sparkling Wine	Brut, Extra Dry, Brut Rosé
	Dry Rosé	Pinot Noir, Syrah, Cabernet
Fish	Dry White	Chardonnay (oaky or not) Sauvignon Blanc, dry Riesling, dry Chenin Blanc, Pinot Blanc
	Sparkling Wine	Brut, Blanc de Blancs, Brut Rosé
	Light Red	Pinot Noir, Pinot Meunier, light-bodied Zinfandel
	Dry Rosé	Pinot Noir, Syrah, Cabernet
Cured Meats/ Picnic Fare	Semi-dry White	Early harvest Riesling or early harvest Gewürztraminer
	Dry White	Chardonnay (less oak), Sauvignon Blanc, dry Riesling
	Sparkling Wine	Brut, Blanc de Blancs, Brut Rosé
	Light Red	Gamay, Pinot Noir, Zinfandel, Sangiovese
	Young Heavy Red	Syrah, Cabernet Sauvignon, Zinfandel, Cabernet Franc, Merlot
	Rosé	Any light Rosé
Red Meat	Dry Rosé	Pinot Noir, Cabernet, Syrah, Blends
	Light Red	Pinot Noir, Zinfandel, Gamay, Pinot Meunier
	Young Heavy Red	Cabernet Sauvignon, Cabernet Franc, Syrah, Grenache, Petite Sirah, Merlot, Blends, Pinot Noir, Cabernet Sauvignon
	Mature Red	Merlot, Syrah, Zinfandel, Meritage, Blends
Fowl	Semi-dry White	Early harvest Riesling, Chenin Blanc, Viognier
	Dry White	Sauvignon Blanc, Chardonnay, Pinot Blanc, dry Riesling
	Sparkling Wine	Extra Dry, Brut, Brut Rosé
	Rosé	Any light Rosé
	Light Red	Pinot Noir, Zinfandel, Blends, Gamay
	Mature Red	Pinot Noir, Cabernet Sauvignon, Merlot, Syrah, Zinfandel, Meritage, Blends
Cheese	Semi-dry White	Riesling, Gewürztraminer, Chenin Blanc
	Dry White	Sauvignon Blanc, Chardonnay, Pinot Blanc, dry Riesling
	Sparkling Wine	Extra Dry, Brut
	Rosé	Pinot Noir, Cabernet, Grenache
	Light Red	Pinot Noir, Zinfandel, Blends, Gamay
	Young Heavy Red	Cabernet Sauvignon, Cabernet Franc, Syrah, Grenache, Petite Sirah, Merlot, Blends
Dessert	Sweet White	Any late harvest White
	Semi-dry White	Riesling, Gewürztraminer, Chenin Blanc, Muscat
	Sparkling Wine	Extra Dry, Brut, Rosé, Rouge
	Dessert Reds	Late harvest Zinfandel, Port

Vintage	1996	1997	1998	1999	2000	2001	2002	2003	2004	2005	2006	2007	2008	2009
Chardonnay **Carneros**	🍇	🍇	🍇	🍇	🍇	🍇	🍇	🍇	🍇	🍇	🍇	🍇	🍇	🍇
Chardonnay **Russian River**	🍇	🍇	🍇	🍇	🍇	🍇	🍇	🍇	🍇	🍇	🍇	🍇	🍇	🍇
Chardonnay **Napa Valley**	🍇	🍇	🍇	🍇	🍇	🍇	🍇	🍇	🍇	🍇	🍇	🍇	🍇	🍇
Sauvignon Blanc **Napa Valley**	🍇	🍇	🍇	🍇	🍇	🍇	🍇	🍇	🍇	🍇	🍇	🍇	🍇	🍇
Sauvignon Blanc **Sonoma County**	🍇	🍇	🍇	🍇	🍇	🍇	🍇	🍇	🍇	🍇	🍇	🍇	🍇	🍇
Pinot Noir **Carneros**	🍇	🍇	🍇	🍇	🍇	🍇	🍇	🍇	🍇	🍇	🍇	🍇	🍇	🍇
Pinot Noir **Russian River**	🍇	🍇	🍇	🍇	🍇	🍇	🍇	🍇	🍇	🍇	🍇	🍇	🍇	🍇
Merlot **Napa Valley**	🍇	🍇	🍇	🍇	🍇	🍇	🍇	🍇	🍇	🍇	🍇	🍇	🍇	🍇
Merlot **Sonoma County**	🍇	🍇	🍇	🍇	🍇	🍇	🍇	🍇	🍇	🍇	🍇	🍇	🍇	🍇
Cabernet Sauvignon **Napa Valley**	🍇	🍇	🍇	🍇	🍇	🍇	🍇	🍇	🍇	🍇	🍇	🍇	🍇	🍇
Cabernet Sauvignon **Southern Sonoma**	🍇	🍇	🍇	🍇	🍇	🍇	🍇	🍇	🍇	🍇	🍇	🍇	🍇	🍇
Cabernet Sauvignon **Northern Sonoma**	🍇	🍇	🍇	🍇	🍇	🍇	🍇	🍇	🍇	🍇	🍇	🍇	🍇	🍇
Zinfandel **Napa Valley**	🍇	🍇	🍇	🍇	🍇	🍇	🍇	🍇	🍇	🍇	🍇	🍇	🍇	🍇
Zinfandel **Southern Sonoma**	🍇	🍇	🍇	🍇	🍇	🍇	🍇	🍇	🍇	🍇	🍇	🍇	🍇	🍇
Zinfandel **Northern Sonoma**	🍇	🍇	🍇	🍇	🍇	🍇	🍇	🍇	🍇	🍇	🍇	🍇	🍇	🍇

🍇 = Outstanding   🍇 = Above Average   🍇 = Average

Peter L. Wrenn/MICHELIN

Napa Valley

Wine is the watchword in this 35 mile-long lush valley, which extends in a northerly direction from San Pablo Bay to Mount St. Helena. Cradled between the Mayacama and the Vaca mountain ranges, Napa Valley boasts some of California's most prestigious wineries, along with a host of restaurants that are destinations in themselves.

A Whirl of Wineries

Reclaimed 19th century stone wineries and Victorian houses punctuate the valley's rolling landscape, reminding the traveler that there were some 140 wineries here prior to 1890. Today, Napa Valley has more than 400 producing wineries (and over 400 brands), up from a post-Prohibition low of perhaps a dozen. They are all clustered along Route 29, the valley's main artery, which runs all the way up the western side of the mountains, passing through the commercial hub of Napa and continuing north through the charming little wine burgs of Yountville, Oakville, Rutherford, St. Helena, and Calistoga.

More wineries dot the tranquil Silverado Trail, which hugs the foothills of the eastern range and gives a more pastoral perspective to this rural farm county. Along both routes, picturesque spots for alfresco dining abound. So pick up some picnic supplies at the **Oakville**

Grocery (on Route 29), or stop by either the **Model Bakery** in St. Helena or **Bouchon Bakery** in Yountville for freshly baked bread and other delectable pastries. Throughout the valley you'll spot knolls, canyons, dry creek beds, stretches of valley

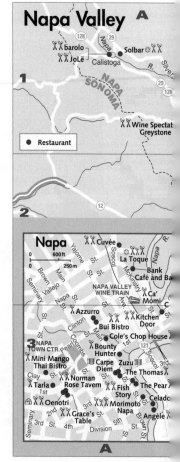

282

floor, and glorious mountain vistas, all of which afford varying microclimates and soil types for growing wine. San Pablo Bay has a moderating effect on the valley's temperatures, while the mountains lessen the influence of the Pacific Ocean. In the valley, powerfully hot summer days and still cool nights provide the ideal climate for cabernet sauvignon grapes, a varietal for which Napa is justifiably famous. Among the region's many winemakers are such well-known names as Robert Mondavi, Francis Ford Coppola, and the Miljenko "Mike" Grgich. Originally from Croatia, Grgich rose to fame as the winemaker at **Chateau Montelena** when his 1973 chardonnay took the top prize at the Judgment of Paris in 1976, outshining one of France's best white Burgundies. This feat turned the wine world on its

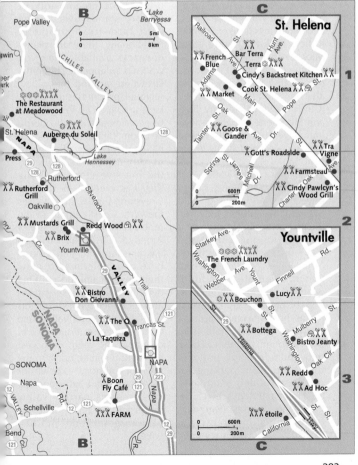

ear, and put California on the map as a bona fide producer of fine wines. Since then, Napa Valley's success with premium wine has fostered a special pride of place. Fourteen American Viticultural Areas (AVAs) currently regulate the boundaries for sub-regions such as Carneros, Stags Leap, Rutherford, and Los Carneros. The boom in wine production has spawned a special kind of food and wine tourism—today tasting rooms, tours, and farm-fresh cuisine are de rigueur here. Along Washington Street, acclaimed chefs like Thomas Keller, Richard Reddington, Michael Chiarello, and Philippe Jeanty frequently rub elbows. Many other well-known chefs also hail from the Napa Valley (Cindy Pawlcyn, Jeremy Fox, and Hiro Sone to name a few) and have successfully raised their local-legend status to the national level.

Those touring the valley will spot fields of wild fennel, silvery olive trees, and rows of wild mustard that bloom between the grapevines in February and March. The mustard season kicks off each year with the Napa Valley Mustard Festival, which celebrates the food, wine, art, and rich agricultural bounty of the region. Several towns host seasonal farmer's markets, generally held from May through October. These may include Napa (held in the Wine Train parking lot on Tuesdays and Saturdays); St. Helena (Fridays in Crane Park); and Calistoga (Saturdays on Washington Street). On Thursday nights in the summer, there's a **Chef's Market** in the Napa Town Center. Opened in early 2008, famed **Oxbow Public Market** is a block-long 40,000-square-foot facility that is meant to vie with the Ferry Building Marketplace across the bay. Oxbow is usually packed with local food artisans and wine vendors, all from within a 100-mile radius of the market. Within this barn-like building you'll find cheeses and charcuterie; spices and specialty teas; olive oils and organic ice cream; and, of course, stands overflowing with farm-fresh produce. Additionally, there are plenty of snacks available after you work up an appetite shopping. Elsewhere around the valley, regional products such as St. Helena Olive Oil, Woodhouse Chocolates, and Rancho Gordo heirloom beans are gaining a national following. Just north of downtown St. Helena, the massive stone building that was erected in 1889 as Greystone Cellars, now houses the West Coast campus of the renowned Culinary Institute of America (CIA). The CIA also has a restaurant, and visitors here are welcome to view their several unique cooking demonstrations—reservations are recommended. With all this going for the Napa Valley, one thing is for sure: from the city of Napa, the region's largest population center, north to the town of Calistoga—known for its mineral mud baths and spa cuisine—this narrow valley represents paradise for lovers of both good food and fine wine.

Ad Hoc

American ✗✗

C3

6476 Washington St. (bet. California Dr. & Oak Circle), Yountville

Phone: 707-944-2487

Web: www.adhocrestaurant.com

Prices: $$$

Lunch Sun
Dinner Thu – Mon

While the world clamors for a taste of Thomas Keller's renowned cooking, lucky Napa locals can make their way down the street from his flagships, to easy breezy Ad Hoc. Hugely homey, this rustic-chic spot with wood residing everywhere is always crammed with locals and tourists.

The set menu is served family-style and may underscore such teasers as an elegant salad of little gem lettuces, romaine hearts, beets, and brioche croutons in a tangy herb vinaigrette. Buttered radishes and pea-and-potato salad finished with bacon crumbles and dill are perfect complements to the best fried chicken *ever*—crisp-skinned, briny, and moist. For the big win, dive into a cheese course revealing tangy cheddar and crisp puff pastry licked with vanilla-pear compote.

Angèle

French ✗✗

A3

540 Main St. (at 5th St.), Napa

Phone: 707-252-8115

Web: www.angelerestaurant.com

Prices: $$

Lunch & dinner daily

Situated in a boathouse on the bend of the Napa River, this restaurant could be notable for its atmosphere alone, from the gabled roof to the whitewashed, reclaimed wood planks that line the bar. The view over the shimmering river is spectacular. The vibe is cozy and casual yet chic with white linen-covered tables, blue-framed windows, and terra-cotta planters.

The food is inspired by French bistros, but options are refined as in a salad of arugula and rabbit confit, silky sautéed petrale sole with potatoes, and a banana custard gratin with an almond crust and vanilla bean ice cream. Surprisingly for a French restaurant, the pasta is also excellent. Be sure to ask a member of the friendly and enthusiastic waitstaff about daily specials.

Auberge du Soleil ✿

Californian 🍴🍴🍴

B1

180 Rutherford Hill Rd. (off the Silverado Trail), Rutherford

Phone: 707-963-1211
Web: www.aubergedusoleil.com
Prices: $$$$

Lunch & dinner daily

Trinette Reed

This casual bistro and upscale spa resort is tucked into miles of picturesque vineyards overlooking the stunning Mayacamas Mountains. Southwestern views from the expansive porch make alfresco dining marvelous and a must. Then again, the entire space seems open and airy, with a high silo-style ceiling and umbrellas raised and lowered to shield guests from the sunset and maximize the vista. Servers are helpful, professional, and make this dining experience seem both grand and relaxed.

The cuisine can make you feel as though you've finally arrived, with food that somehow manages to keep pace with the lush surroundings. Begin with neatly cubed lamb tartare dressed with mustardy vinaigrette in a Parmesan crust as thin and crisp as a potato chip, with soft-cooked quail yolk, pickled yellow mustard seeds, and herb salad. Follow this with a beautifully cooked Kurobuta pork chop fanned over crisped mustard spaetzle, sautéed chard, caramelized apples, and a very pleasant walnut sauce.

Finish with a virtual landscape of torn angel food cake dusted in bright orange pumpkin powder, with squiggles of white chocolate *crémeux*, pumpkin gelato, and coins of candied pumpkin flesh in spiced syrup.

Azzurro

A3

Pizza

1260 Main St. (at Clinton St.), Napa

Phone: 707-255-5552   Lunch & dinner daily
Web: www.azzurropizzeria.com
Prices: $$

This casual, well-executed Napa Italian spot is the perfect place for a pizza and a beer or glass of wine. The setting is semi-industrial with exposed ducts, polished concrete floors, and marble counters. Whether you dine with a group at the large wooden communal table or watch chefs toss arugula salads at the marble counter, you'll feel a brisk, friendly energy here.

Ten kinds of thin, crisp pizza are available, perhaps topped with slices of deliciously salty speck and creamy mozzarella, or the perennially popular *manciata*, a pizza crust topped with salad. (No health points for that one, sadly). Inventive and seasonal antipasti made with local produce and comforting desserts (think double-chocolate brownies) round out the top-notch offerings.

Bank Café and Bar

A2

Contemporary

1314 McKinstry St. (at Soscol Ave.), Napa

Phone: 707-257-5151   Lunch & dinner daily
Web: www.latoque.com/bankbar
Prices: $$

The hotel-like aura at Bank Café and Bar, set off the lobby of the Westin Verasa Napa, does not do this conversation-worthy café any favors. But there is great news: Ken Frank, also of the hotel's La Toque, is notably at the helm here too. Even the casual slant of a Michelin-starred chef tends to inspire, and Chef Frank obliges with upscale bar food and a weekly regional French menu.

Dining in the Languedoc may reveal *brandade de Morue*, chicken with black olives and strawberry *vacherin* for $36. You can also order Cali-flecked items like rock shrimp with a hoisin-lemongrass sauce; or ham-and-cheese sandwiches and pretend that you're gliding along the Seine. Those in the know and with dollars to spare may even pick dishes from the menu at noble La Toque.

barolo

A1

Italian ✗✗

1457 Lincoln Ave. (bet. Fair Way & Washington St.), Calistoga

Phone: 707-942-9900   Dinner nightly
Web: www.barolocalistoga.com
Prices: $$

Set at the base of the Mount View Hotel & Spa in downtown Napa, this cheerful Italian restaurant is easily recognized—there's a Vespa scooter in the middle of the dining room. The pleasant space also combines red walls and white mosaic tiles with large, red-framed posters depicting pasta in all its glory. Local crowds flock to the small, close tables and expansive marble bar, which is perfect for solo dining.

The food spans all regions of Italy, from mozzarella- and pesto-stuffed fried risotto balls to rich spaghetti carbonara and perfectly sautéed pork Milanese with mascarpone and Parmesan risotto and *salsa rossa*. In keeping with the name, the wine list is stocked with sublime (if pricey) barolos, while the bar holds plenty of premium spirits.

Bar Terra

C1

Contemporary ✗✗

1345 Railroad Ave. (bet. Adams St. & Hunt Ave.), St. Helena

Phone: 707-963-8931   Dinner Wed – Mon
Web: www.terrarestaurant.com
Prices: $$

Yes, it shares an address with the more formal Terra next door, but Bar Terra is a solid restaurant in its own right. The rustic stone walls, cozy banquette seating, and friendly servers form a charming respite, where locals love to gather around the L-shaped bar rife with thrilling concoctions.

The menu presents a selection of cocktail accompaniments like *chicharrónes* (fried pork rinds) or *bacalao*, salted cod and potato fritters fried to golden brown gratification. For bigger bites, opt for tender braised beef cheeks in an intense tomato sauce, served with sautéed rapini. Desserts are dreamy here so be sure to save room for a flaky *bisteeya*, crispy layers of phyllo filled with apricot and almond cream and crested with Meyer lemon-rose ice cream.

Bistro Don Giovanni

Italian ✗✗

B2

4110 Howard Ln. (at Hwy. 29), Napa

Phone: 707-224-3300   Lunch & dinner daily
Web: www.bistrodongiovanni.com
Prices: $$

Located just off Highway 29, Bistro Don Giovanni can be easy to pass, but driving by would mean forgoing incredible Napa people-watching and superbly consistent Italian food. Park among the olive trees and grapevines, then take a seat in the airy, flower-decked dining room. If it's sunny, choose one of the rattan chairs on the peerless, postcard-perfect garden terrace.

A *pizzaiolo* mans the wood-burning oven in the front, firing up a selection of seasonal pies that are popular with families. Meanwhile, the more adult set opts for fried olives with warm Marcona almonds, *garganelli* with duck ragù, and seared salmon with tomato-chive butter, all washed down with local wines. Already conquered plenty of wineries? Switch to a cocktail at the buzzing front bar.

Bistro Jeanty 🙂

French ✗✗

C3

6510 Washington St. (at Mulberry St.), Yountville

Phone: 707-944-0103   Lunch & dinner daily
Web: www.bistrojeanty.com
Prices: $$

This cheery bistro in the heart of the culinary mecca that is Yountville is quintessentially French. Envision yellow walls, antiques, full flower boxes, and those woven café chairs and you will get the picture. And yet it also reeks of wine country charm by virtue of its welcoming staff and casual yet elegant demeanor.

The bistro's quality-ridden menu is exemplary, classic, and expertly prepared. For instance, a perfect and balanced rabbit pâté served with Dijon mustard and cornichons is beautifully chased by a supremely tender, slow-roasted pork shoulder paired with butternut squash gratin, caramelized Brussels sprouts, and bacon. One morsel of the crème caramel with a flaky Palmier on the gorgeous patio and you will be instantly transported.

289

Boon Fly Café

American

B3

4048 Sonoma Hwy. (at Los Carneros Ave.), Napa

Phone: 707-299-4870   Lunch & dinner daily
Web: www.thecarnerosinn.com
Prices: $$

Set amid the verdant pastures of the chic Carneros Inn, this rustic red barn is a friendly and unpretentious modern roadhouse, complete with a gracious staff. Fresh and well-made American standards include a classic Caesar with toasted onion, shaved Parmesan, and anchovy vinaigrette; or a generous Margherita flatbread pizza layered with mozzarella, tomatoes, and Italian sausage. Quesadillas and burritos are good, too. Be sure to check the blackboard for daily specials.

Though it's open from breakfast to dinner, Boon Fly Café's most popular meal is brunch, when parties wait on porch swings for eggs Benedict with jalapeño hollandaise. Whether they're locals in the know about its relaxed charm or travelers seeking a break, everybody leaves with a smile.

Bottega

Italian

C3

6525 Washington St. (near Yount St.), Yountville

Phone: 707-945-1050   Lunch Tue – Sun
Web: www.botteganapavalley.com   Dinner nightly
Prices: $$

The crowds flock to the heart of Yountville for a bite of famed Michael Chiarello's signature NapaStyle. Expect striped yellow chairs with lots of stone and wood at the spacious and comfortable Bottega. Reservations are essential.

The menu is Chiarello's take on Cal-Italian cuisine. Plates are oversized, stamped with "bottega," and available for sale. The typically local staff and well-timed kitchen turn out hearty, rustic dishes with big flavors, as in butternut squash *caramelle* with house-made dough; paprika oil-marinated grilled skirt steak with crisp Yukon Gold potato chips; and that ubiquitous side of truffle-Parmesan fries. Bring your appetite for his famed tiramisu and sponge cake gelato in a "cocoa puff" of bittersweet dark chocolate sauce.

Bouchon ⌘

French ✕✕

C3

6534 Washington St. (at Yount St.), Yountville
Phone: 707-944-8037   Lunch & dinner daily
Web: www.bouchonbistro.com
Prices: $$$

Deborah Jones

It's nearly impossible to find fault with Thomas Keller's classic, *très* French bistro. The look alone is a wondrously inviting amalgam of potted palms, polished brass fixtures, burgundy drapes, and cushioned rattan seating. Bouchon is lively, energetic, and has done much to make this little town along Napa's verdant slopes known as one of the country's foremost dining destinations.

Warm, crusty *pain d'epi* (from Bouchon Bakery next door) placed on each table is testament to the fact that the kitchen takes its mission seriously. The menu offers many decadent choices, such as *boudin blanc*, combining white sausage with potato purée and French prunes; or pan-seared skate wing with fennel confit, caramelized onions, and Niçoise olive vinaigrette. Lighter fare might include a fantastic toasted barley salad with artichoke hearts, tart pickled onions, sweet currants, buttery pine nuts, kale, and bits of lemon suprêmes dressed in *barigoule* emulsion.

Dessert absolutely must not be skipped, though take time to contemplate the options over an excellent espresso. Bouchon's crème caramel is silken and sweet, sauced with a generous amount of chilled dark caramel syrup—it is literally perfect.

Bounty Hunter

American American

 A3

975 First St. (at Main St.), Napa

Phone: 707-226-3976
Web: www.bountyhunterwinebar.com
Prices: $$

Lunch & dinner daily

Wine is king at Bounty Hunter, which provides a friendly introduction to the best of the local vineyards with more than 40 wines by the glass (or two-ounce taste) and 400 more by the bottle. No matter what is in the glass, most come here for the spicy, slow-smoked ribs, brisket, and barbecue from the house smoker, fueled by hickory, applewood, and cabernet barrel staves.

Highlights include the "Reubenesque," piling thin slices of pastrami with sauerkraut, Russian dressing, and melting Gruyère on fresh marble rye. The acclaimed beer-can chicken is available at lunch and dinner—a good thing, since you may want it at both meals. Wine pairings are offered with each dish, and the kitchen is open until midnight on weekends to soak up any tasting-room sins.

Brix

Californian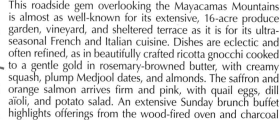

B2

7377 St. Helena Hwy. (at Washington St.), Napa

Phone: 707-944-2749
Web: www.brix.com
Prices: $$$

Lunch & dinner daily

This roadside gem overlooking the Mayacamas Mountains is almost as well-known for its extensive, 16-acre produce garden, vineyard, and sheltered terrace as it is for its ultra-seasonal French and Italian cuisine. Dishes are eclectic and often refined, as in beautifully crafted ricotta gnocchi cooked to a gentle gold in rosemary-browned butter, with creamy squash, plump Medjool dates, and almonds. The saffron and orange salmon arrives firm and pink, with quail eggs, dill aïoli, and potato salad. An extensive Sunday brunch buffet highlights offerings from the wood-fired oven and charcoal grill.

The interior feels like a mountain ranch with stone walls, fireplaces, exposed beams, and clever chandeliers made of cutlery. Service is exceptional.

Bui Bistro

Vietnamese

976 Pearl St. (bet. Main St. & Soscol Ave.), Napa

Phone: 707-255-5417

Web: www.buibistro.com

Prices: 💿💿

Lunch & dinner Mon – Sat

Napa Valley denizens craving the flavors of Vietnam are heading to Chef/owner Patrick Bui's namesake bistro in the wine country where Bui serves the same affordable, flavorful fare for which his former Berkeley location was known.

Inside, gilded mirrors dress up sage green walls and rosewood tables; a small granite bar is well suited to singles lingering over glasses of wine and warm bowls of rice noodles teeming with delicate prawns, scallops, and squid, with plates of condiments. French influences can be found in such dishes as Asian duck confit and beef carpaccio, but the tasty Vietnamese mainstays are also here. Look for shaken beef, pepper tuna, and an array of spicy curries. For dessert, moist tiramisu is both an unexpected and chocolaty surprise.

Ca'Momi

Italian

610 1st St. (at McKinstry St.), Napa

Phone: 707-257-4992

Web: www.camomienoteca.com

Prices: **$$**

Lunch & dinner daily

Local, Organic & Italian is the motto at Ca'Momi. If the ingredients aren't local and organic, rest assured that they are imported from Italy. The authenticity here is praiseworthy as the thin-crust pizzas are VPN (*Verace Pizza Napoletana*) certified—we're talking bona fides. Perhaps small and basic, this Italian treasure also does a large take-out business.

The wood-fired oven turns out thin-crust pizzas capped with super creamy mascarpone, mounds of arugula, and shaved *Parmigiano Reggiano*; or maybe tomato sauce and smoked buffalo mozzarella topped with pancetta and sautéed wild mushrooms. Whatever transpires during a meal, save room for the exquisite *bignè* drizzled with hard caramel and filled with honey-sweetened cream...and go...*molto buono*!

Carpe Diem

A3

American

1001 2nd St. (at Brown St.), Napa

Phone: 707-224-0800
Web: www.carpediemwinebar.com
Prices: $$

Dinner nightly

This wine bar in the heart of Napa has a handful of tables that quickly fill up, so most guests clamor for a seat at the packed bar. With dark stone floors, gleaming wood-covered walls, and a youthful vibe, this is *the* neighborhood spot where thirty and forty-somethings love to hang out in Napa.

Expect a nice selection of wines by the glass and a menu of American dishes that are heavily influenced by global cuisines. Plates range from wild boar salami to shrimp and grits. Ideal with a glass of *vino* is an Italian Stallion, brick-oven flatbread topped with Meyer lemon mascarpone, prosciutto, and caramelized onions; or find a perfect pair in an ostrich burger layered with creamy Brie and a zinfandel reduction. Most can't resist the crispy truffle fries.

C Casa

A3

Mexican

610 1st St. (at McKinstry St.), Napa

Phone: 707-226-7700
Web: www.myccasa.com
Prices: ⊜⊜

Lunch & dinner daily

With a long line that marks it as one of the top destinations in the busy Oxbow Public Market, C Casa may look like a fast-food joint, but it's got serious sustainability credentials—all the more impressive given the reasonable prices.

Unique tacos are made to order and filled with the likes of mahi mahi or ground buffalo, then topped with plenty of fresh vegetables and garlic aïoli. If pork tacos with smashed white beans, cilantro, guacamole, and romaine don't appeal, then check out the daily specials on the small boards above the griddle and stoves. They might include rotisserie chicken with a pile of crisp Caesar salad or a rich duck *tostada*. Throw in a Mexican coffee, fresh juice, or glass of local wine, and you'll still have cash left over.

Celadon

International ✕✕

500 Main St., Ste. G (at 5th St.), Napa

Phone: 707-254-9690
Web: www.celadonnapa.com
Prices: $$

Lunch Mon – Fri
Dinner nightly

Housed in the historic Napa Mill complex on the banks of the Napa River, Celadon is named for the comforting shade of gray-green that permeates its dining room. Inside, small tables, a quaint bar, and framed family photos lend charm, while a heated outdoor atrium with a corrugated aluminum roof allows in natural light by day and serene flickers from the brick fireplace in the evening. Oversized bottles of wine can be found throughout the dining room.

Chef Greg Cole is a Napa fixture, and his signature global cuisine ranges from a nice rendition of classic Caesar salad to plump and gently seared *togarashi*-crusted diver scallops set over creamy mashed potatoes. Friendly service adds to the appeal, as does the wide selection of Napa wines.

Cindy Pawlcyn's Wood Grill

International ✕✕

641 Main St. (bet. Charter Oak Ave. & Mills Ln.), St. Helena

Phone: 707-963-0700
Web: www.cindypawlcynsgrill.com
Prices: $$

Lunch & dinner Wed – Sun

Iconic Chef Cindy Pawlcyn (of Mustards Grill) has reconceived her former seafood home, Go Fish, and launched Wood Grill as a more wide-ranging expression of her global palate. With cabernet-braised short ribs, garden enchiladas, crispy pork belly with Thai chili jam, and a blue cheese burger all on the menu, everyone will find something to like here.

Set at the south end of St. Helena, the restaurant is surrounded by a carefully landscaped edible garden; its patio offers prime seating in the warmer months. The circular dining room is anchored by a large chalkboard mural and is very inviting. If you're a wine fan (and not yet burnt out from tasting), don't miss the CP's Dozen, highlighting 12 small-production local wineries without tasting rooms.

Cindy's Backstreet Kitchen

C1 International ✗✗

1327 Railroad Ave. (bet. Adams St. & Hunt Ave.), St. Helena

Phone: 707-963-1200
Web: www.cindysbackstreetkitchen.com
Prices: $$

Lunch & dinner daily

Cindy's can be found in a historic 1800's house tucked along Railroad Avenue in quaint St. Helena. Locals and families enjoy the welcoming setting—loads of country charm infuses everything from the fruit-motif wallpaper, down to the cushioned banquettes and gracious service.

Under the spin of ceiling fans, a globally influenced menu of small plates, salads, sandwiches, and large plates is divulged. Expect the likes of achiote-roasted pulled pork tacos featuring white corn tortillas, avocado, and kicky red chile salsa; or a delightful duck burger flavored with ginger, topped with a shiitake mushroom reduction, smear of Chinese mustard, and served with crispy fries. But keep room for dessert or just save the homemade honey-glazed cornbread for last!

Cole's Chop House

A3 Steakhouse ✗✗✗

1122 Main St. (bet. 1st & Pearl Sts.), Napa

Phone: 707-224-6328
Web: www.coleschophouse.com
Prices: $$$$

Dinner nightly

Prime meat at prime prices is the modus operandi at Cole's, which gives diners their pick of deeply flavorful cuts like dry-aged California ribeye or 21-day Chicago dry-aged New York strip. Faithful accompaniments like baked potatoes, creamed spinach, and crisp asparagus with hollandaise round out the menu. Traditional desserts like comforting Bourbon bread pudding or a perfect sugar-crusted crème brulée are a satisfying end to the meal. A selection of gutsy red wines, Bourbons, and single-malt Scotches stand up to the steak.

In place of the clubby atmosphere of traditional steakhouses, Cole's (which shares ownership with nearby Celadon) is more refined, with a barn-like stone interior and cozy selection of booths and mezzanine tables inside.

Cook St. Helena

Italian

C1

1310 Main St. (bet. Adams St. & Hunt Ave.), St. Helena

Phone: 707-963-7088
Web: www.cooksthelena.com
Prices: $$

Lunch Mon – Sat
Dinner nightly

On Main Street in chic St. Helena, pull over at Cook where a Carrara marble wine bar awaits with local temptations. This spot reflects its wine country setting with taste and whimsy: antique tin-framed mirrors and black-and-white vegetable prints adorn the walls; dark wood covers the floor; and a playful bovine lantern is mounted like a trophy on the wall. While solo diners may prefer a spot at the bar, white linen topped with butcher paper make the close-knit tables a cozy place to dine. With pride, the kitchen brings to you reasonably priced Cal-Italian fare, with daily specials on the blackboard. Sample steamed mussels in spicy tomato broth; red trout stuffed with roasted fennel and fingerlings; and a flourless chocolate cake dusted with grey sea salt.

Cuvée

American

A2

1650 Soscol Ave. (at River Terrace Dr.), Napa

Phone: 707-224-2330
Web: www.cuveenapa.com
Prices: $$

Lunch & dinner daily

In downtown Napa on a Thursday night, head to Cuvée for half-priced bottles of wine and (if lucky) live music. When the evening is warm, find the large retractable doors thrown open to a tree-lined courtyard; when cooler, look for a bit of the outdoors inside, where vine clippings make for rustic wall art beneath contemporary chandeliers.

Next door to the River Terrace Inn, Cuvée is a favorite among hotel guests and locals hungry for American fare such as pinot noir-braised short ribs and Atlantic salmon wrapped in paper-thin potatoes. For a subtle taste of Asia, try the tuna tartare with crunchy slaw and crisp rice crackers. In true old-world style, the wine selection includes several locally made options on tap, as a barrel tasting.

étoile

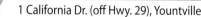

Contemporary

1 California Dr. (off Hwy. 29), Yountville

Phone: 707-204-7529 | Lunch & dinner Thu – Mon
Web: www.chandon.com
Prices: $$$$

The barrel-like curved wood ceilings at this lovely sanctum serve as a reminder of its owner—the famed sparkling wine producer Domaine Chandon. Tourists with cheeks flushed from wine tasting flock here for a glass of their rosé, perhaps selecting a treat from the oyster and caviar menu, before sampling artistic plates like Colorado lamb loin over Israeli couscous and eggplant.

Each dish at étoile contains a wealth of ingredients like sunchoke, spinach, beets, chard, orange, and brown butter that interplay beautifully with fleshy, pan-seared arctic char. The informed staff can help navigate both the menu and 5,000+ bottles on the iPad-based wine list, but don't let them steer you away from a classic caramelized pear mille-feuille for dessert.

FARM

California n

4048 Sonoma Hwy. (at Old Sonoma Rd.), Napa

Phone: 707-299-4882 | Dinner Wed – Sun
Web: www.thecarnerosinn.com
Prices: $$$

Just off a main road at the Carneros Inn, FARM exudes wine country style with cathedral ceilings, romantic banquettes, trendy fixtures, and the requisite fireplaces. Expect a mixed clientele of fancy locals, tourists, and hotel guests filling the main dining room and watching the chefs through the glassed-in kitchen.

Whether settling into a cushioned wicker seat in the outdoor lounge to sip local wines by the half-glass, noshing at the indoor bar, or going for the tasting menu in the dining room, the gorgeous surrounds will not disappoint. On the menu, expect interesting compositions like lobster risotto with Parmesan and Meyer lemon. Seasonal desserts can be a highlight, as in pumpkin pudding cake with sugar-sweet pumpkin and butternut frosting.

Farmstead

Californian

C2

738 Main St. (at Charter Oak Ave.), St. Helena

Phone: 707-963-9181   Lunch & dinner daily
Web: www.longmeadowranch.com
Prices: **$$**

Local winemakers love to dine at this former nursery barn, owned by the 650-acre Long Meadow Ranch, which also supplies all of its olive oil, beef, and other produce. Spacious and airy, with a cathedral ceiling and an open kitchen, it's a lively spot to savor a great glass of wine from Long Meadow or another local producer. As a result, the 100-seat dining room is nearly always full.

The sustainable, Southern-accented fare changes with the seasons, but might include light and smooth tomato soup with tart goat cheese *crema*, generously portioned bone-in pork chops flanked by jalapeño grits, and a hearty wedge of Scharffenberger chocolate cream pie. Recreate the experience by taking home some fresh produce and flowers from the outdoor farm stand.

Fish Story

Seafood

A3

790 Main St. (at 3rd St.), Napa

Phone: 707-251-5600   Lunch & dinner daily
Web: www.fishstorynapa.com
Prices: **$$**

Ahoy, seafood lovers! This is a yarn about a true fish house on the banks of the Napa River, where a heated patio thaws the bones and a nip from the horseshoe bar warms the belly. Never mind the chill cast from the local maritime temperatures posted on the wall—documented local fishing stories and photos posted in the hall do plenty to authenticate the experience.

Fish Story never veers from its course: silver lures and hooks hang from above, and the day's fresh catch is displayed on ice. Those large kettles are used for brewing the namesake beer, perfect for washing down towers of raw seafood from oysters to ceviche; ahi tuna tartare with Asian pear and avocado mousse; plump grilled Florida shrimp; and Half Moon petrale sole swimming in a saffron broth.

French Blue

Californian ✗✗

1429 Main St. (bet. Adams & Pine Sts.), St. Helena

Phone: 707-968-9200

Web: www.frenchbluenapa.com

Prices: $$

Lunch & dinner Wed – Sun

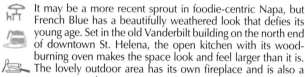

It may be a more recent sprout in foodie-centric Napa, but French Blue has a beautifully weathered look that defies its young age. Set in the old Vanderbilt building on the north end of downtown St. Helena, the open kitchen with its wood-burning oven makes the space look and feel larger than it is. The lovely outdoor area has its own fireplace and is also a very cozy option.

The food is as well-seasoned and carefully plotted as the décor with dishes like perfectly plump grilled Monterey sardines; an exquisite puffed and wood-scented flatbread topped with rotating local produce; and simple, ingredient-driven salads. In addition to local wines, the extensive cocktail menu (including a "twice the booze" category—watch out!) is varied and refreshing.

Goose & Gander

American ✗✗

1245 Spring St. (at Oak Ave.), St. Helena

Phone: 707-967-8779

Web: www.goosegander.com

Prices: $$

Lunch & dinner daily

In keeping with the proliferation of more casual restaurants in this upscale area, the former Martini House has been transformed into this British-inspired gastropub. The wooden floors, red walls, and leather banquettes upstairs give it the vibe of a mountain lodge crossed with a gentlemen's club. The downstairs bar is cozier and centered around a large fireplace.

The simple, rustic fare includes shared plates like cheese and charcuterie boards or sticky-moist Medjool dates stuffed with Gorgonzola; as well as entrées like moist, tender roast chicken or rich Scottish salmon. Though the upstairs closes at 10:00 P.M., a limited bar menu is available until midnight—perfect for soaking up the array of local wines and handcrafted cocktails on offer.

The French Laundry ✿ ✿ ✿

Contemporary ✗✗✗✗

C2

6640 Washington St. (at Creek St.), Yountville

Phone: 707-944-2380

Web: www.frenchlaundry.com

Prices: $$$$

Lunch Fri – Sun
Dinner nightly

Deborah Jones

Set in a quiet commercial district near Chef Thomas Keller's other venerable properties, The French Laundry is synonymous with impeccable service and exceptional food. No longer a brothel or launderer, this building is firmly footed at the height of the civilized world and surrounded by three acres of lush gardens. The ratio of server to guest seems to increase each visit, as if to ensure that any whim can be met.

Known for being both a perfectionist and a purist, Chef Keller helms a kitchen that has defined the idea of understated elegance in ten-course tasting menus (and by 10, we mean 13 and counting). To begin, fresh cornets may arrive filled with sweet red onion crème fraîche, topped with a scoop of minced beets and chives. Beneath an abundant amount of premium caviar, *oeufs en gelée* are prepared as lobster *salpicon* suspended in lobster-tarragon gelée over a gently cooked quail egg. Rabbit sirloin is beautifully prepared, dredged in Sicilian pistachios, and placed over cauliflower purée with tiny florets, apricots, and sorrel.

At dessert, chocolate and kumquat vol-au-vents are served with thick vanilla *chiboust*, poppy-seed ice cream, and 100-year aged balsamic vinegar.

Gott's Roadside

American

 C2

933 Main St. (at Charter Oak Ave.), St. Helena

Phone: 707-963-3486   Lunch & dinner daily
Web: www.gotts.com
Prices:

For a change of pace from Napa's upscale restaurants, tourists flock to this roadside burger joint just outside of St. Helena. Their long lunchtime lines lead to delicious beef patties topped with the best local cheese and produce, all accompanied by crisp fries. Other popular choices include hot dogs, onion rings, veggie burgers, and the famed ahi tuna sandwich.

Though prices are high for a burger joint, top-notch ingredients are sustainable, and the staff is friendly and engaging. Just be sure not to save a visit for a rainy day—all the seating is outdoors, at clean and abundant picnic tables. Additional locations at the Oxbow Public Market, the San Francisco Ferry Building, and Palo Alto satisfy the burger urge whenever it strikes.

Grace's Table

International

A3

1400 2nd St. (at Franklin St.), Napa

Phone: 707-226-6200   Lunch & dinner daily
Web: www.gracestable.net
Prices: $$

Named for Mother Nature's fabulous bounty, Grace's Table is just as you might expect—a little earthy. Recycled materials in green and brown hues come together for a low-key vibe, while potted plants breathe life onto wooden tables.

Couples and singles can grab a beer and nosh at the 10-seat bar, while tables are preferred for dinners and weekend brunch. The global menu leans toward European comfort fare like tender pork osso buco with wild mushroom risotto, but it's the seasonal tamale that has become a local legend. If the short rib-stuffed tamale isn't wicked enough, try a slice of the old-fashioned devil's food cake with dark chocolate frosting, Chantilly cream, and a sprinkling of Maldon salt—this dessert is the sweet work of Gaia.

JoLē

Mediterranean XX

1457 Lincoln Ave. (bet. Fair Way & Washington St.), Calistoga

Phone: 707-942-5938 — Dinner nightly
Web: www.jolerestaurant.com
Prices: $$

Located in the heart of Calistoga, JoLē is owned and operated by a husband (chef) and wife (pastry chef) team. The dining room may be simple but it is never silent. Dressed with wood furnishings, a small bar lined with solo diners, and an exhibition prep area, this Mediterranean marvel is always jamming with locals and visitors.

The farm-to-table food is prepared with seasonal and flavorful ingredients. A tasting menu unveils shredded kale stew, salty from ham and creamy from potatoes and a Parmesan *fonduta*; while bruschetta is topped with fine fixings like wilted spinach, buttery chanterelles, and a quail egg. A glazed duck breast with eggplant and tofu is as tender as the cubes of lamb in a flavorful stew of carrots finished with pillows of gnocchi.

Kitchen Door

International XX

610 1st St. (at McKinstry St.), Napa

Phone: 707-226-1560 — Lunch & dinner daily
Web: www.kitchendoornapa.com
Prices: $$

A novel kid on the Oxbow Public Market block, Kitchen Door preens a roster of internationally inspired and reasonably priced dishes. Enter this mighty, bright space through swinging red kitchen doors and place your order at the counter. Then fetch your flatware, find a seat in the dining room or on the patio, and await the rest.

Large communal tables face the open kitchen while private booths allow for cozy reunions. Sealing the family-friendly deal are sky-lit ceilings, hanging pots and pans, and shelves of foodstuffs. As if that weren't enough, there is a dish for every palate—from simple beef carpaccio with Himalayan truffle purée, potatoes, and lemon aïoli, to an exhilarating candy cap mushroom bread pudding with golden raisins and maple anglaise.

La Taquiza

Mexican 🍴

B3

2007 Redwood Rd., Ste. 104 (at Solano Ave.), Napa

Phone: 707-224-2320   Lunch & dinner Mon – Sat
Web: www.lataquizanapa.com
Prices: 💰

For sustainable *sabor* that doubles as a budget-saver in pricey Napa, La Taquiza's upscale take on Mexican fast food is well worth a visit. Whether you prefer your fish California-style (flame-grilled) or Baja-style (battered and fried), you'll find no end of spicy, tangy, and savory options, available in heat levels from mild to spicy and in configurations from tacos to burritos to rice bowls.

However, the adventurous shouldn't stop at crisp corn tortillas—there's also a fine selection of snappy ceviches, grilled octopus, beer-battered oysters, and other delights of the sea. Counter service is friendly and prompt, and massive, colorful paintings from a local artist give the room a vibe almost as bright as the delicious strawberry *agua fresca*.

Lucy

Californian 🍴🍴

C2

6526 Yount St. (bet. Finnell Rd. & Mulberry St.), Yountville

Phone: 707-204-6030   Lunch & dinner daily
Web: www.bardessono.com
Prices: $$$

This modern restaurant in the eco-chic Bardessono hotel offers more adventure than many of its Napa neighbors, while retaining the area's strict adherence to farm-to-table bonafides (including many ingredients grown in its own garden). Expect attractive compositions like a salad of orange and yellow carrots, some cooked until tender, some shaved into ribbons, all dressed in a curried carrot-shallot emulsion. Other dishes might include matcha-infused diver scallops, and a yuzu-accented strawberry shortcake with vanilla sorbet.

The sleek terrace features a Japanese aesthetic, overlooking verdant bamboo and a pond. The wine list highlights the area's best producers, while the courteous staff gladly helps hotel guests and tourists navigate the options.

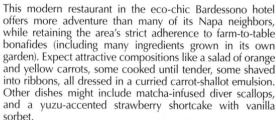

La Toque ✿

Contemporary 🍴🍴🍴

1314 McKinstry St. (at Soscol Ave.), Napa

Phone: 707-257-5157   Dinner nightly
Web: www.latoque.com
Prices: $$$

La Toque

Though it's located within the Westin Verasa Napa, La Toque is far from the standard hotel dining room. Done in elegant shades of brown and cream, with large windows and leather booths, it's a stunning destination for market-driven seasonal cuisine with global flavor. Start with one of the in-house riffs on classic cocktails like the martini and Manhattan, before settling into a smartly set, leather-topped table.

The three- or four-course prix-fixe might start with a perfectly grilled portobello mushroom topped with arugula pesto, onion *soubise*, and shards of Parmesan, then shift to sweet Nantucket Bay scallops with orange and fennel *gastrique*. Outstanding Niman Ranch ribeye gets a unique accompaniment in toothy pearl tapioca bathed in a creamy local white cheddar sauce, accented by sweet Thumbelina carrots.

The wine list is extensive and California-centric. For those who don't want a whole bottle, each menu item features a suggested pairing. The staff knows their vintages well, and their warm service keeps things humming until the last bite of ginger semifreddo sandwiched in a gingersnap crust. With food like this, even those who aren't guests of the Verasa could be tempted to stay.

Market

American ✕✕

1347 Main St. (bet. Adams St. & Hunt Ave.), St. Helena

Phone: 707-963-3799   Lunch & dinner daily
Web: www.marketsthelena.com
Prices: $$

Chef/owner Eduardo Martinez is sharing his American dream at Market, where classics like mac 'n' cheese dressed up with aged Fiscalini cheddar, mingle with little tastes from his Mexico City home—think buttermilk fried chicken and peppery cheddar-jalapeño cornbread, or blackened chicken rolls spiced with chipotle chiles.

There are many reasons to love Market, including pristine oysters on the half shell; zinfandel-braised lamb shank with creamy mashed potatoes and mint remoulade; and a sinfully fabulous butterscotch pudding made with real Scotch, ahem, and served in a waffle cone bowl. Slip into a plush brown leather banquette and get comfy with your latest prize from wine tasting: an anomaly in the Valley, Market generously forgoes corkage fees.

Mini Mango Thai Bistro

Thai ✕

1408 W. Clay St. (bet. Franklin and Seminary Sts.), Napa

Phone: 707-226-8884   Lunch Tue – Sat
Web: www.minimangonapa.com   Dinner Tue – Sun
Prices: 🅒🅒

In an area where moneyed travelers seek Californian flavors and fine wines, good esoteric restaurants can be hard to come by. So while this sweet, no-frills Thai spot may lack the proper heat level of a Bangkok street feast, it still earns its stripes for Napa.

Affordable favorites include tender seabass topped with creamy panang curry; steamed and seared radish cakes; and brightly flavored prawn, spinach, and lettuce wraps.

Though the dining room is small and comfortable, with fresh plants and bamboo-covered walls, most diners head for the covered outdoor patio, all the better to enjoy the pristine wine country weather. Don't miss the chocolate-stuffed wontons with coconut ice cream for dessert—far from authentic, they're still close to divine.

Morimoto Napa

Japanese ✗✗✗

A3

610 Main St. (at 5th St.), Napa

Phone: 707-252-1600
Web: www.morimotonapa.com
Prices: $$$

Lunch & dinner daily

Beautiful Morimoto draws tourists and locals for its sleek industrial style and contemporary cuisine. The front room is best for groups and sports a sushi bar, stylish lounge, and large communal tables. While the back nook with its smooth wood tables and cushioned banquettes is ideal for a private party.

The innovative kitchen encourages sharing in dishes like sashimi towers (crafted from toro, salmon, eel, and tuna) painted with yuzu juice or barbecue eel sauce. Homemade tofu is prepared tableside and expertly coupled with mushroom sauce and bonito flakes; while a hearty pot pie of stewed abalone is comfort food at its best. Come with friends so you don't miss out on a fantastic sticky toffee pudding made with kabocha and topped with poached Asian pear.

Mustards Grill

American ✗✗

B2

7399 St. Helena Hwy. (at Hwy. 29), Yountville

Phone: 707-944-2424
Web: www.mustardsgrill.com
Prices: $$

Lunch & dinner daily

Well before Thomas Keller staked his flag in Yountville, local favorite Cindy Pawlcyn was serving luxe "truckstop" fare at her already iconic Mustards. Opened in 1983, this wine country roadhouse still draws the crowds for new American fare (think oak-smoked barbecue ribs) and bargain sips from the list of Too Many Wines.

Soak up your favorite California varietal with one of the various daily specials scribbled on the blackboard. Or try such old favorites as Dungeness crab cakes; and grilled quail accented with herbs and vegetables from the restaurant's own gardens. Venture out for a stroll and you just might encounter the chef. If reservations aren't available at Mustards, pick up one of Pawlcyn's many cookbooks and try your hand at home.

Norman Rose Tavern

Wine Country ▶ Napa Valley

 A3

Gastropub

1401 1st St. (at Franklin St.), Napa

Phone: 707-258-1516
Web: www.normanrosenapa.com
Prices: 🅴🅴

Lunch & dinner daily

For everyone who is lagging after the dragging from winery to winery and just wants an ice-cold pint at the end of a hoity-toity day, this place is for you. Those of you who just perked up should cruise over to Norman Rose Tavern, one of the few spots in the Valley with a true-blue penchant for a burger and a PBR (or micro-brew on tap). Plentiful bar seating, walls lined with reclaimed barn wood, and a ceiling of empty "decorative" beer bottles leave no one doubting the theme.

Chef Michael Gyetvan gets it—never mind that his resume includes stints at One Market and Tra Vigne. At his approachable American pub, find plump all-beef hot dogs with tangy relish; milk-braised pork shoulder with gravy and sausage grits; and highbrow junk food at its very best.

Oenotri

 A3

Italian

1425 1st St. (bet. Franklin & School Sts.), Napa

Phone: 707-252-1022
Web: www.oenotri.com
Prices: $$

Lunch & dinner daily

The pizza ovens at Oakland's Oliveto have seasoned more than a handful of talented chefs, including Curtis Di Fede and Tyler Rodde who are now blistering their pies in an oven imported from Naples to Napa. Be warned, locals are happy to wait for a taste of that almond- and cherry-wood fire-licked pie.

With sunny textiles, exposed brick, and concrete floors, Oenotri—from an ancient word for "vine cultivator"—is a mix of practicality and pretty. But the design is just a side dish to standout Italian food including the smoky pizza Napoletana; porcini *fidei* pasta with grated tuna heart; and Silverado Trail strawberry *crostata* with Meyer lemon cream. With 30 wines for under $25, Oenotri is ideal for cultivating your palate without breaking the bank.

Press

Steakhouse ☓☓☓

B2

587 St. Helena Hwy. (near Inglewood Ave.), St. Helena

Phone: 707-967-0550　　　　　　　　　　Dinner Wed – Mon
Web: www.pressthelena.com
Prices: $$$$

Here at Press, there are no sub-par cuts of meat. Those toppings—blue cheese, truffle butter, a fried organic egg—and bounty of tasty sauces may be delicious but are certainly not required on such perfectly prepared beef. Deeper pockets should go for the Wagyu from Idaho.

The gorgeous St. Helena space fashions a bucolic vibe with its black walnut floors reclaimed from a Midwestern mill, and bar crafted from a trio of walnut trees. A roaring fireplace warms the contemporary yet rustic interior, while a second hearth and candles add to the patio's ambience and make for an ideal spot to sit and sip a rich, steak-worthy cabernet. The raw bar and many seasonal offerings are just as wonderful and will please those who shy away from the main attraction.

The Q

Barbecue ☓☓

B3

3900 D, Bel Aire Plaza (at Trancas St.), Napa

Phone: 707-224-6600　　　　　　　　　　Lunch & dinner daily
Web: www.barbersq.com
Prices: $$

With its tight space in the congested Bel Aire shopping plaza, the busy Q makes the most of its location by offering as much seating outside as in. Potted hedges help separate the umbrella-topped patio tables from the parking lot, while the interior is more luxe with Italian marble, beveled mirrors, and black-and-white photos of local suppliers (namely, farmers and vintners).

"American heritage" cooking is on the menu, as in the Memphis-style brisket barbecue sandwich with slaw; Southern skillet of cornbread with honey butter; or Cajun hush puppies with cheddar and pickled peppers. Each table has a caddy of various hot sauces, and a bottle from the all-California wine list is ready to cool the burn.

Takeout is also a good option if waits are long.

Redd

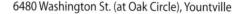

C3

6480 Washington St. (at Oak Circle), Yountville

Phone: 707-944-2222　　　　　　　　Lunch & dinner daily
Web: www.reddnapavalley.com
Prices: $$$$

At the far end of Yountville's restaurant row, Redd immediately stands out for its modern, polished exterior. However, its food leans more towards contemporary comfort than cutting-edge, with upscale takes on meat-and-potatoes classics like prime New York strip steak with crispy potato cakes. The updated childhood favorites continue at dessert, from apple tart with apple sorbet to s'mores panna cotta.

Redd's lovely courtyard is accented by a gently gurgling fountain, while inside, the sleek, urban-chic atmosphere draws locals to the bar for top-notch cocktails. As is to be expected in wine country, the Franco-Californian list here is remarkable, and the helpful staff is happy to suggest pairings for the popular five-course tasting menu.

Redd Wood

B2

6755 Washington St. (bet. Madison & Pedroni Sts.), Yountville

Phone: 707-299-5030　　　　　　　　Lunch & dinner daily
Web: www.redd-wood.com
Prices: $$

This newcomer from Richard Reddington (of bigwig Redd down the street) is not just any old neighborhood pizzeria. Bespeaking a sophisticated-slash-industrial décor are high ceilings, dark-stained walls, tufted black leather banquettes, and a spectacularly lit bar area.

The Italian roster fulfills your wine country noshing needs. For a super start, indulge in golden brown salt cod fritters served with batons of *panisse* and streaked with *harissa* aïoli; then move on to a thin-crust pizza topped with taleggio, prosciutto, and a farm-fresh egg. Bookend fluffy potato gnocchi joined by tender pieces of duck meat and caramelized pancetta, with a super sweet butterscotch semifreddo capped in a heady Bourbon sauce. Sleep it off at the adjoining North Block hotel.

The Restaurant at Meadowood ✿ ✿ ✿

B1

Contemporary 𝗫𝗫𝗫𝗫

900 Meadowood Ln. (off Silverado Trail), St. Helena

Phone: 707-967-1205   Dinner Mon – Sat
Web: www.therestaurantatmeadowood.com
Prices: $$$$

The Restaurant at Meadowood

Not to be confused with the less formal Grill, The Restaurant is located on the same resort property that reflects a certain country-style comfort and prosperity. The circular dining room features leather furniture, beamed ceilings, and windows overlooking the flora, patios, and landscape. A sense of masculine sophistication extends to the front lounge and stone fireplace.

Service is beyond reproach—a standard that may have been set in Chef Christopher Kostow's extraordinary kitchen. This deeply inspired cuisine promises intelligence, flow, and pleasure through every meal.

There can be no doubt of their dedication to local ingredients when a small gardener's book is the serving vessel for a Meadowood garden crudité starring baby radishes and carrots "planted" in whipped romaine mousse and crème fraîche beneath tomato-water vinaigrette "snow." Later, small mounds of oyster tartare arrive topped with golden trout roe, sea lettuce, and sunchoke-infused milk to combine natural brine with earthy sweetness. A neat, bronze square of coal-roasted sturgeon with fermented pear purée, marrow bones, and braised kale is downright sensational— as are *mignardises* presented as "stages of the grape."

311

Rutherford Grill

B2

American ⚔️

1180 Rutherford Rd. (at Hwy. 29), Rutherford

Phone: 707-963-1792   Lunch & dinner daily
Web: www.hillstone.com
Prices: $$

Temptation starts in the parking lot at Rutherford Grill, where aromas from the wood-fired rotisserie make impatient bellies growl. Just don't arrive too hungry; this popular hangout nearly guarantees a wait. Sidle up to the bar in the meantime for a glass of something local and you might find yourself rubbing elbows with notable Napa Valley oenophiles.

Once summoned from your bar stool, step up to a red leather booth and sink into the warm ambience primed for hearty fare. The open kitchen aces menu staples such as artichoke dip; buttery skillet cornbread; and slabs of fall-off-the-bone pork ribs served with shoestring fries and slaw. Rutherford Grill mingles so well with wine country charm that its chain restaurant roots are all but forgotten.

Tarla

A3

Mediterranean ⚔️

1480 1st St. (at School St.), Napa

Phone: 707-255-5599   Lunch & dinner daily
Web: www.tarlagrill.com
Prices: $$

A stacked stone façade and orange sign indicate that you've found Tarla. This casual Mediterranean restaurant in Napa's hub boasts a modern décor with hints of rusticity—bright orange barn door panels line the walls. Guests can eat at the bar, or at tables along a banquette. But, when the sun is out, alfresco seats on the sidewalk are most coveted.

Expect to see a mix of local business sorts at lunch and families for dinner devouring items that range in influence from Greek to Turkish. These have included a juicy lamb *kofte* burger layered with fava bean spread and white cheddar cheese, coupled with herb-strewn fries; or tasty beef *doner*, shavings of Turkish spit-roasted beef served on a pita coated with spicy mayonnaise and topped with a sumac salad.

Solbar ✿

Californian 🍴🍴

A1

755 Silverado Trail (at Rosedale Rd.), Calistoga

Phone: 707-226-0850
Web: www.solagecalistoga.com
Prices: $$$

Lunch & dinner daily

Solage Calistoga

The Solage Calistoga's restaurant has become a destination of its own for Napa's young and hip, who join hotel guests on the lively terrace for a plate of the "locally world-famous" beet salad with green goddess dressing. The airy indoor dining room has a barn-meets-loft vibe with high ceilings and enormous windows that make the glorious view of the vineyards and mountains feel even closer. A chic lounge, where locals congregate for sips and bites on black leather couches, offers its own carte and cocktails. On sunny days, however, it's all about that terrace for some post-meal exploration. Splendid vistas aside, it is the food—dinner mainly—that excels here.

Solbar offers a pleasurable trip into healthy eating, and the menu is structured accordingly with lighter dishes (maybe steamed Alaskan halibut with basil, artichokes, and chickpeas) nestled beside indulgences like crisp, piquant "sol fries" with lemon aïoli.

If you follow the virtuous path, however, you'll have room left over for one of their exquisite desserts like honey-soaked baklava with local walnuts and espresso cream; or a rich chocolate *crémeux* accented by devil's food cake and impossible-to-resist hazelnut ice cream.

Terra ✿

Contemporary 🍴🍴🍴

C1

1345 Railroad Ave. (bet. Adams St. & Hunt Ave.), St. Helena

Phone: 707-963-8931
Web: www.terrarestaurant.com
Prices: $$$

Dinner Wed – Mon

Hiro Sone

Hiro Sone and Lissa Doumani's long-running St. Helena restaurant is actually two restaurants in one: Terra and its more relaxed sister, Bar Terra (which offers a separate menu). Although Terra is the upscale half, exposed beams, stone walls, and built-in wine storage lend an ancient, earthy feel that is far from stuffy. A sense of timeless romance and quietude attracts couples celebrating special occasions.

The food shares the low-key aesthetic, using excellent ingredients to achieve an elegance and simplicity in dishes like a perfectly grilled duck breast with garlicky duck sausage wrapped in dark, leafy greens with plumped wheatberries, broad beans, and sunchokes finished with elderberry jus. Portions are moderately sized, allowing diners to curate their own four- five- or six-course tasting. Tempting options commence with crisp pig trotter croquettes with shredded Brussels sprouts and sauce *gribiche*, and conclude with a flaky phyllo *bisteeya* filled with soft-cooked apples and nested atop tangy crème fraîche and fragrant cinnamon.

Along the way, the gracious staff will happily suggest wine pairings from the extensive list, which boasts many high-end options, including fine sakes.

The Pear

Southern   🍴🍴

720 Main St. (at 3rd St.), Napa

Phone: 707-256-3900
Web: www.thepearsb.com
Prices: $$

Lunch & dinner daily

The Pear is the brainchild of celebrated chef, Rodney Worth. He continues his love affair with Southern food at this Napa outpost, rife with stunning views of the promenade and river, a pristine exposed kitchen, and large dark wood tables. Speaking of *amour*, the Blues play in the background, further enhancing this sense of romance; look for the trumpet, violin, and saxophone, all hanging on pistachio-hued walls.

Generous portions of great food including a creamy crab dip crusted with Parmesan and studded with baby artichokes plays into the Southern bent. Gumbo *ya ya* is an intensely flavorful stock bobbing with chicken and seasoned with andouille, tomato, and garlic. Bourbon-glazed baby back ribs with crushed peanuts evoke Louisiana in all its glory.

The Thomas

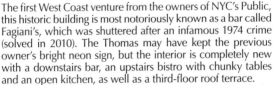

Californian   🍴🍴

813 Main St. (bet. 2nd & 3rd Sts.), Napa

Phone: 707-226-7821
Web: www.thethomas-napa.com
Prices: $$$

Lunch & dinner daily

The first West Coast venture from the owners of NYC's Public, this historic building is most notoriously known as a bar called Fagiani's, which was shuttered after an infamous 1974 crime (solved in 2010). The Thomas may have kept the previous owner's bright neon sign, but the interior is completely new with a downstairs bar, an upstairs bistro with chunky tables and an open kitchen, as well as a third-floor roof terrace.

The seafood-centric menu is varied, perhaps including fleshy grilled squid, an extensive raw bar, and wood-grilled salmon. The brined and crusted pork chop is succulent and notable. The bar is popular for cocktails and serves the full menu. Sunday is a good day to visit, with a well-regarded brunch and a $45 evening prix-fixe.

Tra Vigne

Italian ✕✕

C2

1050 Charter Oak Ave. (off Hwy. 29), St. Helena

Phone: 707-963-4444   Lunch & dinner daily
Web: www.travignerestaurant.com
Prices: $$$

It's impossible not to love Tra Vigne, the St. Helena retreat evocative of Tuscany with its rugged stone building and vineyard surrounds. On balmy nights, head to the garden patio where tables intertwine with olive trees and white lights twinkle overhead. Cooler weather? No matter. The spacious interior is just as cozy for enjoying rustic Italian fare as it makes its way from the exhibition kitchen.

Tra Vigne is best known for its dishes from the wood-burning oven in hearty portions that highlight seasonal ingredients, as in the cracker-crisp fig pizza topped with spicy arugula and Gorgonzola. The signature and über-creamy mozzarella *al minuto* deserves its buzzing popularity. After dinner, join the locals in savoring a cabernet at the bustling bar.

Wine Spectator Greystone

Californian ✕✕

A1

2555 Main St. (at Deer Park Rd.), St. Helena

Phone: 707-967-1010   Lunch & dinner Tue – Sun
Web: www.ciarestaurants.com
Prices: $$$

The kitchen is the classroom at the Culinary Institute of America's West Coast training restaurant, housed (along with the school) in the former Christian Brothers château. The big, visually impressive room—with stone walls, copper lighting, and display of oversized spoons and whisks—is a comfortable perch in which to watch students at work in the open kitchen.

Each day's three-course prix-fixe is conceived and prepared solely by students, while an à la carte menu is more focused. Though dishes will change daily, expect the likes of roast quail, moist with lightly crisped skin, served with carrot-parsnip purée and squash ribbons. Swordfish arrives fresh and meaty, accompanied by lemon risotto and a bisque-like sea urchin broth packed with flavor.

Zuzu

829 Main St. (bet. 2nd & 3rd Sts.), Napa

Phone: 707-224-8555
Web: www.zuzunapa.com
Prices: $$

Lunch Mon – Fri
Dinner nightly

Napa Valley

Wine Country ►

There's a sultry authenticity to this delightful tapas spot, which blends Mediterranean and South American influences with skill and care. Dishes include the signature *boquerones*, stuffed with the flavors of white anchovy, egg, and remoulade; or tender lamb chops in a minty-sweet Moroccan barbecue glaze. Daily specials might include a rich and spicy seafood stew. At a recommended three plates per diner, there are opportunities to sample numerous dishes.

The space is better than ever after a brief closure for earthquake retro-fitting, with a colorful, brightly tiled floor and artfully rusted Mexican tin tiles on the ceiling. Other attractions include the extensive list of sherry or wines by the glass, and dinner served until 11:00 P.M. on weekends.

Sonoma County

Often eclipsed as a wine region by neighboring Napa Valley, this canton that borders meandering Marin County claims 76 miles of Pacific coastline, as well as over 250 wineries that take advantage of some of the best grape-growing conditions in California. Agoston Haraszthy established northern California's first premium winery, **Buena Vista**, just outside the town of Sonoma in 1857. Today, thirteen distinct wine appellations (AVAs) have been assigned in Sonoma County, where vintners produce a dizzying array of wines in an area slightly larger than the State

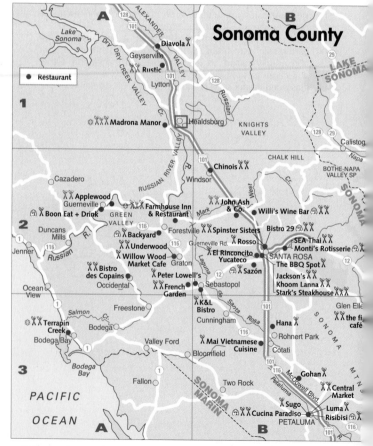

of Rhode Island itself. Along Highway 12 heading north, byroads lead to out-of-the-way wineries, each of which puts its own unique stamp on the business of winemaking. For instance, the Russian River Valley edges the river named for the early Russian trading outposts that were set up along the coast. This is one of the coolest growing regions in Sonoma, thanks to the river basin that offers a conduit for cool coastal climates. Elegant and well-liked pinot noir and chardonnay headline here, but syrah is quickly catching up.

At the upper end of the Russian River, the Dry Creek Valley yields excellent sauvignon blanc as well as more chardonnay and pinot noir. This region is also justly famous for its zinfandel, a grape that does especially well in the valley's rock-strewn soil. Winery visits in Dry Creek are a study in contrasts. Palatial modern wineries rise up along the same rural roads that have

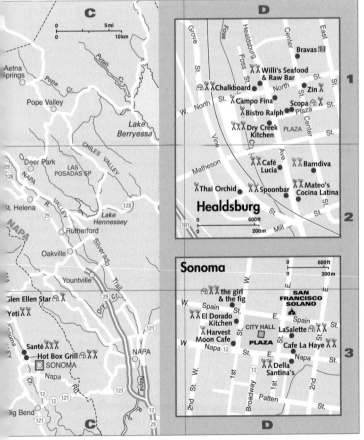

been home to independents for generations; and young grapevines trained into laser-straightened rows are broken up by the dark, gnarled fingers of old vines.

Sonoma County's most inland AVAs are Knights Valley and Alexander Valley. These two warm regions both highlight cabernet sauvignon. Nestled between the Mayacamas and Sonoma ranges, the 17-mile-long Sonoma Valley dominates the southern portion of the county. At its center is the town of Sonoma, site of California's northernmost and final mission also known as the San Francisco Solano Mission, founded in 1823. At one time, the mission included a thriving vineyard before secularization and incorporation into the Sonoma State Historic Park system 102 years ago, when the vines were uprooted and transplanted elsewhere in Sonoma.

The town's eight-acre plaza continues to be surrounded by 19th century adobe buildings, most of them now occupied by shops, restaurants, and inns. Of epicurean note is the fact that building contractor Chuck Williams bought a hardware store in Sonoma in 1956. He gradually converted its stock from hardware to unique French cookware, kitchen tools, and other novelty items. Today, **Williams-Sonoma** has more than 200 stores nationwide, and is a must-stop among foodies around the world. Just below Sonoma lies a portion of the Carneros district, named for the herds of sheep (*los carneros* in Spanish) that once roamed its hillsides.

Carneros is best known for its cool-climate grapes, notably pinot noir and chardonnay.

Pastoral Pleasures

Throughout this scenic and bucolic county—also referred to as SoCo by savvy locals—vineyards rub shoulders with orchards and farms that take advantage of the area's fertile soil to produce everything from apples and olives, to artisan-crafted cheeses. The words "sustainable" and "organic" are key here at local farmer's markets, which herald the spring (April or May) in Santa Rosa, Sebastopol, Sonoma, Healdsburg, and Petaluma. Within these open-air smorgasbords, you can find it all from just-picked heirloom vegetables to sea urchin plucked out of the water so recently that they may still be wiggling. Artisanal olive oils, chocolates, baked goods, and jams count among the many homemade products that are also in store. In addition, ethnic food stands cover the globe with offerings that have their roots as far away as Mexico, India, and Afghanistan. Thanks to the area's natural bounty, farm-to-table cuisine takes on new heights in many of the county's restaurants. Some chefs need go no farther than their own on-site gardens for fresh fruits, vegetables, and herbs. With easy access to local products such as Dungeness crab from Bodega Bay, poultry from Petaluma, and cheeses from the Sonoma Cheese Factory, it's no wonder that the Californian cuisine in this area has attracted such major national attention.

Applewood

 Californian

A2

13555 Hwy. 116, Guerneville

Phone: 707-869-9093
Web: www.dineatapplewood.com
Prices: $$$

Dinner Wed – Sun

With a sweeping view over well-manicured orchards, a top-notch spa, and 19 romantic rooms, Applewood is as much an appealing getaway as it is a destination restaurant. The talented kitchen prepares each dish with care, resulting in delightful starters like seared scallops set over fresh Mendocino uni in sumptuous, tangy saffron-butter sauce. Follow this with cocoa nib-coated lamb chops over lardons of sherry-braised chorizo and mint *chimichurri*. Dine à la carte or explore the tasting menu with wine pairings.

The dining room is quiet and barnlike with soft music, fireplaces, and couples soaking in the views of an interior courtyard from the enclosed sun porch. After sampling the well-curated list of local bottles, many choose to check in for the night.

Backyard 😊

Californian ✗

A2

6566 Front St. (bet. 1st & 2nd Sts.), Forestville

Phone: 707-820-8445
Web: www.backyardforestville.com
Prices: $$

Lunch & dinner Wed – Mon

Centered in the sleepy main drag of serene Forestville, this hyper-local restaurant from a husband-and-wife team aims to make the most of Sonoma's seasonal and sustainable foods. Even some of the serving dishes are made from salvaged hazelnut and redwood. With credits for purveyors taking up more than half its length, the menu prominently features house-made pasta, sausage, and *salumi*. Begin with starters like deliciously creamy chicken liver mousse with sourdough points.

The butter-yellow walls of the open dining room display old window frames and hanging succulents. The red-brick courtyard offers seating under a giant oak and live music on weekends. Family-style fried chicken Wednesdays are popular, as is the succinct list of local wines.

Barndiva

Californian ✗✗

231 Center St. (bet. Matheson & Mills Sts.), Healdsburg

Phone: 707-431-0100
Web: www.barndiva.com
Prices: $$

Lunch & dinner Wed – Sun

It's all kinds of wine country-chic here at Barndiva. From the rising vaulted ceilings and rustic wood tables in the dining room, to the gorgeous tree-shaded patio, this beguiling little number is the epitome of California-style sophistication. It's no surprise that many a wedding and private party take place here, so call ahead for reservations.

The exquisite menu has featured delights like creamy lobster risotto and luscious pork belly with bean cassoulet. Dig into crispy young chicken, perfectly prepared, seasoned, and served over roasted artichoke hearts, root vegetables, and smoky pancetta, with a soft ricotta-egg yolk *raviolo* perched on top. The warm peach- and almond-frangipane tart with vanilla bean-thyme ice cream is a dream come true.

The BBQ Spot

Barbecue ✗

3448 Santa Rosa Ave. (bet. Robles Ave. & Todd Rd.), Santa Rosa

Phone: 707-585-2616
Web: www.thebbqspot.net
Prices: 👛👛

Lunch & dinner Tue – Sun

This Santa Rosa respite has a no-frills locale and is situated next to a tattoo parlor, but don't let the lack of ambience dissuade you—the little restaurant is turning out some seriously good barbecue. Its bill of fare has all the heavy hitters like succulent, falling-off-the-bone pork ribs that are smoky and caramelized with a sweet glaze; and tender pulled pork that is delicious on its own or drizzled with house-made spicy sauce. With sides like homemade baked beans and coleslaw to choose from, your barbecue sampler is complete. The restaurant is simple and causal with colorful linoleum floors, flat-screen TVs on the walls, and disposable utensils. Expect a low-key, local crowd, but as the word gets out, this place may get super busy.

Bistro des Copains

French

 A2

3782 Bohemian Hwy. (at Occidental Rd.), Occidental

Phone: 707-874-2436
Web: www.bistrodescopains.com
Prices: $$

Dinner nightly

In the quaint town of Occidental, in a small cottage off of the main street, is Bistro des Copains. Take in the cheery yellow walls, wood burning oven, and red floral tablecloths. Vintage photos of the French countryside will have you instantly transported to Roquefort, where one of the owners spent part of his childhood at his grandparent's sheep farm.

Perfecting the setting is very traditional French bistro fare that might include onion soup to start; followed by *poisson du jour*, perhaps a simple and deliciously browned pan-roasted halibut, served over a pool of beurre blanc, and paired with a potato galette. One bite into raspberry shortcake filled with sweet whipped cream and plump berries, and you might even believe those memories are your own.

Bistro Ralph

Californian

D1

109 Plaza St. (bet. Center St. & Healdsburg Ave.), Healdsburg

Phone: 707-433-1380
Web: www.bistroralph.com
Prices: $$

Lunch daily
Dinner Mon – Sat

Set on the square in Healdsburg's central plaza, Chef/owner Ralph Tingle's California-French charmer draws plenty of locals for a light lunch or laid-back dinner. Though the menu is seasonal, afternoon standbys include crisp and spicy Sichuan calamari, a classic salad *Lyonnaise*, and a succulent lamb burger. In the evening, braised rabbit with egg noodles and a chocolate-caramel-espresso "animal-style" sundae are among the more substantial options.

Though there are two patio tables, the prime seating is inside, with whitewashed brick walls and an open kitchen with a concrete bar. Martinis are a special focus, with a big selection of vodkas and gins for mixing. Local wines, including some nice late-harvest dessert options, are also represented.

Bistro 29

B2 ━━━━━━━━━━━━━━━━━━━━━━━━━━ French ✕✕

620 5th St. (bet. D St. & Mendocino Ave.), Santa Rosa

Phone: 707-546-2929   Dinner Tue – Sat
Web: www.bistro29.com
Prices: **$$**

This charming French bistro-meets-crêperie in downtown Santa Rosa specializes in the authentic dishes of Bretagne in the northwest of France. Bistro 29 has a traditional look to match the menu with deep red-painted walls, dark-framed mirrors, and crisp white linen. It is popular with locals and families and the diminutive spot is hopping at sundown.

Expect such faithful bistro items as a half head of butter lettuce massaged with a creamy *fromage blanc* dressing and then liberally sprinkled with chopped herbs. This is best trailed by a savory crêpe *Lyonnaise* filled with smoked lardons, caramelized onions, and melting cave-aged Gruyère. A runny egg tops this classic rendition and may leave you wondering how you got here without a passport.

Boon Eat + Drink

A2 ━━━━━━━━━━━━━━━━━━━━━━━━━━ Californian ✕

16248 Main St. (bet. Armstrong Woods Rd. & Church St.), Guerneville

Phone: 707-869-0780   Lunch Thu – Tue
Web: www.eatatboon.com   Dinner nightly
Prices: **$$**

The cat's out of the bag. Boon Eat + Drink might be a bit off the radar (tucked in the picturesque town of Guerneville) but its seasonal Californian fare attracts connoisseurs from miles around. The modest storefront features a covered patio for outdoor dining, and a quaint interior where aluminum chairs and simple wood tables allow the local, sustainable fare to shine.

When in season, Boon's flash-fried Brussels sprouts with olive oil and red chili flakes may be the best you've had. You may say the same of the grilled calamari set atop peppery arugula mingled with white beans; or Gleason Ranch-braised pork belly with black-eyed peas and sautéed garlicky greens. For dinner, try the grilled halibut with fennel braised *gigante* beans and basil *pistou*.

Bravas

D1

Spanish

420 Center St. (bet. North & Piper Sts.), Healdsburg

Phone: 707-433-7700   Lunch & dinner daily
Web: www.starkrestaurants.com
Prices: $$

This latest project from Willi's Wine Bar legends Mark and Terri Stark is named for the classic Spanish potato dish. Given their longstanding expertise with small plates, a truly Spanish tapas spot is right in their wheelhouse. Located in a small, quaint cottage two blocks north of Healdsburg's central plaza, the orange-walled dining room draws lines for first-come first-serve seats at the metal bar. Psychedelic posters and a beaded curtain evoke the '70s.

Bites are traditional yet flaunt California flair, perhaps beginning with a refreshing yet bold tuna belly salad with squid-ink vinaigrette, or a rich *jamón Serrano* and Manchego *bocadillo*. Spanish wines and sherries figure prominently, and soft-serve ice cream provides a fun end to the lively meal.

Cafe La Haye

D3

Californian

140 E. Napa St. (bet. 1st & 2nd Sts.), Sonoma

Phone: 707-935-5994   Dinner Tue – Sat
Web: www.cafelahaye.com
Prices: $$

Cafe La Haye is the curious yet wonderful collision of a bespectacled former college music teacher with seasonal ingredients and a charming house off Sonoma's town square. A local favorite since 1996, the bi-level dining room with a revolving art collection is constantly packed: make reservations or hold out hope for a seat at the tiny kitchen-facing counter.

The open kitchen provides an unobstructed view of the local produce that comprises the Californian cuisine. Be sure to ask for the daily risotto before embarking on such dishes as smoked trout with lemon-horseradish cream and shaved fennel; or roasted chicken frilled with grilled zucchini and oven-dried tomatoes. Seal your meal with a throwback and delicious butterscotch pudding.

Café Lucia

D2

Spanish ✗✗

235 Healdsburg Ave., Ste. 105 (bet. Matheson & Mill Sts.), Healdsburg

Phone: 707-431-1113
Web: www.cafelucia.net
Prices: $$

Lunch & dinner daily

Tucked just outside of Healdsburg's main plaza, this sibling to LaSalette shares its emphasis on authentic Portuguese ingredients, like seafood, stewed meats, tomatoes, garlic, and olive oil. Day boat scallops seared with a thin crust of *chouriço* sausage set over mashed Japanese sweet potatoes, and tender wood-oven roasted sea bass are among the delicious options.

A serene, plant-lined, interior courtyard leads to an airy dining room with a dark-red horseshoe bar and prints of the owners' hometown, São Jorge, in the Azores. Settle into one of the espresso leather banquettes and be rewarded with cumin- and cinnamon-tinged dinner rolls, just like the chef's mother used to make—perfect for savoring over generous flights of Portuguese or Sonoma wine.

Campo Fina

D1

Italian ✗

330 Healdsburg Ave. (bet. North & Plaza Sts.), Healdsburg

Phone: 707-395-4640
Web: www.campo-fina.com
Prices: ⬟⬟

Lunch & dinner daily

Just as card games inspire Scopa, this sister restaurant features a highly coveted patio for backyard bocce during the sunny months (expect a wait). The long, narrow dining room combines brick walls, Edison bulbs, and a wood-burning pizza oven, then gives way to the patio's arched twig roof for a lovely balance of sun and shade.

An antipasto like roasted and chilled spicy-sweet cherry peppers stuffed with tuna salad or *burrata* with grilled bread are great for savoring with a Negroni or black-walnut Manhattan. Sandwiches like *il Nonno* with house-made *soppressata*, rapini, fried egg, salsa *verde*, and "Calabrian chilies" make for a hearty lunch. At dinner, the Neapolitan pies take center stage, while a rich *shakerato* iced coffee is perfect anytime.

Central Market

M e d i t e r r a n e a n ✗✗

B3

42 Petaluma Blvd. N. (at Western Ave.), Petaluma

Phone: 707-778-9900

Web: www.centralmarketpetaluma.com

Prices: $$

Dinner nightly

♿ This is a relaxed but packed spot in downtown Petaluma where huge painted canvases of cows adorn the walls. Chef Tony Najiola is the welcoming proprietor walking through the dining room chatting with guests, many of whom are regulars. He is clearly passionate about his menu which includes first-rate ingredients sourced from his own farm.

Foodies aim for seats facing the open kitchen where the chef can be seen creating Mediterranean-inspired dishes with care and precision. Starring local ingredients is a kale salad dressed in a light vinaigrette, tossed with shaved Parmesan, walnuts, and topped with a superbly fresh farm egg; or rainbow trout stuffed with wilted spinach, olives, and garlic, served with crispy paprika-seasoned potatoes.

Chalkboard ☺

C o n t e m p o r a r y ✗✗

D1

29 North St. (bet. Foss St. & Healdsburg Ave.), Healdsburg

Phone: 707-473-8030

Web: www.chalkboardhealdsburg.com

Prices: $$

Lunch Fri – Sun
Dinner nightly

♿ The space that long housed Cyrus now presents Chalkboard—enter Hotel Les Mars, pass by a gracious hostess, and head straight to this contemporary bistro adorned with vaulted ceilings, hardwood floors, casual banquettes, and very snug tables. The open kitchen may be ubiquitous but fits in beautifully with California's sensibility.

This small plates venue underlines an organic, seasonal menu capped off by local ingredients. The result is an excellent marriage of technique and flair as seen in hamachi crudo accented with fruity olive oil, sea salt, and ruby red grapefruit; or well-executed *strozzapretti* twirled with spicy sausage and leafy *broccolini*. A warm vanilla bean cake crested with Cointreau-and-crème fraîche sherbet makes for a perky finish.

Chinois

B2

186 Windsor River Rd. (at Bell Rd.), Windsor

Phone: 707-838-4667   Lunch Mon – Fri
Web: www.chinoisbistro.com   Dinner Mon – Sat
Prices: $$

Pan-Asian fare is given the fresh, seasonal California treatment at this Windsor bistro. The menu offers everything: plump, flavorful Filipino *lumpia*; Chinese dim sum; calamari and prawns in a peppy Cambodian garlic sauce. Thai curries, Taiwanese honey prawns, and even Indian *roti prata* are also represented, but the dance between cuisines is elegant and streamlined, not muddled.

The entry features a small wine bar that's great for solo dining, while the modern dining room is marked by red and white barrel light fixtures. The wine list is respectable (thanks to the surroundings); beer and sake or *sochu* cocktails are also strong. Happy hour, with $5 dishes and drinks, packs in crowds until 6:20 P.M. on the dot—get there early to savor it all.

Cucina Paradiso

B3

114 Petaluma Blvd. N. (bet. Washington St. & Western Ave.), Petaluma

Phone: 707-782-1130   Lunch & dinner Mon – Sat
Web: www.cucinaparadisopetaluma.com
Prices: ⊜⊜

Nestled in downtown Petaluma, Cucina Paradiso kills with kindness. Chef/owner Dennis Hernandez and his wife, Malena, run their homey mainstay with a strong sense of family: the staff is a tight-knit group, regulars are greeted with kisses and hugs, while the rest of us are simply friends they haven't met yet.

Once a well-kept secret, Cucina Paradiso is flourishing in this spacious dining room bathed in sunny yellow with Gerbera daisies smiling from each table, all a far cry from its strip mall origins. The menu of homemade specialties is informed by the chef's Italian training, so as arias fill the air, find harmony in such dishes as rigatoni with spicy pork, red peppers, and creamy tomato sauce; or pillowy Gorgonzola gnocchi with chopped walnuts.

Della Santina's

Italian ✗✗

D3

133 E. Napa St. (bet. 1st & 2nd Sts.), Sonoma

Phone: 707-935-0576
Web: www.dellasantinas.com
Prices: $$

Lunch & dinner daily

Just a few steps off the main square, through an iron gate, and down a brick pathway lies Della Santina's—a family-owned and operated Italian restaurant where guests are treated like part of the family. Coziness abounds from the garden patio with wisteria and olive trees, to the simple furnishings and family photographs.

The home-style dishes are prepared with skill and may be exactly what your Italian grandmother would make. And you'd happily heed her urge to *mangia* with dishes such as the restaurant's signature *gnocchi della nonna* (super soft gnocchi in an herbaceous tomato sauce), and a hearty *panino* of garlicky pork sausage and roasted peppers, served with a side of rosemary potatoes. Have a glass of wine and enjoy the warmest of welcomes.

Diavola

Pizza ✗

A1

21021 Geyserville Ave. (at Hwy. 128), Geyserville

Phone: 707-814-0111
Web: www.diavolapizzeria.com
Prices: $$

Lunch & dinner daily

Folks far and wide know to come to Geyserville for Dino Bugica's artisan-cured meats and pizzas. Once a brothel, the room's original wood floors, tin ceilings, and exposed brick exude history. And as for its decidedly tamer wares, find artisan hams, with whole legs hanging up front, as well as fresh sauces, sausages, and imported cheese available to take home.

A rosy pizza oven from Italy is hard at work at the end of the lengthy marble bar, where thin-crust pizzas are one-size-fits-all and decked with toppings ranging from the simple Margherita to smoked pork belly, meatballs, pine nuts, and raisins. Salads may include pomegranate, persimmon, and *ricotta salata*. Roasted bone marrow or crispy beef tongue are at the ready if pizza isn't your thing.

Dry Creek Kitchen

D1

Californian ✗✗✗

317 Healdsburg Ave. (bet. Matheson & Plaza Sts.), Healdsburg

Phone: 707-431-0330
Web: www.charliepalmer.com
Prices: $$$

Lunch Fri – Sun
Dinner nightly

Housed in Hotel Healdsburg, just off of the town's central square, Dry Creek Kitchen is the very picture of elegance. Its dining room is bedecked with sweeping flower arrangements, gorgeous arching pillars, towering windows, and smart linen-topped tables; round, banquet-style tables are perfect for families and larger parties.

Tasty dishes like porcini *velouté* garnished with prosciutto chips, topped with cognac foam, and drizzled with a scallion oil; or Petaluma chicken with local squash and padrón pepper fondue with piquillo pepper beurre blanc show off the kitchen's Californian aesthetic. Don't forget to gratify your sugar craving with a rich and dense Meyer lemon cheesecake finished with sweet lemon curd and refreshing mint sorbet.

El Dorado Kitchen

D3

Californian ✗✗

405 1st St. W. (at Spain St.), Sonoma

Phone: 707-996-3030
Web: www.eldoradosonoma.com
Prices: $$

Lunch & dinner daily

A stone's throw from the grassy Sonoma town square and tucked away in the El Dorado Inn, this stylish yet always casual canteen is a wine country hot spot, and deservedly so. Dressed in earthy shades, the spacious and attractively rustic dining room contrasts dark wood furnishings with bright white walls and isn't the slightest bit cliché. Meanwhile, a central communal table beloved by large groups offers a view into the busy exhibition kitchen.

Utilizing the region's bounty, the kitchen turns out the likes of fried green tomatoes with pineapple salsa, or flaky Alaskan halibut with corn pudding, pea shoots, and shaved asparagus. The cheese plate sticks to West Coast producers, and desserts like warm rhubarb crisp make a strong case for seasonality.

El Rinconcito Yucateco

Mexican 🍴

3935 Sebastopol Rd. (bet. Campoy St. & Wright Rd.), Santa Rosa

Phone: 707-526-2720
Web: N/A
Prices: 💰

Lunch & dinner Tue – Sun

This small dining room specializes in dishes from the Yucatán region of Mexico. The spot may be fuss-free, casual, and basic, but the family who runs the place is super welcoming and convivial.

All meals start with homemade chips and spicy roasted chili salsa for dipping. *Auténtico* is to be found in the Yucatán specialty, *cochinita pibil panuchos*—black been purée sandwiched between two corn tortillas and topped with deliciously tender achiote-marinated roasted pork. Fresh tomato and pickled onions complete the flavorful creation. Fine fixings abound in the pineapple- and chili-marinated *al pastor panucho*; while the grilled chicken topped with cool, creamy avocado is simply *delicioso!* For those in a hurry, there is a weekend taco stand out front.

French Garden

French 🍴🍴

8050 Bodega Ave. (at Pleasant Hill Ave.), Sebastopol

Phone: 707-824-2030
Web: www.frenchgardenrestaurant.com
Prices: $$

Lunch & dinner daily

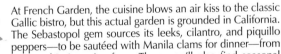

At French Garden, the cuisine blows an air kiss to the classic Gallic bistro, but this actual garden is grounded in California. The Sebastopol gem sources its leeks, cilantro, and piquillo peppers—to be sautéed with Manila clams for dinner—from its own bio-intensive farm. There you'll also find seasonal ingredients for such expertly adapted plates as a traditional frisée salad with bacon and poached egg.

As you would expect, French Garden boasts soft blue paint and large white columns; on cooler nights find a seat in the dining room or near the hearth in the lounge. Desserts are excellent here so don't miss out. With pistachio pastry crust, cranberry coulis, and toasted meringue, the lemon tart may be the most refined you've ever had.

Farmhouse Inn & Restaurant

A2

Californian

7871 River Rd. (at Wohler Rd.), Forestville

Phone: 707-887-3300
Web: www.farmhouseinn.com
Prices: $$$

Dinner Thu – Mon

Farmhouse Inn & Restaurant

Surrounded by miles of forest and vineyards, this quaint yellow farmhouse not only offers lodging but an exquisite culinary experience that draws locals and travelers alike. The emphasis on nature extends inside, with a flowing mural depicting farm life, high ceilings, large wooden chandeliers, and a crackling fireplace.

The seasonal, uncomplicated cooking here bursts with flavor, from the tangy dressing that tops a hamachi tartare with tiny green daikon sprouts to the plump octopus tentacles, alternately crispy and tender, that splay over plump beans and a flavorful tomato-chorizo vinaigrette. The most talked-about dish is the "rabbit rabbit rabbit," a trio of leg confit bathed in mustard cream, a delicious roasted rack, and a tender loin wrapped in applewood-smoked bacon.

The small staff is on-point and professional, offering insightful advice on selecting dishes from the three- and four-course menus and wines from the largely Californian list. Don't miss the delightful take on a "fig Newton," wrapping fresh fig in delicate pastry drizzled with Port-caramel sauce—the result is a vast improvement on the original (especially with the accompanying cinnamon brittle ice cream).

Glen Ellen Star

Californian

C3

13648 Arnold Dr. (at Warm Springs Rd.), Glen Ellen

Phone: 707-343-1384
Web: www.glenellenstar.com
Prices: $$

Lunch Sat – Sun
Dinner nightly

The country charm of this quaint cottage belies the level of culinary chops that will impress even a hardened city slicker. With knotty pine tables, well-worn plank floors, and a wood-burning oven, the space is delightful. A perch at the chef's counter affords a great view of the selections.

Seasonal dishes can include large and plump wood-roasted asparagus with thin shards of *lavash* crackers and shaved radish over a tangy hen egg emulsion; or chicken cooked under a brick with creamy coconut curry and sticky rice. The daily pizzas like the tomato-cream pie with Turkish chilies, are also a must. Save room for the excellent, freshly churned house-made ice cream in flavors like vanilla maple Bourbon, salted peanut butter, and peach verbena.

Gohan

Japanese

B3

1367 N. McDowell Blvd. (at Redwood Way), Petaluma

Phone: 707-789-9296
Web: www.gohanrestaurant.com
Prices: $$

Lunch Mon – Fri
Dinner nightly

Sushi may be an unexpected choice of fuel while shopping at Pier 1 or Michael's, but Gohan is the pride and joy of its strip mall surrounds at Petaluma's Redwood Gateway Shopping Center. With crisp linen-topped tables, lovely high ceilings, and an LCD fire in the high-tech hearth, this is an undeniably cool spot for lunch.

Serving classics like tender ribeye teriyaki and fresh hamachi sashimi, Gohan's menu has something for everyone. Fans of creative maki, though, have truly come to the right place. For a view of the chef in action, slip up to the sushi counter and watch as your fish is neatly sliced and expertly displayed. Don't miss the Kryptonite roll with tuna, hamachi, salmon, cucumber, and creamy avocado topped with *tobiko*.

Hana

Japanese ✗

B3

101 Golf Course Dr. (at Roberts Lake Rd.), Rohnert Park

Phone: 707-586-0270
Web: www.hanajapanese.com
Prices: $$

Lunch Mon – Sat
Dinner nightly

For the full experience, park it at the sushi bar where the obliging chefs can steer you through the best offerings of the day. Rohnert Park denizens are wising up to this little gem of a spot, tucked in a hotel plaza next to the 101, and run by affable owner, Chef Ken Tominaga, who sees to his guests' every satisfaction.

Traditional, fresh sushi and Japanese small plates are the secret to Hana's success, though simply exquisite items like pan-seared pork loin with ginger-soy jus, and pots of steaming udon also hit the spot. Chef's omakase is a fine way to go—six pieces of nigiri which could include toro, hamachi belly, kampachi, *tai* snapper, halibut with ponzu sauce, or sardine tangy from lemon juice and sprinkled with Hawaiian lava salt.

Harvest Moon Cafe

Californian ✗

D3

487 1st St. W. (bet. Napa & Spain Sts.), Sonoma

Phone: 707-933-8160
Web: www.harvestmooncafesonoma.com
Prices: $$

Dinner Wed – Mon

Harvest Moon Cafe is located on the main town square in Sonoma. Without an obvious façade, this place has become popular by word of mouth. Featuring a pleasant crowd of locals, connoisseurs, and tourists, the café serves Californian fare made from local, seasonal ingredients. Some may choose to start a meal with gypsy pepper and potato soup with crème fraîche and sage. Others may embark with a crisp chicory salad tossed in tangy blue cheese dressing with caramelized grilled onions and smoky-salty bacon; before moving on to the likes of house-made *boudin blanc* with collard greens and whole grain mustard sauce.

Adorned with wildflowers, this charming café features an open kitchen and bar, as well as an outdoor patio for warm summer evenings.

Wine Country ▶ Sonoma County

334

Hot Box Grill 😊

American ✕✕

C3

18350 Sonoma Hwy. (bet. Calle Del Monte & Hawthorne Ave.), Sonoma

Phone: 707-939-8383
Web: www.hotboxgrill.com
Prices: $$

Dinner Wed – Sun

Hot Box Grill is Sonoma County's definition of down-home family dining. Chef/owner Norm Owens can be spotted daily in the kitchen working side-by-side with his sous chef brother; while his wife is responsible for their fantastic pastries and sister-in-law is credited with creating those linoleum prints around the room.

Flower boxes line the front windows with views of the open kitchen, and the back wall doubles as a blackboard boasting the day's dressed-up comfort food specials. Each dish makes the most of local ingredients as evident in plump duck confit ravioli in spiced broth, or succulent fried Cornish game hen with shells and cheese. With sweet bites like the deliciously campy Valhrona S'mores tart, dessert should be mandatory.

Jackson's

American ✕✕

B2

135 4th St. (at Davis St.), Santa Rosa

Phone: 707-545-6900
Web: www.jacksonsbarandoven.com
Prices: $$

Lunch & dinner daily

Chef/owner Josh Silver's menu is created with families in mind. Still, the room is mighty sleek and curvy, adorned with soaring ceilings; while an espresso brown and deep crimson shade the walls. Contemporary wood tables and chairs look upon bright paintings, many of which were actually done by one of the chefs.

The open kitchen with its shiny fire-engine red wood-burning oven is loved for more than just pizza. An oven-roasted Cornish game hen shares the menu with a daily changing hot dog, and sandwiches too. Lamb meatballs, mac and cheese, oysters, and mussels all get the roaring fire treatment.

While the kids enjoy a giant carrot cake cupcake for dessert, moms and dads can choose from their list of Scotch, Ports, and stickies.

335

John Ash & Co.

B2

Californian XX

4330 Barnes Rd. (off River Rd.), Santa Rosa

Phone: 707-527-7687

Web: www.vintnersinn.com

Prices: $$$

Dinner nightly

The Vintner's Inn's restaurant—where the terra-cotta walls, wrought-iron chandeliers, and a flickering fireplace lead to acres of vineyards—exudes the romance of a Tuscan farmhouse. Yet even solo diners can enjoy a taste of John Ash thanks to the clubby Front Room, where the hunting-lodge vibe meets a chic bar menu of sweet-and-sour meatballs or avocado fries.

The food here emphasizes seasonal ingredients, and on-site gardens provide much of the produce. Expect the likes of zippy tuna tartare with *sriracha* aïoli and house-pickled ginger, or chorizo-crusted sea bass over beans and roasted cauliflower. Noted Sonoma winery Ferrari-Carano may own the inn and dominate the wine list, but other fine local and international selections are also available.

Khoom Lanna

B2

Thai XX

107 4th St. (bet. Davis & Wilson Sts.), Santa Rosa

Phone: 707-545-8424

Web: www.khoomlannathai.com

Prices: $$

Lunch & dinner daily

Although this Thai jewel might seem pricey to some, Khoom Lanna's generous use of fresh vegetables and unique ingredients in each of its dishes merits the expense. A brick façade (flanked by a wood awning adorned with windows and greenery) marks the entry into this charming yet rustic Asian burrow.

Countering its vibe (mauve walls, linen-lined tables, lush flower arrangements, and Thai artifacts), servers are candid and casual. If *pad si ew* (noodles stir-fried with vegetables, tofu, eggs, and splashed with dark soy); or *plah gung* (succulent, smoky prawns tossed in tangy lime juice and dusted with toasted rice powder) aren't as fiery as you'd hoped, up the spice ante in a hearty dish of basil lamb glazed with garlic and red chilies.

K & L Bistro

French

B2

119 S. Main St. (bet. Burnett St. and Hwy. 12), Sebastopol

Phone: 707-823-6614
Web: www.klbistro.com
Prices: $$

Lunch & dinner Tue – Sat

Chefs, owners, and spouses, Karen and Lucas Martin split time at the stoves at this quaint bistro. Servers and a loyal clientele (of a certain age) take great pride in their neighborhood gem. The mesquite grill crackles from the open kitchen; exposed brick and paper-topped tables complete the cozy vibe.

At the center of this intimate space is a rustic blend of Californian, Italian, and French cuisines. Locally focused dishes include the delicious house-made *boudin blanc* with apple-endive salad. Meals may start with a rich braised beef terrine with a mound of celery root tossed in mustardy rémoulade, followed by petrale sole meunière with a mound of fries. Sunday suppers with pairings from featured wineries are a budget-friendly delight.

LaSalette

Portuguese

D3

452-H 1st St. E. (bet. Napa & Spain Sts.), Sonoma

Phone: 707-938-1927
Web: www.lasalette-restaurant.com
Prices: $$

Lunch & dinner daily

LaSalette is a passage to Portugal just off Sonoma's town square. While wooden Port wine crates and pumpkin-hued walls may aim to transport, you'll feel right at home thanks to Chef/owner Manuel Azevedo and his wife, Kimberly, who bring the flavors of his native Azores Islands to wine country. Peek into the open kitchen where a wood-burning oven roasts a variety of small plates for sharing. Try the linguiça with *queijo fresco*—a piece of pork-and-garlic sausage crowned with farmer's cheese and a Portuguese olive. A lunch special of *caldeirada* (fisherman's stew) unveils a fragrant lobster-saffron broth teeming with fresh seafood and fingerling potatoes; while *piri piri* fries are dusted with chile powder and served with a creamy garlic-herb aïoli.

Luma

 B3

 C a l i f o r n i a n

500 1st St. (at G St.), Petaluma

Phone: 707-658-1940 Lunch & dinner Tue – Sun
Web: www.lumapetaluma.com
Prices: $$

The milk chocolate and caramel color palette isn't the only thing sweet and delicious about Luma, a Californian eatery that offers after-school specials and crayons for kiddos on the industrial side of Petaluma. Luma is also parent-approved with a small wine counter and plenty of savory fare to snack on before that creamy key lime pie arrives.

Pizzas and pears hold court on a menu featuring the Pear & Blue, a thin-crust pie topped with the obvious. Lunch delights include fish tacos starring corn tortillas stuffed with dandelion greens and homemade salsa; and a wood oven-roasted vegetable calzone. Dinner may bring ancho-seared skirt steak over cannellini beans and *chimichurri*, or a roasted half-chicken served with mushroom bread pudding.

Mai Vietnamese Cuisine

 B3

 V i e t n a m e s e

8492 Gravenstein Hwy. (bet. Cotati Ave. & Hwy. 101), Cotati

Phone: 707-665-9628 Lunch & dinner Tue – Sun
Web: www.maivietnamesecuisine.com
Prices: 🪙🪙

The cheery yellow walls, the delightful servers, the abundance of hospitality—this lovely Cotati spot is practically a mood enhancer. Tucked into the corner of a small shopping plaza next to Highway 101, this place is packed with loyal regulars craving fresh, tasty Vietnamese classics.

Items like lemongrass chicken and scallop curry share the menu with vermicelli and rice dishes, as well as a list of refreshing Vietnamese shakes, including mango and durian (if you dare). *Pho* lovers can choose from several types, like *pho tai* with thinly sliced steak, vermicelli, white onions, scallions, and cilantro swimming in a ginger-clove broth. Or go with a hearty barbecue plate of prawns, smoky-glazed pork, and egg rolls served over rice noodles.

Madrona Manor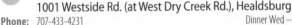

A1

Contemporary ✕✕✕

1001 Westside Rd. (at West Dry Creek Rd.), Healdsburg

Phone: 707-433-4231

Dinner Wed – Sun

Web: www.madronamanor.com

Prices: $$$

Madrona Manor

Tucked away yet hard to miss, this very charming destination offers lodging and fine dining in a Victorian mansion built in 1881. The sunny yellow structure is nestled among eight acres of bucolic grounds, where citrus trees and vegetable patches flourish. The look is decidedly romantic throughout the intimate spaces, each elegantly enhanced by pastel walls, white crown moldings, floral prints, heavy drapery, and soft lights from crystal chandeliers. Better still, choose to sit outside on the wraparound porch and bask in the glow of the sun setting over Dry Creek Valley.

Madrona Manor's timeless scene is an intriguing contrast to the contemporary menu that lets California ingredients be the star of the show. In fact, Sonoma-raised Chef Jesse Mallgren uses many vegetables plucked fresh from the surrounding gardens.

The tasting menus showcase the kitchen's brilliance with items that have included *suzuki* crudo expertly dressed with fresh wasabi, sea salt, and olive oil; Yukon gold potato gnocchi with *Manchego* and estate-grown greens; and seared veal loin with bone marrow and black walnuts. Save room for the incredible bread…and stunning desserts…and a sip from the exceptional wine list.

Mateo's Cocina Latina

D2

 Mexican

214 Healdsburg Ave. (bet. Matheson & Mill Sts.), Healdsburg

Phone: 707-433-1520
Web: www.mateoscocinalatina.com
Prices: $$

Lunch Thu – Tue
Dinner nightly

Skip the Mexican street-style food prominent in the Bay Area and head to this slam-dunk of a spot, where organic ingredients get whipped-up into a stunning array of succulent goodness. Credit is due to Chef/owner Mateo Granados for his serious cooking chops, Yucatán heritage, and devotion to healthy eating. Stone floors, mosaic-tiled tabletops, rustic wood tables, marigold walls, and sky lights create a gorgeous atmosphere, so snag a seat and get feasting.

Here you'll find tamales and tortillas made with olive oil instead of lard, and several scorching-hot varieties of homemade sauce—made from habaneros picked off the family's tree. These are also a delicious complement to smoky lamb carne asada; tender suckling pig *tamal*; or olive oil-guacamole *tacone*.

Monti's Rotisserie

B2

 American

714 Village Court (at Sonoma Ave.), Santa Rosa

Phone: 707-568-4404
Web: www.starkrestaurants.com
Prices: $$

Lunch & dinner daily

A mirrored room with wrought-iron accents, colorful hanging antique doors, and a quirky collection of decorative roosters give Monti's Rotisserie an unusual Mediterranean-cum-Southwest vibe where spit-roasted meats are the common denominator. Since opening in 2004, Monti's long wooden bar has beckoned shoppers to Santa Rosa's Montgomery Village for snacks like house-made charcuterie, Tunisian-flavored crab "briks," and to-die-for homemade fries.

Of course, it's the smoky meats turned over smoldering coals that give the place its name. On Wednesdays, belly up for a spit-roasted leg of lamb; and Fridays bring the roast rack of nature-fed veal. On Saturdays, dive into such delish protein as a crispy duck special coupled with sweet and sour duck jus.

Peter Lowell's

Italian

B2

7385 Healdsburg Ave. (at Florence Ave.), Sebastopol

Phone: 707-829-1077   Lunch & dinner daily
Web: www.peterlowells.com
Prices: $$

You may refer to this Sebastopol eatery as a "sleeper." Once just a little known spot to lunch, Peter Lowell's is now enjoying a renaissance thanks to their skilled kitchen championing the local, sustainable ethos and taking it to new heights with seasonal Cal-Italian cuisine made from organic ingredients sourced in Sonoma County.

Dine inside or out and be patient with the service—remember, good things come to those who wait. Meals might bring a bowl of beans and greens tossed in olive oil, lemon juice, salt, and pepper; cracker-thin pizza topped with squash blossoms and Calabrian chilies; and veal paired with saffron risotto. End on a sweet note with a light, moist, and spongy olive oil cake layered with ripe strawberries and mascarpone cream.

Risibisi

Italian

B3

154 Petaluma Blvd. N. (bet. Washington St. & Western Ave.), Petaluma

Phone: 707-766-7600   Lunch & dinner daily
Web: www.risibisirestaurant.com
Prices: $$

Though it's named for a comforting dish of rice and peas, Risibisi's seafood-heavy take on Italian cuisine is a bit more sophisticated. A meal here might begin with tissue-thin morsels of fresh salmon carpaccio with julienned celery, or blanched potato salad in orange-herb vinaigrette and zesty horseradish cream. Gnocchi with chunky wild boar ragù are so light and tender that it somehow seems easy to finish the generous portion. Finish with house-made tiramisu or cannoli, and you'll feel like you've been transported to Italy. The $14.95 three-course lunch prix-fixe is a steal.

A makeshift picture gallery constructed out of salvaged Tuscan chestnut window frames, wine barrels, and wagon wheels bring character to the brick-walled dining room.

Rosso

P i z z a ✗

53 Montgomery Dr. (at 3rd St.), Santa Rosa

Phone: 707-544-3221   Lunch & dinner daily
Web: www.rossopizzeria.com
Prices: $$

Wood-fired pizzas are the name of the game at this Santa Rosa pizzeria. Italian wines live in total harmony at Rosso with the urban décor that spotlights a wine bar, simple wood details, and an exhibition kitchen.

While the sports channel may suit its strip mall locale, their crisp, chewy, and blistered Neapolitan-style pizza with smoky chorizo and garlic-tomato sauce is a divine departure abroad. Most start with a range of small plates—braised Brussels sprouts with pancetta cream are a coveted choice—before moving on to a hearty pizza *salsiccia* with spicy sausage, mushroom-tomato sauce, and olives. Others may prefer a walk to the wild side by way of a white pizza *funghi di limone* topped with roasted mushrooms, shaved artichokes, and lemon oil.

Rustic

I t a l i a n ✗✗

300 Via Archimedes (off Independence Ln.), Geyserville

Phone: 707-857-1485   Lunch & dinner daily
Web: www.franciscoppolawinery.com
Prices: $$

With every turn up the vineyard-lined hill that leads to the Francis Ford Coppola Winery, visitors begin to breathe deeply and relax a little more. At its peak, discover a Mediterranean château that feels like a swanky getaway, with a cabana-lined pool designed for daytime relaxation and a restaurant, Rustic, that's as luxe as it is homey—if you are Coppola himself, you are in fact right at home.

Themed around "Francis' Favorites," Rustic is a hodgepodge of wine ephemera, movie memorabilia, and foods from the director's past. From the *parilla* (an Argentine grill), look for sweet-savory ribs inspired by a Polynesian restaurant from the filmmaker's college days; as well as Mrs. Scorsese's lemon chicken with organic herbs and chocolate mousse "al Francis."

Wine Country ▶ Sonoma County

Santé

C3

Californian XXX

100 Boyes Blvd. (at Hwy. 12), Sonoma

Phone: 707-939-2415   Dinner nightly
Web: www.santediningroom.com
Prices: $$$

A renovation has transformed the Fairmont Sonoma's restaurant (now featuring black walls and espresso leather chairs) giving the dining room a polished edge. It's a fine match for the contemporary and original cuisine with dishes like rabbit presented three ways: roast loin chops, supremely tender rillettes, and bacon-wrapped roulade sliced into coins and fanned across the plate.

Diners are encouraged to build their own four-course menu, but with choices like seared scallops with crispy sweetbreads, choosing is tough. Then think about a layered tranche of lychee and raspberry *chiboust* redolent of green tea and find your temptation mounting.

The keen service staff provides adept service as well as a huge wine list rife with provocative options.

Sazón

B2

Peruvian X

1129 Sebastopol Rd. (at Roseland Ave.), Santa Rosa

Phone: 707-523-4346   Lunch & dinner daily
Web: www.sazonsr.com
Prices: ☜

Take a chance on Santa Rosa's divey-looking Sazón, and the only broken heart will be the Peruvian *anticucho de corazón*, or traditional skewered beef heart from the busy open kitchen. It may be a tiny spot in an awkward locale, but know that all this leaves little room for disappointment. Elbow up to the granite counter or slip into a small corner table set atop painted concrete floors and amid mustard-hued walls.

On warm days, a cold Inca Cola will help keep things cool. Know that you may need it: spicy *rocoto* and jalapeño peppers enliven the *causas limena*—spheres of mashed potato infused with *aji amarillo* and topped with Dungeness crab. Also try creamy prawn chowder (*chupe de camarones*) and *pollo a la brasa*, rotisserie chicken with hand-cut fries.

Scopa 😋

D1

Italian 🍴

109A Plaza St. (bet. Center St. & Healdsburg Ave.), Healdsburg
Phone: 707-433-5282   Dinner nightly
Web: www.scopahealdsburg.com
Prices: $$

♿ Like the lively Italian card game that gives Scopa its name, this Healdsburg hottie is one big, boisterous family meal brought to the table by Chef Ari Rosen and his wife (and resident oenophile), Dawnelise. The space is pint-sized, but the vibe is bustling, especially on Winemaker Wednesdays, when local vintners work the room and pour their wares at the six-seat marble bar.

Framed Scopa cards set the scene for dinners designed to share. Fill up on antipasti like spicy meatballs and crispy, piping-hot *arancini*. Try splitting a crusty artisanal pizza topped with wafer-thin prosciutto or the seasonal ravioli, but *nonna's* tomato-braised chicken is a dish that heartier appetites keep to themselves.

Check out baby sis Campo Fina just a few steps away.

SEA Thai

B2

Thai 🍴🍴

2323 Sonoma Ave. (at Farmers Ln.), Santa Rosa
Phone: 707-528-8333   Lunch & dinner daily
Web: www.seathaibistro.com
Prices: $$

♿ SEA Thai is a sought-after reprieve perched on a cozy corner in the bustling Montgomery Village outdoor mall. Flanked by plenty of parking and authentic, upscale food, this Thai bistro attracts an army of patrons from small groups to families with children in tow. Here, crimson walls crawl along a narrow dining space, and Californian ingredients get a top-notch spin in starters like firecracker shrimp with jalapeño, mango chutney, and *sriracha*.

There are many goodies to choose from, but holy basil chicken with beans and bell peppers; or street fair noodles with bacon and egg are nothing short of holy moly amazing. The staff is compliant so make sure to state your spice preference in a fiery red pumpkin coconut curry laced with mushrooms and basil.

Spinster Sisters

B2

American   ✗✗

401 S. A St. (at Sebastopol Ave.), Santa Rosa

Phone: 707-528-7100   Lunch & dinner Tue – Sun
Web: www.thespinstersisters.com
Prices: $$

This terra cotta-tinged bungalow is housed on a residential block off the city center, and flaunts a very hip and modern vibe as evidenced in concrete walls and a large circular wood counter. The urban respite also reeks of good taste—not only in design but also in their delicious range of food crafted from local Californian produce.

Open from breakfast to dinner, Sonoma County crowds come swarming in for Spinster Sisters' enticing cocktails impeccably paired with updated but serious American cuisine. A crunchy, wilted kale salad tosses creamy goat cheese, smoky bacon, pickled onion, and moist slices of chicken. The well-priced wine selection is as luring as a flaky quiche with gooey fontina, spicy sausage, and lemon vinaigrette.

Spoonbar

D2

Mediterranean   ✗✗

219 Healdsburg Ave. (bet. Matheson & Mill Sts.), Healdsburg

Phone: 707-433-7222   Lunch Sat – Sun
Web: www.spoonbar.com   Dinner nightly
Prices: $$

The restaurant of the hip and sustainable h2hotel draws locals and tourists for its elevated and inventive fare. Expect the likes of a knockout beet tartare wrapped in crispy pastry and served with sliced beets in a rich miso dressing, an artistic kampachi sashimi, or an addictive take on crispy rock shrimp with a "granola" of sesame seeds.

A smart cocktail menu incorporates local ingredients and creative touches, as in St. George whiskey, lemon, ginger, and Thai coconut foam in the John Chapman. The spacious bar and communal table are often packed with diners and drinkers, while the quieter, loft-like dining room blends indoor and outdoor with its big floor-to-ceiling windows. In warmer weather, the bar scene on the lovely terrace is young and vibrant.

Stark's Steakhouse

Steakhouse

 B2

521 Adam St. (at 7th St.), Santa Rosa

Phone: 707-546-5100
Web: www.starkrestaurants.com
Prices: $$$

Lunch Mon – Fri
Dinner nightly

This Railroad Square steakhouse is part of the Stark group of restaurants and is hitting its stride as a sophisticated den for carnivores. Make your way into the handsome retreat that entices with dark wood, smoky accent walls, and a baby grand. Flesh rules here and a vast choice of Bourbon and Scotch fit the menu choices from mini burgers to substantial steaks.

Happy hour is hopping and small plates like Moroccan chicken meatballs or crisp calamari are full of pizzazz. You can't go wrong with the burger but the 28 day house-aged steaks are excellent, especially when married with such novel sauces—whole grain mustard béarnaise? Tempting steak toppings like roasted bone marrow, truffle fried egg, or blue cheese butter sate those with meat on the mind.

Sugo

Italian

 B3

5 Petaluma Blvd. S. (at B St.), Petaluma

Phone: 707-782-9298
Web: www.sugopetaluma.com
Prices: $$

Lunch & dinner daily

Sugo is a quaint trattoria housed behind an ordinary brick façade in the center of Petaluma. Its casual interior is bedecked with tightly spaced tables and a small open kitchen. The latter offers a comely take on dinner, perhaps with a movie—classic films are projected on one wall and add visual interest to the space.

If this art house vibe doesn't distract from Sugo's strip mall locale, a trio of bruschetta or panzanella salad with peppers, tomatoes, and red onion should be enough to transport you at last. And while there are many mains, pastas truly shine here as the name suggests. So, arrive early to revel in such iconic dishes as pappardelle with rotisserie chicken and pistachios; or penne tossed with creamy pesto *verdura*, asparagus, and peas.

Terrapin Creek ❀

1580 Eastshore Rd. (off Hwy. 1), Bodega Bay

Phone: 707-875-2700
Web: www.terrapincreekcafe.com
Prices: $$

Lunch & dinner Thu – Sun

Terrapin Creek

Wine Country ▶ Sonoma County

While Napa and Sonoma have excellent culinary destinations, few can match the hospitality of a meal at Terrapin Creek, which feels incredibly personal—as if you were dining in the home of a close friend. Set in picturesque Bodega Bay, this quiet, unassuming restaurant wins hearts with its flavor-packed food (which transcends at dinner) and engaging, thoughtful service.

Done in yellow and orange, the clean, uncluttered room draws the eye to the open kitchen, where Asian, French, and American flavors blend seamlessly. Begin with a delightfully fresh and clean-tasting tuna tartare, accented by delicate soy-yuzu vinaigrette and cucumbers. This may seem like a ubiquitous dish, but it is rarely as fine as here. The painterly baby beet salad topped with fresh baby greens and goat cheese is almost too pretty to eat. You'll long to sop up the juices from deliciously grilled octopus over warm potato salad, but save room for the tender Liberty duck breast over forbidden fried rice instead.

The selection of local wines and a few sakes is small but well curated. Regardless of your chosen drink, you'll want to finish with dessert. Buttery, flaky banana cream pie is one of many exquisite options.

Thai Orchid

D2

1005 Vine St. (at Mill St.), Healdsburg

Phone: 707-433-0515
Web: N/A
Prices: 🐷

Lunch Mon – Sat
Dinner nightly

Rocking a no-frills vibe and nestled inside a bustling shopping center, this under-the-radar gem does Thai food right. Bold, delicious flavors may as well be the motto here at Thai Orchid, where local families can be found chowing on select favorites like spicy basil duck, pumpkin red curry, and *pad see ew.*

The simply appointed space shows off photos of the Thai royal family, artsy carved screens, and bamboo plants. Amid such ease, start on complex items like tangy *tom kha kai,* spicy coconut and lemongrass broth brimming with chicken, cilantro, and green chilies. The pork *pad ka prow*—a sumptuous platter of spicy garlic-basil pork with onions and red peppers—is a fine choice, as is the *kai-yang,* grilled smoky-sweet chicken with jasmine rice.

the fig café

B3

13690 Arnold Dr. (at O Donnell Ln.), Glen Ellen

Phone: 707-938-2130
Web: www.thefigcafe.com
Prices: $$

Lunch Sat – Sun
Dinner nightly

The fig café is so much a fixture in Glen Ellen that she is practically a landmark. And with a deluge of natural light from plenty of windows to illuminate the vaulted ceilings, a glorious open kitchen, and a friendly crowd, it's simple to see why the fig is a favorite among locals. The interior is casual and comfy and the Californian cuisine is consistent, approachable, and beautifully prepared.

Dinners frequently feature local ingredients and might include, you guessed it, a fig and chèvre salad with caramelized pancetta, pecans, and spicy arugula; crispy duck confit with glazed turnips over earthy French green lentils; butcher's steak with blue cheese butter; and fluffy lemon bread pudding with macerated berries and a bit of crème fraîche.

the girl & the fig

Californian ✗✗

D3

110 W. Spain St. (at 1st St.), Sonoma

Phone: 707-938-3634
Web: www.thegirlandthefig.com
Prices: $$

Lunch & dinner daily

It is easy to see why this restaurant is a favorite with both locals and tourists. Her fresh and seasonal Californian fare is prepared with top ingredients and not a ton of fuss. Frilled with a beautiful garden patio, the quaint country house décor features pastel-hued walls and mini lamp sconces. A beautiful carved wood bar completes the experience with inventive cocktails.

A California-and-French influenced menu may divulge a delicate smoked trout salad—moist, flaky, and mingled with pea tendrils and baby red and golden beets; or pastis-scented steamed mussels with crispy frites. If you're looking for the fluffiest quiche Lorraine ever (studded with bacon and Gruyère and served with ultra-thin herbed matchstick fries), you've come to the right spot.

Underwood

International ✗✗

A2

9113 Graton Rd. (at Edison St.), Graton

Phone: 707-823-7023
Web: www.underwoodgraton.com
Prices: $$

Lunch Tue – Sat
Dinner Tue – Sun

Graton may be little more than a cluster of restaurants and shops, but Underwood is where local winemakers gather to celebrate the harvest or make deals over good food and wine. The nickel bar has a saloon feel, especially when laden with classic cocktails and oysters; and red, riveted banquettes alongside zinc-topped tables in the dining room conjure a French bistro. Yet, the cuisine is decidedly international.

The menu ranges from cheeses and salads to an eclectic selection of globe-trotting small plates like hoisin-glazed baby back ribs, or Thai lettuce cups full of lemongrass- and mint-seasoned pork, served with cucumbers, roasted peanuts, and rice noodles.

The Willow Wood Market Café across the street has the same owner and is a bit more rustic.

Willi's Seafood & Raw Bar

D1

Seafood XX

403 Healdsburg Ave. (at North St.), Healdsburg

Phone: 707-433-9191   Lunch & dinner daily
Web: www.starkrestaurants.com
Prices: $$

Healdsburg locals have all new reason to clink glasses of Sonoma County wines: their beloved haunt, Willi's Seafood & Raw Bar, now has room enough for everyone. A few years since their expansion, Willi's rustic-chic interior continues to burst at the seams with regulars and tourists who come for seafood-focused small plates. Not to worry, the fab alfresco dining patio is still perfectly intact.

Ideal for sharing with a jovial bunch of friends, Willi's savory nibbles include fresh hamachi ceviche tossed with *pepitas* and *rocoto* chilies in zesty lime juice; salty, deep-fried Ipswich clams with shisito peppers and citrus aïoli; uni "mac & cheese" with Sweet Bay scallops; and clam, mussel, or oyster "steamers" with green garlic butter and PBR.

Willi's Wine Bar

B2

International XX

4404 Old Redwood Hwy. (at Ursuline Rd.), Santa Rosa

Phone: 707-526-3096   Lunch Tue – Sat
Web: www.starkrestaurants.com   Dinner nightly
Prices: $$

This roadhouse is easily missed when racing down the old tree-lined highway, if not for the packed parking lot. The name comes from a spot in Paris that pioneered serving American wines to the French 30 years ago. Nowadays, Willi's serves over 40 wines by the glass and an eclectic menu of smaller plates. Inside, find a series of small, wood-accented rooms with a romantic and a ruby-red glow.

The multi-cultural menu is divided into Surf, Earth, and Turf—and if the Iberico pork loin is on offer, get it. In addition, try the skewed brick chicken with *harissa*, *tzatziki* sauce, and fried onion salad; Moroccan lamb chops; or goat-cheese fritters with smoked paprika and lavender honey.

Aspiring oenophiles should belly up to the bar for a real wine education.

Willow Wood Market Cafe

A2

Californian ✗

9020 Graton Rd. (at Edison St.), Graton

Phone: 707-823-0233
Web: www.willowwoodgraton.com
Prices: $$

Lunch daily
Dinner Mon – Sat

Hospitality always pairs well with food—especially in California where that casual and cozy comfort is a distinct local pleasure. And stepping into the Willow Wood Market Cafe feels like returning to a welcoming home, or maybe a quirky sundries store stocked with good wine. Obscure specialty items for foodie friends and revolving local artworks hanging on the buttery yellow walls all combine to enhance this quaint eatery's charms.

Salads and sandwiches are tasty, but the menu focuses on many different homey renditions of piping-hot polenta. This creamy cornmeal goodness has many guises including garlicky rock shrimp with roasted peppers, or simple with goat cheese, sweet-roasted red onions, and pesto. Just about everything comes with garlic bread.

Yeti

C3

Nepali ✗✗

14301 Arnold Dr., Ste. 19 (in Jack London Village), Glen Ellen

Phone: 707-996-9930
Web: www.yetirestaurant.com
Prices: $$

Lunch & dinner daily

Historic Jack London Village, with its gristmill from the mid-1800s, may seem like an unlikely spot for a Nepali restaurant, but somehow, this odd combination works. Pass a 25-foot water wheel to find the quaint Yeti. Inside, large barn-windows open for fresh air and garden-views, while Himalayan and some Indian influences are patent in the artifacts and fabrics—and cooking, of course.

This is a peaceful spot to enjoy superlative Nepali preparations like *momo*, heart-warming Himalayan-style dumplings filled with ground meat and spices; trailed by a Himalayan pepper pot soup. Their version of chicken *tikka masala* (yogurt- and *garam masala*-marinated chicken in creamy tomato sauce) is above par, especially when paired with that piping-hot garlic naan.

Zin

D1

American ✗

344 Center St. (at North St.), Healdsburg

Phone: 707-473-0946
Web: www.zinrestaurant.com
Prices: $$

Dinner nightly

A narrow window at the door lined with jars packed with preserved goodies is a portent to the homemade goodness inside. Casual with polished concrete floors and walls hung with bright agrarian scenes, high ceilings overlook cork-lined tables below. The co-owners are sons of farmers, and that upbringing has not been forgotten in the cuisine.

The seasonal menu is laced with fresh spins on American classics, and their tempura-fried green beans with mango salsa are legendary in these parts. Southwestern zeal is evident in the crispy duck leg with pepper jelly or shrimp and grits with andouille sausage. Different blue-plate specials every night celebrate Americana.

There are always zinfandel tasting flights, with a half-dozen available by the glass.

Look for our new category 🥟, small plates.

LIVE
IN
ITALIAN

Where to **Eat**

Indexes

Alphabetical List of Restaurants

Indexes ▶ Alphabetical List of Restaurants

Indexes ▶ Alphabetical List of Restaurants

Restaurants by Cuisine

Afghan

Helmand Palace	✗✗	98
Kabul	✗✗	229
Kamdesh	✗	179

American

Ad Hoc	✗✗	285
Blue Plate	✗✗	77
Bluestem Brasserie	✗✗	138
Boon Fly Café	✗	290
Bounty Hunter	✗	292
Brick & Bottle	🏵 ✗✗	202
Brown Sugar Kitchen	✗	165
Buckeye Roadhouse	✗✗	202
Bungalow 44	✗✗	203
Carpe Diem	🍲	294
Corner Store (The)	✗	27
Cuvée	✗✗	297
Duarte's Tavern	✗	225
Fish & Farm	✗✗	47
FIVE	🏵 ✗✗	174
Goose & Gander	✗✗	300
Gott's Roadside	✗	302
Hot Box Grill	🏵 ✗✗	335
Jackson's	✗✗	335
Market	✗✗	306
Mason Pacific	🏵 ✗✗	101
Maverick	✗	84
Mission Beach Café	✗✗	85
Monti's Rotisserie	🏵 ✗✗	340
Mustards Grill	✗✗	307
Nick's Cove	✗✗	209
Nick's Next Door	✗✗✗	265
900 Grayson	✗	182

Park Chow	✗	126
Park Tavern	✗✗✗	113
Prospect	✗✗✗	148
Richmond (The)	✗✗	127
Rutherford Grill	✗✗	312
Salt House	✗✗	149
Sauce	✗✗	34
Sir and Star	🏵 ✗✗	213
Spinster Sisters	✗✗	345
Tavern at Lark Creek	✗✗	214
Terrapin Crossroads	✗✗	215
1300 on Fillmore	✗✗✗	36
Town Hall	✗✗	152
Wexler's	✗	54
Zin	✗	352

Argentinian

Lolinda	✗✗	84

Asian

Betelnut	✗✗	60
Champa Garden	✗	167
Chinois	✗✗	328
Hawker Fare	✗	177
house (the)	✗	110
Mingalaba	✗	234

Austrian

Leopold's	✗✗	101
Naschmarkt	✗✗	265

Barbecue

BBQ Spot (The)	✗	322
Cathead's BBQ	✗	138

Cuban

La Bodeguita del Medio	✗	262

Eastern European

Bar Tartine	✍	✗✗	76

Ethiopian

Café Colucci	✗	166
Zeni	✗	275

French

Angèle		✗✗	285
Artisan Bistro	✍	✗✗	161
Bistro des Copains		✗✗	323
Bistro Jeanty	✍	✗✗	289
Bistro Liaison		✗✗	163
Bistro 29	✍	✗✗	324
Bouchon	❀	✗✗	291
Café de la Presse		✗✗	43
Café Jacqueline		✗	108
Chapeau!	✍	✗✗	122
Chevalier	✍	✗✗	168
Fleur de Lys		✗✗✗	47
French Garden		✗✗	331
Fringale	✍	✗✗	142
Keiko à Nob Hill	❀	✗✗✗	99
K & L Bistro		✗	337
La Folie	❀	✗✗✗	100
L'Ardoise		✗✗	20
Le Charm		✗✗	143
Left Bank		✗✗	207
Le Garage	✍	✗	207
Pastis		✗	267

Fusion

Chaya Brasserie	✗✗	140
Va de Vi	✗✗	192

Gastropub

Alembic (The)		🍺	16
Magnolia Pub		✗	20
Martins West		✗✗	233
Norman Rose Tavern		✗✗	308
Sidebar		✗	188
Tipsy Pig (The)		✗✗	72
Tribune Tavern		✗✗	191
Village Pub (The)	❀	✗✗✗	243
Wayfare Tavern		✗✗	53

Greek

Dio Deka		✗✗	257
Evvia	✍	✗✗	259
Ikaros		✗✗	178
Kokkari Estiatorio	✍	✗✗	112

Indian

All Spice	❀	✗✗	220
Ark Grill		✗✗	221
Arti		✗	200
Curry Up Now		✗	224
Dosa	✍	✗✗	62
Gajalee	✍	✗✗	80
Kabab & Curry's		✗	261
Mela Tandoori Kitchen		✗✗	30
Rangoli		✗✗	268
Sakoon		✗✗	270
Viva Goa		✗	72

International

Bridges		✗✗	165
Celadon		✗✗	295
Cin-Cin		🍺	257
Cindy Pawlcyn's Wood Grill		✗✗	295
Cindy's Backstreet Kitchen		✗✗	296
Foreign Cinema		✗✗	80
Grace's Table		✗✗	302
Kitchen Door		✗✗	303

Southern

Boxing Room	✗✗	27
CreoLa	✗✗	223
Dixie	✗✗✗	62
Picán	✗✗✗	184
The Pear	✗✗	315

Spanish

Bocadillos	▤	41
Bravas	▤	325
Café Lucia	✗✗	326
César	✗	167
Contigo	⊕ ✗✗	17
Coqueta	✗✗	46
Duende	✗✗	173
Gitane	✗✗	48
Iberia	✗✗	228
Zuzu	▤	317

Sri Lankan

1601 Bar & Kitchen	⊕ ✗✗	151

Steakhouse

Alexander's Steakhouse	✗✗✗	252
Bourbon Steak	✗✗✗	42
Cole's Chop House	✗✗✗	296
El Paseo	✗✗	204
Epic Roasthouse	✗✗	141
Lark Creek Steak	✗✗	143
LB Steak	✗✗✗	263
Press	✗✗✗	309
Stark's Steakhouse	✗✗✗	346

Thai

Anchalee	✗	160
Arun	✗	200
Bangkok Jam	✗✗	161
Basil Canteen	✗✗	136
Blackwood	✗✗	61
Grand Avenue Thai	✗✗	175
Khan Toke Thai House	✗	124
Khoom Lanna	✗✗	336
Lers Ros	✗✗	29
Manora's Thai Cuisine	✗	145
Mini Mango Thai Bistro	✗	306
Modern Thai	✗	102
R'Noh Thai	✗✗	212
SEA Thai	✗✗	344
Sweet Basil	✗	239
Thai House	⊕ ✗✗	190
Thai Orchid	✗	348
Thep Phanom	✗	36

Vegan

Millennium	✗✗	51

Vegetarian

Encuentro	✗	173
Greens	✗	64
Plant (The)	✗	67

Vietnamese

Bui Bistro	✗✗	293
Bun Bo Hue An Nam	✗	255
Mai Vietnamese Cuisine	✗	338
Slanted Door (The)	⊕ ✗✗	53
Tamarine	✗✗	273
Thiên Long	✗	274
Vanessa's Bistro	✗✗	193
Vung Tau	✗✗	275

Cuisines by Neighborhood

Indexes ▶ Cuisines by Neighborhood

Indexes ▲ Cuisines by Neighborhood

Indexes ▶ Cuisines by Neighborhood

375

MARIN

WINE COUNTRY

Napa Valley

Starred Restaurants

Within the selection we offer you, some restaurants deserve to be highlighted for their particularly good cuisine. When giving one, two, or three Michelin stars, there are a number of elements that we consider including the quality of the ingredients, the technical skill and flair that goes into their preparation, the blend and clarity of flavours, and the balance of the menu. Just as important is the ability to produce excellent cooking time and again. We make as many visits as we need, so that our readers may be assured of quality and consistency.

A two or three-star restaurant has to offer something very special in its cuisine; a real element of creativity, originality, or "personality" that sets it apart from the rest. Three stars – our highest award – are given to the choicest restaurants, where the whole dining experience is superb.

Cuisine in any style, modern or traditional, may be eligible for a star. Due to the fact we apply the same independent standards everywhere, the awards have become benchmarks of reliability and excellence in over 20 countries in Europe and Asia, particularly in France, where we have awarded stars for 100 years, and where the phrase "Now that's real three-star quality!" has entered into the language.

The awarding of a star is based solely on the quality of the cuisine.

Exceptional cuisine, worth a special journey

One always eats here extremely well, sometimes superbly. Distinctive dishes are precisely executed, using superlative ingredients.

Excellent cuisine, worth a detour

Skillfully and carefully crafted dishes of outstanding quality.

A very good restaurant in its category

A place offering cuisine prepared to a consistently high standard.

Bib Gourmand

This symbol indicates our inspectors' favorites for good value. For $40 or less, you can enjoy two courses and a glass of wine or a dessert (not including tax or gratuity).

Artisan Bistro	XX	161	flour + water	X	79
A16	XX	58	Fringale	XX	142
Backyard	X	321	Gajalee	XX	80
Bar Tartine	XX	76	Gather	XX	175
Bellanico	XX	163	Glen Ellen Star	X	333
Bistro Aix	XX	60	Hachi Ju Hachi	X	260
Bistro Jeanty	XX	289	Happy Noodles	X	227
Bistro 29	XX	324	Hot Box Grill	XX	335
Boon Eat + Drink	X	324	Insalata's	XX	206
Brick & Bottle	XX	202	Ippuku	X	178
Burma Superstar	X	122	Izakaya Yuzuki	X	81
C Casa	X	294	Kappou Gomi	X	123
Chalkboard	XX	327	Kokkari Estiatorio	XX	112
Chapeau!	XX	122	La Costanera	XX	231
Chevalier	XX	168	LaSalette	XX	337
Chu	X	169	Le Garage	X	207
Comal	XX	169	Mamacita	XX	66
Contigo	XX	17	Marinitas	XX	208
Cook St. Helena	XX	297	Marlowe	XX	146
Corso	X	171	Mason Pacific	XX	101
Cotogna	XX	110	Monti's Rotisserie	XX	340
Crouching Tiger	XX	224	M. Y. China	XX	147
Cucina Paradiso	XX	328	Oenotri	XX	308
Delfina	XX	79	Old Mandarin Islamic	X	125
Domo	X	28	Osteria Coppa	XX	235
Donato Enoteca	XX	225	Perbacco	XX	52
Dosa	XX	62	Plum	XX	185
Ebisu	X	123	Ramen Shop	X	186
Evvia	XX	259	Redd Wood	XX	310
Fey	XX	226	Regalito	X	90
FIVE	XX	174	Rich Table	XX	33

Under $25

Brunch

Indexes ▶ Brunch

Late Dining

YOU ALREADY KNOW THE MICHELIN GUIDE,
NOW FIND OUT ABOUT THE MICHELIN GROUP

The Michelin Adventure

It all started with rubber balls! This was the product made by a small company based in Clermont-Ferrand that André and Edouard Michelin inherited, back in 1880. The brothers quickly saw the potential for a new means of transport and their first success was the invention of detachable pneumatic tires for bicycles. However, the automobile was to provide the greatest scope for their creative talents. Throughout the 20th century, Michelin never ceased developing and creating ever more reliable and high-performance tires, not only for vehicles ranging from trucks to racing cars but also for underground transit systems and airplanes.

From early on, Michelin provided its customers with tools and services to facilitate mobility and make travelling a more pleasurable and more frequent experience. As early as 1900, the Michelin guide supplied motorists with a host of useful information related to vehicle maintenance, accommodation and restaurants, and was to become a benchmark for good food. At the same time, the Travel Information Bureau offered travellers personalised tips and itineraries.

The publication of the first Michelin road map, in 1910, was an instant hit! In 1926, the first regional tourist guide to France was published, devoted to the principal sites of Brittany, and before long each region of France had its own Green Guide. The collection was later extended to more far-flung destinations, including New York in 1968 and Iceland in 2012.

In the 21st century, with the growth of digital technology, the challenge for Michelin maps guides and digital services is to continue to develop alongside the company's tire activities. Now, as before, Michelin is committed to improving the mobility of travellers.

MICHELIN TODAY

- 69 production sites in 18 countries
- 113,400 employees from all cultures and on every continent
- 6,000 people employed in the Michelin Technology centre
- A commercial presence in more than 170 countries

Moving
for a world

Moving forward means developing tires with better road grip and shorter braking distances, whatever the state of the road.

CORRECT TIRE PRESSURE

RIGHT PRESSURE

- Safety
- Longevity
- Optimum fuel consumption

-0,5 bar

- Durability reduced by 20% (- 8,000 km)

-1 bar

- Risk of blowouts
- Increased fuel consumption
- Longer braking distances on wet surfaces

forward together
where mobility is safer

It also involves helping motorists take care of their safety and their tires. To do so, Michelin organises "Fill Up With Air" campaigns all over the world to remind us that correct tire pressure is vital.

WEAR

DETECTING TIRE WEAR

MICHELIN tires are equipped with tread wear indicators, which are small blocks of rubber molded into the base of the main grooves at a height of 1.6 mm. When tread depth is the same level as indicators, the tires are worn and need replacing.

Tires are the only point of contact between vehicle and the road, a worn tire can be dangerous on wet surfaces.

NEW TIRE

WORN TIRE
(1,6 mm tread)

The photo shows the actual contact zone on wet surfaces.

Moving forward
means sustainable mobility

By 2050, Michelin aims to cut the quantity of raw materials used in its tire manufacturing process by half and 99.8% of the company's tires are produced in ISO 14001 certified factories. The design of MICHELIN tires has already saved billions of liters of fuel and, by extension, millions of tons of CO_2.

Similarly, Michelin prints its maps and guides on paper produced from sustainably managed forests and is diversifying its publishing media by offering digital solutions to make travelling easier, more fuel efficient and more enjoyable!

The group's whole-hearted commitment to eco-design on a daily basis is demonstrated by ISO 14001 certification.

Chat with Bibendum

Go to www.michelin.com/corporate/EN/home
Find out more about Michelin's
history and the latest news.

QUIZ

Michelin develops tyres for all types of vehicles. See if you can
match the right tyre with the right vehicle…

Notes

Notes

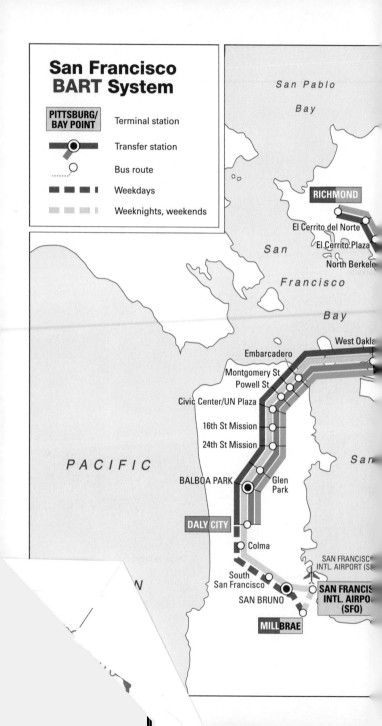

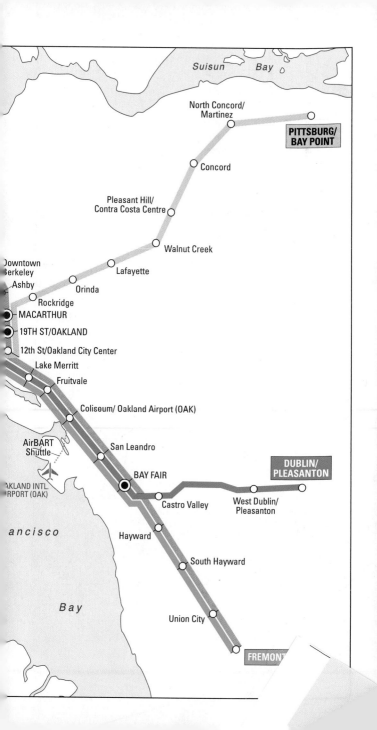

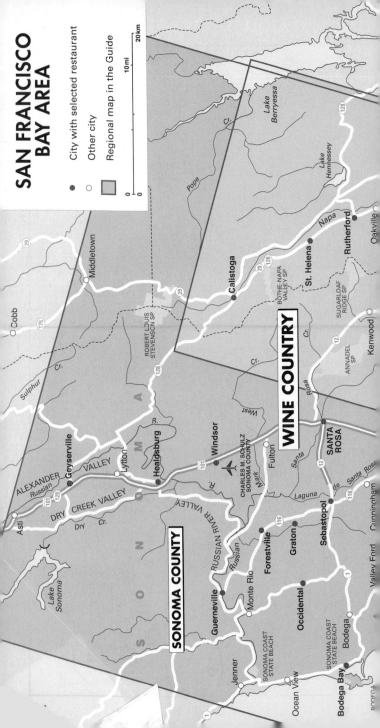

SAN FRANCISCO BAY AREA

- ● City with selected restaurant
- ○ Other city
- ▢ Regional map in the Guide

20km
10mi
0
0

Middletown

Cobb

(175)
(29)

Sulphur   Cr.

Pope

Cr.

Lake
Berryessa

(128)

Lake
Hennessey

ROBERT LOUIS
STEVENSON SP

(128)

(29)

Callistoga

(29) (128)

BOTHE-NAPA
VALLEY SP

St. Helena

Napa

SUGARLOAF
RIDGE SP

Rutherford

Oakville

Kenwood

Asti

ALEXANDER   VALLEY

Russian
(101) (128)

Geyserville

DRY   CREEK VALLEY

Dry   Cr.

Lake
Sonoma

Lytton

Healdsburg

R.

Windsor

(101)

CHARLES M. SCHULZ
SONOMA COUNTY

Mark
West

Cr.

Rosa

(12)

ANNADEL
SP

SANTA
ROSA

Santa

(12)

de   Santa Rosa

Cunningham

Fulton

Laguna

Russian   River   Valley

Monte Rio

Guerneville

Russian   Rio

Forestville

(116)

Graton

Sebastopol

(116)

(116)

SONOMA COUNTY

WINE COUNTRY

SONOMA

Occidental

(1)

Bodega

Bodega Bay

BODEGA

Valley Ford

SONOMA COAST
STATE BEACH

SONOMA COAST
STATE BEACH

Ocean View

Jenner

Cr.

(1)